The NAPA VALLEY Book

EVERYTHING
You Need to Know
About California's
Premium Wine Country

Wineries, restaurants, hotels,
sightseeing, historic attractions,
shopping, recreation, tours,
and much, much more

Mick Winter

Westsong Publishing
Napa, California
www.westsongpublishing.com

THE NAPA VALLEY BOOK

EVERYTHING
You Need to Know
About California's
Premium Wine Country

Copyright © 2003, 2007 by Mick Winter

Published by
Westsong Publishing
PO Box 2254
Napa CA 94558
www.westsongpublishing.com
nvbook@westsong.com

First print edition published 2003
ISBN 0-9659000-1-0
Updated and expanded 2004
Third print edition published 2007
ISBN 978-0-9659000-7-2

Library of Congress Control Number: 2007928689

Printed in the United States of America

Cover photos (courtesy of):
Hot air balloon (Napa Valley Conference and Visitors Bureau)
Wine Train (Napa Valley Wine Train)
Sculptures at Artesa Winery (Gordon Huether)
Welcome sign (Napa Valley Conference and Visitors Bureau)

Dedicated to Kathryn
and to all those who fought—and fight—to preserve
the beauty of the Napa Valley.

And to Joanna, because it's her home.

It's Online, Too

All of the information in this book, plus color photographs and active links, is also online at

www.NapaNow.com

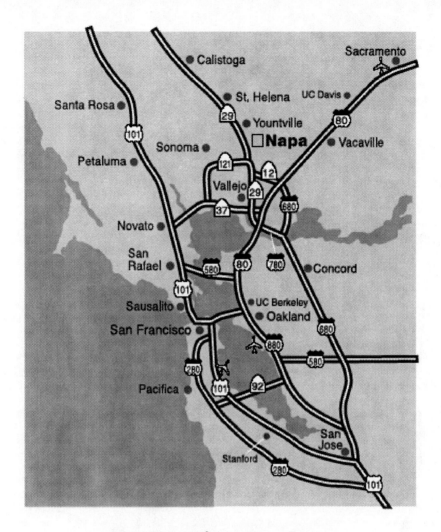

San Francisco Bay Area
(Map courtesy of Napa Downtown Association)

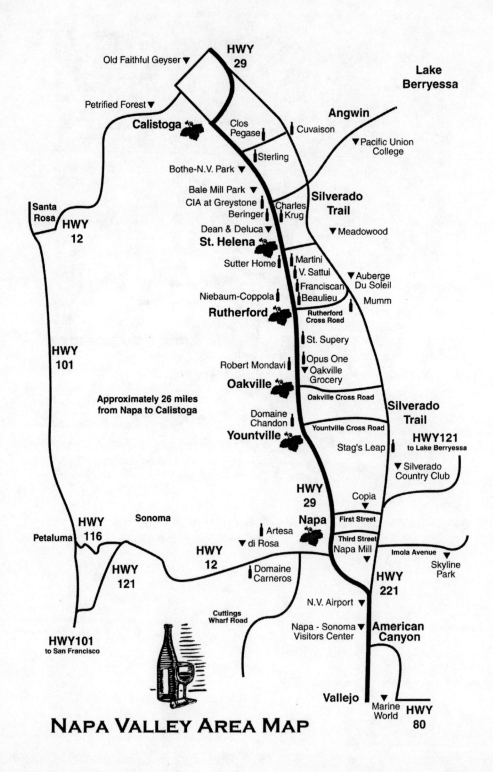

NAPA VALLEY AREA MAP

Table of Contents

Welcome to the Napa Valley

Hello—and welcome.

If you're here for only a day or two, as are 90% of the visitors to our valley, you don't have time to visit every one of the more than 300 wineries, or to eat at each of our fine restaurants. And then there's shopping, hiking, golf, ballooning, spas, music, gliding, entertainment and more.

To make your visit easier, we've listed what we feel are the very best, most unusual, most interesting, most enjoyable and most varied Napa Valley experiences. The rest is up to you.

The first half of the book offers a section on each town or region, moving south to north up the valley and then dealing with surrounding areas. Each section includes wineries, resorts, restaurants, shopping, events and sightseeing attractions. You'll find lodging and spas, recreation and other activities and information in their own sections further on in the book. There's also a section of local information that is particularly helpful to new residents.

The last major section is on wine and covers such areas as grapegrowing, winemaking, wine tasting, and the wines of the Napa Valley, as well as a glossary of wine terms, tips on pronunciation of wine names, and answers to frequently asked questions about wine.

Of course, just because something isn't included in the book, doesn't mean it isn't worth seeing. Almost all wineries in the Napa Valley make wine that's well worth tasting. We've focused on the wineries that are perennial visitor favorites and that are open for drop-in visitors. We've also included many others that have a unique quality or offering we felt you would enjoy.

The same with restaurants. We may be a small rural area, but we're blessed with a large number of truly first-class restaurants. Here again, we've listed all of the best known, and added many others known largely only to locals. You'll find it a very comprehensive list.

Because this guide has no paid advertising, you can be sure that all of the listings are based totally on what we believe is their value to you, the visitor to the Napa Valley. We hope we're able to make your visit more enjoyable, whether it's for a day, a weekend, or longer.

We welcome any comments, suggestions and recommendations you have. If you found one of the listings unsatisfactory, we definitely want to know. And if you discovered a place or activity you feel should be included in the next edition, we want to know that, too. You can email us at nvbook@westsong.com.

Thanks for buying the book. We wish you great enjoyment as you visit our home—the beautiful Napa Valley.

Mick Winter

Getting Here

You can reach the Napa Valley by air, land or water, although almost all visitors come by auto or tour bus.

Air

There is no scheduled air service to the Napa Valley but visitors with private planes can fly into Napa Valley Airport.

Napa Valley Airport
2030 Airport Road
Napa CA 94558
707.253.4300
www.napacountyairport.org

Located 6.5 miles south of the city of Napa, Napa Valley Airport is a general aviation airport operated by the County of Napa. It was originally established by the U.S. Army in 1942 as the Napa Auxiliary Air Defense Field. The Army turned it over to the county in 1945. It can accommodate aircraft up to a Gulfstream V. Its FAA-manned control tower is operated seven days a week from 7 a.m. to 7 p.m.

Evans Airporter
4075 Solano Avenue
Napa CA 94558
707.255.1559 944.2025 (upvalley)
www.evanstransportation.com

Evans has frequent, regularly scheduled trips to and from both San Francisco and Oakland Airports with a stop at Vallejo. Their local terminal is at the north end of Napa just off Highway 29. Evans is how those of us who live here usually get to the airport.

Wine Country Helicopters
2030 Airport Road
Napa CA 94558
707.226.8470
www.winecountryhelicopters.com

Helicopter transportation to/from Bay Area airports, wineries, resorts. Also tours and various commercial services such as aerial photography.

Boat

Few visitors come to the Napa Valley by water, although if you have a small boat it's possible to motor up the Napa River as far as the city of Napa.
  You can also stop south of the city of Napa and dock your boat in the Carneros region at the Napa Valley Marina.

Napa Valley Marina
1200 Milton Road (Off Cuttings Wharf Road)
Napa CA 94559
707.252.8011
www.napavalleymarina.com

Ferry

There's a very enjoyable ferry that takes you from the San Francisco Ferry Building to Vallejo, which is about 20 miles south of Napa. It's about a one-hour trip with a great view of San Francisco, the Golden Gate and Bay Bridges, Angel Island, and areas you'll never see when driving. From Vallejo, you can take the Napa Valley Transit bus to the valley, but this is not yet a highly traveled method. Someday, there will be train service between the Vallejo ferry terminal and Napa, but it's not here yet.

BayLink Ferries
877.64-FERRY
www.baylinkferry.com

Cruise Ship

Cruise West
2401 4th Avenue, Suite 700
Seattle, WA 98121
800.888.9378 Fax: 206.441.4757
www.cruisewest.com

A private cruise line with low-draft ships that sail up the lower Napa River to dock in the Carneros area. Ships hold about 100 passengers. Three and four-night cruises let passengers visit wineries in both Napa and Sonoma Valleys.

Train

Amtrak
800.USA.RAIL
www.amtrak.com

Amtrak buses to and from the Amtrak train station in Martinez stop at the downtown Napa transit center as well as at the Wine Train station.

Car

Since over 90% of our visitors come by car (or tour bus), we'll focus on driving to the Napa Valley.

The Golden Gate Bridge between San Francisco and Marin County (photo courtesy of Wine Institute)

Via Golden Gate Bridge

Drive north over the Golden Gate Bridge on Highway 101 and continue through Marin County almost to Novato. Take the Napa 37 East turnoff to the east and continue following the signs to Napa. The trip takes just under an hour in good traffic, considerably more at rush hour. But as a visitor you shouldn't be driving at rush hour anyhow. Enjoy the views, the cows, the vineyards, and the oak trees. It's by far the most scenic way to drive to the Napa Valley.

Shortly before you reach the Napa Valley, you'll pass (on the right side of Highway 12/121—the Carneros Highway) Domaine Carneros winery. Continuing east, you'll see a sign for "Napa River Resorts" on the south side of the road. The sign has been there a long time, and no transportation officials know for sure why it's there, since there are no resorts and have been none in recent memory. (There are, however, a number of homes, vineyards and wineries as well as the Napa Valley Marina and Moore's Landing restaurant.)

A short time after passing the "resort" turnoff, you'll find yourself at Highway 29, the main highway running north-south in the valley. Turn left (north) toward Napa and Calistoga.

Via San Francisco-Oakland Bay Bridge

Take the Bay Bridge east towards Oakland, then head north on Highway 80 (although it says "East") towards Sacramento. If you're staying in downtown San Francisco, driving to the Napa Valley is usually quicker over the Bay Bridge than going over the Golden Gate Bridge. Going up the East Bay isn't pretty, but it's fast.

Once through Vallejo, turn off Highway 80 at the exit marked "Napa" and head toward the Napa Valley. North of the town of American Canyon you'll pass the intersection of Highway 29 and Highway 12. At the southeast corner of this intersection, across from the Napa Valley Airport, is a large three-story stone building nestled among oak trees that looks like it just has to be winery. It isn't. It's a medical malpractice insurance company— *The Doctors Company*. Sorry; no wine, no visitors, and no picnicking.

On the other (west) side of Highway 29 is the Napa Valley Airport (www.mynapa.info/departments/air port). The largest facility there belongs to Japan Air Lines. JAL provides basic flight training for almost all its pilots at this airport. More than 150 student pilots are undergoing training at any given time.

Continuing north on Highway 29, you'll come to a fork. You can either go right onto Soscol Avenue (forking off to the right just before the traffic light) and on into the downtown area of Napa, or stay on Highway 29 and pass over the Southern Crossing (George F. Butler Bridge) and continue north on Highway 29 toward Calistoga. (Along Highway 29 there are a number of exits into Napa.)

If you follow the "Calistoga" sign and stay on 29, you'll cross over the bridge and be able to look down on the meandering Napa River.

You're now in the Napa Valley.

Getting Around

Traffic Information

For online traffic information for the entire San Francisco Bay Area, including the North Bay and Napa Valley, we recommend:
www.sfgate.com/traffic/

Caltrans

Caltrans, the State of California's Department of Transportation, has up-to-the-minute online information on state highways. Here's information on Highway 29, which runs north-south through the Napa Valley.
www.dot.ca.gov/hq/roadinfo/sr29

For toll-free information on significant delays on California State Highways, call 1.800.427.ROAD (7623).

Caltrans District 4
www.dot.ca.gov/dist4/

Information on District 4, which covers the entire Bay Area including Napa County.

511
www.511.org

Toll-free hotline from all area codes in the San Francisco Bay Area that provides complete Bay Area public and private transportation information, including up-to-the-minute traffic information on 37 freeways, eight bridges and all major roads. Includes information on public transit, paratransit, carpools, vanpools, parking and biking. Just dial 511 from your phone.

Automobile Rental

If you didn't arrive by car, you can rent one in Napa.

Budget
407 Soscol Ave
Napa CA 94559
800.527.7000

Enterprise
230 Soscol Ave
Napa CA 94559
707.253.8000

Hertz
686 Soscol Ave,
Napa CA 94559
707.265.7575

Tour/Limousine Services

Antique Tours Limousine Service
707.226.9227
www.antiquetours.net

Fully restored 1947 convertible Packard limousines.

California Wine Tours
800.294.6386
www.californiawinetours.com

Five-hour Napa Valley tour and tasting $49/person.

Classic Limousine

572 Lincoln Avenue
Napa CA 94558
707.253.0999 800.259.8401
www.classiclimousine.50megs.com

Limos include a 1949 Packard and a 1969 Silver Cloud Rolls Royce.

Esperya

101 Old Vine Way
Napa CA 94558
707.255.7517
www.winecountryesperya.com

Personal and corporate tours, including winery visits, barrel tastings, restaurants, picnics and cave dinners.

Group Outings

4225 Solano Avenue #575
Napa CA 94558
Fax 707.226.8652
www.groupoutings.com

Limos include a town car and 120" stretch limousine. A special tour offers barrel tastings and discounts at top wineries.

Royal Coach Limousine Service

1850 Imola Avenue
Napa CA 94558
800.995.7692
www.royalcoachlimousine.com

Napa Valley's oldest service—since 1985.

Taxis

Taxi service is available throughout the valley, but only by telephone. It's very unlikely you'll be able to wave one down on the street. These two services offer vehicles that are much more luxurious than the average.

Black Tie Taxi

707.259.1000 888.544.8294
www.blacktietaxi.com

Winery Shuttle

Napa Winery Shuttle

707.257.1950
www.wineshuttle.com

The shuttle is a great service if you'd like to spend the day touring and tasting and have someone else do the driving. The shuttle leaves from most Napa Valley hotels and travels on a fixed route, stopping at seven well-known wineries. You can get off and on when and where you wish. Because they stop at each location every 30-40 minutes, you can do a tasting, then conveniently catch the next shuttle to the next winery.

The shuttle also stops at two upvalley restaurants for lunch. Price, which does not include winery tasting fees or food purchases, is $38 per person, which includes unlimited stops per day. Plus they'll pick up your wine at the winery and deliver it to your hotel.

Train

Napa Valley Wine Train

1275 McKinstry
Napa CA 94559
707.253.2111. 800.427.4124 Fax: 707.253.9264
www.winetrain.com

For full information on the Wine Train, see page 64.

About the Napa Valley

The Napa Valley is in Northern California at the northeastern tip of San Francisco Bay (actually called San Pablo Bay up that far), about an hour's drive north of San Francisco. To the west is the Sonoma Valley, to the north is Lake Country, and to the east is the Sacramento Valley.

The Napa Valley is actually just one of many valleys in Napa County, but it's by far the largest and best known. The valley itself is about 30 miles long and ranges from one to five miles in width.

Napa County has a population of about 125,000 people, including five incorporated cities. North to south, they are: Calistoga, St. Helena, Yountville, Napa and, at the southern end, American Canyon. Angwin, Deer Park, Pope Valley, Rutherford and Oakville are communities with post offices but aren't actual towns.

The county's primary industries are winegrape growing, wine production and tourism. Thanks to stringent and ongoing efforts by a number of dedicated agriculturalists, environmentalists, elected officials, and concerned citizens, and the support of the vast majority of the voters, there is little development in the unincorporated area of the county. Most commercial and residential development is in the cities. This preserves a huge amount of agricultural land, allowing Napa County to avoid the urban sprawl that has affected almost all other San Francisco Bay Area counties. The result is an attractive place for residents to live and for tourists to visit.

Napa River

The Napa River is one of four navigable rivers in California and one of only three surviving free-flowing rivers. It's a major source of freshwater to San Francisco Bay, and offers excellent fishing for striped bass and sturgeon. There's even peaceful canoeing right in the heart of the city of Napa.

"Friends of the Napa River" (www.friendsofthenapariver.org), is a local organization that was formed to preserve the river, which has a tendency to frequently flood downtown Napa. Of course, building a city on a flood plain wasn't a great idea to begin with, but now that it's here, citizens decided to create ways to save both the river and the city by turning out a river that's developed and flood-safe, yet still natural and free-flowing.

Voters approved a bond issue and construction is now well underway to restore the river to a more natural state, as well as one that will not flood populated areas.

For more information on the river, see the special Napa River section (page 58).

Mount St. Helena

That extinct volcano you see at the north end of the valley—Mount St. Helena—is not extinct. But don't worry; it isn't a volcano either. Despite the beliefs of many locals, it's just a mountain, in fact the highest part of the Mayacmas Mountains—frequently misspelled "Mayacamas"—that also extend into Sonoma, Lake and Mendocino

Counties. It is, however, one (and the highest at 4,343 feet) of the four dominant mountains of the San Francisco Bay Area. Mount St. Helena at the north, Mount Hamilton at the south—near San Jose; Mount Diablo at the east—near Concord; and Mount Tamalpais at the west in Marin County.

Even if Mount St. Helena was never a volcano, there is a great deal of geyser activity just below it in the hot springs town of Calistoga, and to the northwest in an area known as The Geysers, currently used as a source of thermal energy.

History

The original inhabitants of the valley were the Wappo. The name Wappo was given by the Spanish and probably derived from the Spanish word "guapo" meaning "handsome." The natives were here at least 4,000 years before the Spaniards arrived. In 1831 there were an estimated 10,000 to 12,000 Wappo living in the valley. Most later lost their lives to cholera and smallpox, as well as to attacks by white men. There are still surviving Wappo in Napa, Sonoma and Lake counties.

The first American settler in the Napa Valley was George Yount. He arrived in 1831, became friends with General Mariano Vallejo, and was given an 11,000-acre Mexican land grant. He built the first wooden structure in the county, a two-story Kentucky blockhouse. He also planted the first grapevines in the Napa Valley. The vines were from Mexico; it was not until 1860 that the higher-quality European winegrapes were introduced.

The wealth of post-Gold Rush San Francisco created a huge demand for wine, and by 1891 there were 619 vineyards throughout the valley. Many of wines produced were receiving awards in European wine competitions. The wineries survived economic depression and the disease of phylloxera but were no match for Prohibition, the United States' "Great Experiment" of declaring alcoholic beverages not just immoral but illegal.

Prohibition closed almost every Napa Valley winery. The few that survived provided medicinal wine or sacramental wine for churches. Vineyards were ripped out to be replaced by prune and walnut orchards.

Prohibition ended in 1933, but it was not until 1951 that a new winery was finally built in the Napa Valley. It was Stony Hill, a small family winery that is still actively producing excellent wine. Sixteen years later, in 1967, the next winery opened. It is a much larger winery, located in Oakville. Its founder, Robert Mondavi, launched a wave of winery construction—and wine promotion—that has not yet stopped.

Since that time more than three hundred wineries have been built, as the Napa Valley was rediscovered as a premium wine region, recapturing its earlier pro-Prohibition fame.

Napa County is one of the 27 original counties that were established on February 18, 1850 and therefore part of California when it became a state on September 9, 1850. In 1861, Lake County, including Clear Lake, was formed from the northern part of Napa County. Some additional land was given to Lake County in the 1860s but returned back to Napa County in

1972. In addition, some land in Solano and Sonoma Counties was also added to Napa County in 1855.

Napa Valley Today

Today the Napa Valley is one of the most popular tourist attractions in California, and world-renowned for its wines. The fame of its wineries is matched by the reputation of its restaurants. Combined with the beauty of the area, and the gentleness of its climate, they provide a vacation holiday without equal anywhere in the country.

Although many locals bragged for years that the Napa Valley received as many visitors as Disneyland, the reality is that Disneyland has about 14 million visitors a year and the Napa Valley nearly five million.

Five million is enough—particularly because most of them come during the summer, "Crush"—the harvest in September and October, or the Mustard Festival in the early spring. Come visit us in the off periods and you'll find far fewer people and have much more time to chat with winery staff.

The valley is beautiful all year long, just different from season to season. The wine and food are always delicious.

Best Time to Visit

Winter tends to be the quietest time of the year in the Napa Valley, although February and March are now lost to the Mustard Festival (www.mustardfestival.org). This festival was initiated because restaurants and lodging facilities weren't getting enough business during the slow months. (It also meant they had to lay off staff during this time.) This is a beautiful season with mustard flowers in the vineyards and early-blooming trees.

The quietest time is November, December and January—except over the Christmas holidays. It's easier then to get a room reservation and, who knows, you may even be able to get a reservation at the French Laundry. Many hotels and bed and breakfast inns offer lower rates from November through March.

Summer is very busy, as are September and October during "Crush"—the time of harvest.

Most Visited Attractions

(Courtesy of the Napa Valley Conference and Visitors Bureau)

St. Helena—Main Street, Beringer Winery and Culinary Institute of America

Calistoga—Lincoln Ave, Sterling Vineyards and Old Faithful Geyser

Rutherford—Rubicon Estate, Beaulieu Vineyard, St. Supéry Wine Discovery Center

Oakville—Robert Mondavi Winery and Oakville Grocery

Yountville—Domaine Chandon Winery, Vintage 1870 and Washington Street restaurants

Napa—Premium Outlets and Napa Town Center (Napa Valley Visitors Center)

Reasons to Visit
(Courtesy of the Napa Valley
Conference and Visitors Bureau)

Here are the reasons for visiting
given by a cross-section of visitors in
a survey:

1. Wine/wineries
2. Food
3. Friends
4. Family
5. Relaxation
6. Scenery
7. Weather
8. Beauty
9. Vacation
10. Business
11. Wedding
12. Close by
13. Birthday
14. Honeymoon

And here are the most visited
wineries according to that same
survey:

1. Beringer
2. V. Sattui
3. Sterling
4. Domaine Chandon
5. Robert Mondavi
6. Rubicon
7. Mumm
8. Cakebread
9. BV
10. Peju
11. Rutherford Hill
12. Franciscan

And the most visited restaurants
(according to survey respondents):

1. Bouchon
2. Mustard's Grill
3. CIA (Wine Spectator)
4. Tra Vigne
5. Bistro Jeanty
6. V. Sattui
7. Julia's Kitchen
8. Rutherford Grill
9. Brix
10. N. V. Wine Train
11. Don Giovanni

Climate

In short, it's Californian–very
Mediterranean. It's a great place to
be a grape, and a very good one to be
a human. The Napa Valley is far
enough inland to escape most of the
fog that lingers along the California
coast during summer. Yet, unlike
California's Central Valley, it's close
enough to the ocean to take
advantage of the cooling effect of
that fog.

It can get hot in the summer, but
usually not too hot. We can expect a
week or two during the summer
when the temperatures are around
100° F, usually in July or August,
which are the hottest months. The
southern end of the valley, where the
city of Napa is located, is cooler. It's
closer to the northern tip of San
Francisco Bay, known as San Pablo
Bay. Winds come through the
Golden Gate, move upward and cool
off the southern end of Napa County
as far as Yountville. They also come
over the hills from the west and
Sonoma County's coast.

North of Yountville the valley doglegs to the left (west). The late afternoon wind from the bay doesn't make the turn, so the St. Helena and Calistoga areas tend to be much warmer. During the summer, the temperature upvalley can be ten to twenty degrees (F) warmer than in the Napa area.

In the winter, it rains—but not a lot. The county's average annual rainfall for the entire year is less than 24 inches, with over half of that in December, January and February. And it's not unusual to have temperatures in the 70s and 80s (F) around Christmas time.

The western side of the valley—the Mayacmas Mountains—gets more rain, apparent by the redwood and fir forests and numerous streams and waterfalls. The eastern side of the valley—the Vacas Mountains (named for the Vaca family that settled here in 1841)—tends to be more desert-like in many areas, with scrub brush and even cactus.

Average Temperatures by Season (Fahrenheit)

Season	Min	Max
Spring	64°	78°
Summer	81°	92°
Fall 7	4°	85°
Winter	61°	72°

Average Rainfall for Napa County

Month	MM	Inches
Jan	117.3	4.6
Feb	84.8	3.3
Mar	79.5	3.1
Apr	50.2	2.0
May	13.6	0.5
Jun	5.9	0.2
Jul	0.4	0.0
Aug	3.1	0.1
Sep	6.0	0.2
Oct	32.6	1.3
Nov	72.3	2.8
Dec	132.9	5.2
Year	599.3	23.6

Weather Report

For current weather conditions in the Napa Valley, and the forecast for the following week, we recommend:
www.sfgate.com/weather
Click on "Napa" on the map.

The Best and Worst

Best Things About The Napa Valley

1. The natural beauty of the valley

2. Wonderful weather

3. Outstanding restaurants

4. Superb wines

5. The relatively slow pace of small town life

6. Friendly people

7. The ease of finding a parking place and the low traffic compared to the rest of the Bay Area

8. Closeness to San Francisco

9. County-wide cooperation on important issues

10. The proximity of both beach and mountains

Worst Things About The Napa Valley

1. Expensive restaurants

2. Expensive wines (and the markup on wine in most restaurants)

3. The traffic on Highway 29

4. Ugly ego-driven "mansions on steroids" on top of hills and ridges

5. High cost of housing

6. Low wages

7. Snobs (See 1, 2 and 4 above)

8. Box chain stores in the city of Napa

9. Wealth disparity and the disappearing middle class.

Best Ideas That Actually Happened

1. Ending Prohibition

2. Agricultural Preserve. In 1968 Napa Valley vintners and other community leaders enacted the country's first Agricultural Preserve, protecting over 30,000 acres of open space

3. "Measure A". Vote of the people in 1980. It saved agriculture in the Napa Valley by restricting growth in the unincorporated areas to 1% a year, with 25% of that having to be affordable housing. (The affordable housing never happened, but at least it further restricted the expensive housing)

4. Measure J. Vote of the people in 1990. This further protected agriculture by requiring all currently agricultural-zoned land to be rezoned to non-agricultural use only with the approval of the voters

5. Flood control on Napa River - Vote of the people in 1998 that approved a bond measure to restore much of the Napa River to its natural state, increase and protect wetlands, prevent frequent flooding of homes and businesses through the valley, and help revitalize the downtown Napa business area.

Of course there's a downside, too. Many small businesses and low-income residents are being displaced, a few property owners will make a lot of money, and the slow and easy character of downtown Napa is likely to be significantly changed. Whether that's for the better remains to be seen.

In fact, we can't yet tell whether this was a really good idea, a really bad idea, or somewhere in the middle. In the meantime, we'll list it under "Good Ideas", but keep a space open for it under "Best Bad Ideas That Actually Happened."

Worst Ideas That Actually Happened

1. Stopping passenger train service between Napa and Calistoga in 1929. Long-gone are the days when you could take the train from Calistoga all the way to Napa and then take the ferry to San Francisco.

2. Prohibition

3. "Redeveloping" downtown Napa by tearing down most of its historical buildings.

4. Allowing Wal-Mart, Home Depot, Target and other box stores into the valley.

5. Building "trophy homes/homes on steroids" on top of hills and ridges in the valley.

6. Bulldozing thousands of beautiful old valley oaks and replacing them with vineyards.

Worst Ideas That Were Fortunately Avoided

1. Building a freeway on the east side of the Napa Valley. (This one still pops up occasionally.)

2. Making Highway 29 a four-lane freeway all the way up the valley and into Lake County.

3. Expanding the city of Napa to a population of 198,000 by the year 2000. (Or 558,000 by 2020.) Fortunately we're only at 72,000, which many feel is bad enough.

4. Cementing the Napa River in the city of Napa area in order to prevent flooding. This was another brilliant idea from the Army Corps of Engineers, who brought us the now dead Los Angeles River (but whose reputation was saved by their support of the environmentally-focused Napa River project).

Top Misconceptions About The Napa Valley

1. Mt. St. Helena is an extinct volcano. (It's not extinct because it never was a volcano.)

2. Mt. St. Helena is the highest point in Napa County. (It's the highest point in *Sonoma* County, 4,343 feet.) The highest point in *Napa* County is Sugarloaf Mountain, 2,988 feet, northeast of Calistoga.

3. Napa Valley gets more tourists than Disneyland. (Napa Valley gets less than 5 million visitors, Disneyland approximately 14 million. This was a rumor promoted by the local daily newspaper and chamber of commerce.)

4. Robert Mondavi Winery was the first winery built in the Napa Valley after Prohibition. (The first one was Stony Hill, built in 1951. Mondavi was the second, opening in 1967.)

Most Uniquely Napa Valley Things To See And Do

1. Artesa Winery (Carneros)

2. Bale Grist Mill Historic State Park (St. Helena)

3. Beringer Vineyards (St. Helena)

4. Bothé-Napa Valley State Park (Calistoga)

5. Bridgeford Flying Services (Napa County Airport)

6. Buy a good bottle of wine (everywhere)

7. California State Historical Landmarks (throughout the county)

8. Veterans Home of California (Yountville)

9. Calistoga spas (Calistoga)

10. City of Napa walking tours (Napa)

11. Copia—American Center for Wine, Food and the Arts (Napa)

12. DiRosa Art Preserve (Carneros)

13. Downtown Calistoga (Calistoga)

14. Eating in a good restaurant (everywhere)

15. French Laundry (Yountville)

16. Greystone—Culinary Institute of America (St. Helena)

17. Hot air balloons (Yountville)

18. Napa Valley Museum (Yountville)

19. Oxbow Market (Napa)

20. Rubicon Estate (Rutherford)

21. Old Faithful Geyser (Calistoga)

22 Petrified Forest (Calistoga)

23. Robert Louis Stevenson State Park (Calistoga)

24. Robert Mondavi Winery (Oakville)

25. Scenic drives (throughout the county)

26. Sharpsteen Museum (Calistoga)

27. Silverado Museum (Calistoga)

28. Sterling Vineyards Airtram (Calistoga)

29. Wine Train (Napa)

30. Wine-tasting fund raisers (all towns)

Best Things That You Probably Don't Have Back Home

1. Hot air balloons

2. Mud baths

3. The French Laundry

4. Internationally known wineries

5. Small towns filled with gourmet restaurants

6. Vineyards instead of subdivisions

7. Copia

8. Culinary Institute of America at Greystone

9. The Wine Train

10. Napa Valley Opera House

11. Oxbow Market

12. Uptown Theater (once it's open)

Best Broadway Show Set In The Napa Valley

"Most Happy Fella." 1956. Music, lyrics & book by Frank Loesser based on Sidney Howard's "They Knew What They Wanted." Ran for 676 performances. Cast: Robert Weede, Jo Sullivan, Art Lund. Best known song: "Standing on the Corner (Watching All the Girls Go By)."

Best TV Melodrama Set In The Napa Valley

"Falconcrest." Starring Jane Wyman (first wife of Ronald Reagan), and a bunch of others. The winery shown in the series was Spring Mountain Winery, which still exists (see page 107).

Best Books on Napa Valley Politics

Napa: The Story of an American Eden and the more recent *The Far Side of Eden: The Ongoing Saga of Napa Valley*. Both books are by James Conaway and both are available at Napa Valley bookstores, and at www.napavalleybooks.com. They describe the players and events in the ongoing land-use battles in the Napa Valley. Grapegrowers, vintners, developers, politicians and environmentalists all appear in fascinating detail. Not everyone liked how they were portrayed in the books, but they all read them. We highly recommend both books if you'd like to know the behind-the-scenes story of life in the valley.

Photo Opportunities

You can take beautiful photographs anywhere in the Napa Valley. Here are some of the most popular locations for photos.

1. Artesa Winery (Carneros)

2. Beringer Vineyards (St. Helena)

3. Culinary Institute of America - Greystone (St. Helena)

4. diRosa Preserve (Carneros) - outside only.

5. Old Faithful Geyser (Calistoga)

6. Robert Mondavi Winery (Oakville)

7. Sterling Vineyards (Calistoga)

8. The "wine is bottled poetry "sign between Yountville and Oakville on the west side of Highway 29. (There's another one on the east side of Highway 29 between Calistoga and St. Helena).

The welcome sign quotes Robert Louis Stevenson—who was actually talking about France when he said "...and the wine is bottled poetry". But he liked the Napa Valley, too.

Websites

NapaNow
www.napanow.com

The most comprehensive and up-to-date guide to the valley.

Napa Life
www.napalife.com

Napa Valley Register columnist Paul Franson's excellent guide to wining, dining and events in the valley.

American Canyon Online
www.americancanyon.com

Online site for the American Canyon community.

Napa Valley Register
www.napavalleyregister.com

The valley's only daily newspaper, based in Napa and founded in 1863. Website includes the latest edition.

St. Helena Star
www.sthelenastar.com

St. Helena's weekly newspaper, founded in 1874, offers an online version of the latest edition.

Weekly Calistogan
www.weeklycalistogan.com

Online version of Calistoga's weekly newspaper that has been publishing for over 120 years.

Napa Valley Today
www.wineviews.com

The webcam of award-winning Napa Valley photographer Charles O'Rear shows a St. Helena Cabernet Sauvignon vineyard. O'Rear's latest book is *Napa Valley, The Land, The Wine, The People.*

Drive-Yourself Tours

Here are some ideas for "off-the-shelf" drive-it-yourself tours. The attractions in each tour are similar; only the length of time varies—from a quick journey through the valley to a more leisurely one or two-night stay. They focus on places that can handle large numbers of drop-in visitors. Ideally you'll have even more time to visit and you'll be able to put together your own personalized tour, based on the hundreds of listings you'll find in this book.

"I'm Just Passing Through"

If you're just passing through the Napa Valley, heading north or south to get somewhere else, try this tour. It's set up for those driving south to north through the valley. Simply reverse it if you're heading in the other direction.

However you approach the valley from the south, head north on Highway 29. Continue north till you come to Yountville. Take the Washington Street turnoff, turn right at the stop sign, then immediately left at the next stop sign. Continue into town, staying on the left at the fork. You'll find yourself at Vintage 1870, 40 shops in a three-story brick building on the west side of Washington Street. Stop, park, shop and/or have lunch. (If there's no time, just keep on driving through Yountville and pick up the directions in the next paragraph.) You can eat lunch at Pacific Blues at Vintage 1870, across the street at Bouchon, Bistro Jeanty or Hurley's, or at the north end of town at the Napa Valley Grille.

After lunch, continue north on Washington Street. Turn left at Madison Street (there's a stop sign there) to Highway 29. At the traffic light, very carefully turn right on the highway and head north. Approximately two miles ahead, just past Oakville, you'll see Robert Mondavi Winery on the left. Go into the left turn lane, then head into the winery. Park in the visitors' area. If there's time, take a tour. Otherwise just taste a few wines, take a few photographs, and head north again. Be careful as you make a left turn onto Highway 29.

A few miles further north and you'll be in Rutherford. On the right, just past the Rutherford Cross Road and the Rutherford Grill restaurant, pull into the Beaulieu Vineyard (BV) parking lot. Taste a few wines from this more than 100-year old winery. If you have the time, and the next tour is soon, take it. It's an excellent tour of wonderfully wine-smelling cellars and aging areas.

After BV, head north and drive through the town of St. Helena. Admire the quaintness of the town and overlook the fact that having a main highway through your quaint town is a traffic nightmare.

Continue through town, taking pictures out the window as you pass Beringer Vineyards and the Culinary Institute of America at Greystone on your left just north of town.

Continue a few more miles till you reach Calistoga. Turn right on Lincoln Avenue and drive into the heart of Calistoga's main shopping area. Here you can window shop, have an ice cream cone or cold beer (it's not all wine here), or, if you've suddenly decided you're not in so much of a hurry, visit a spa and have a mud bath and massage. Your *I'm Just Passing Through* tour is over and you're on your own.

"Five Hour"

Head up Highway 29 until you're just north of Oakville. Visit Robert Mondavi Winery on the left (west) side of the highway. Take a tour, taste some wine. It's the first of the major new Napa Valley wineries; that is, it opened in 1967, the first large winery built in the valley after Prohibition. Since Mondavi, several hundred others have appeared.

Leave Mondavi, turn left on Highway 29 and continue north. Just past the Rutherford Cross Road, turn right into Beaulieu Vineyard. This is the true monarch of the valley, built in 1900 and famous for its wines, particularly its Cabernet Sauvignon. Taste a variety of their wines, then tour the winery and experience the 100-year-old buildings. This place looks and smells like a winery. It's wonderful.

After BV, keep your car in the parking lot and walk into the Rutherford Grill for lunch. Good food, extremely varied menu, and very casual and comfortable. Good place for kids, too.

After lunch, continue to the north on Highway 29 and go into St. Helena. Wander around, enjoy the windowshopping, maybe even buy something. There are top-notch stores for all tastes.

Leave St. Helena and head back south. If you still have time, you can visit another winery, shop at Vintage 1870 in Yountville, or visit Moët et Chandon's Domaine Chandon sparkling wine facilities (also in Yountville but on the west side of the highway).

We mentioned the view? It's everywhere. Highway 29 is an incredibly scenic highway and you'll see wineries and vineyards galore on the entire stretch.

Enjoy.

"First Timer All Day"

Most first-time visitors tend to start at the bottom of the valley and work their way north, generally visiting wineries on the right-hand (east) side of the road. We suggest you skip the crowds and drive directly (but enjoy the view) to Rutherford. Visit Beaulieu Vineyard (outstanding wines, historic winery facility, excellent tour guides), then drive through St. Helena to Sterling Vineyards (beautiful winery, self-guided tour, and an air tram ride up and down the hill—there is a charge) just south of Calistoga.

After Sterling, drive to Calistoga, walk around town, and have lunch. Then do a leisurely drive back downvalley, drive through St. Helena (stop for a little window shopping if you wish), then visit Robert Mondavi Winery just north of Oakville. Mondavi is perhaps the best known winery in the Napa Valley. The tour is optional; take it if you have time and are interested in yet another winery tour.

After Mondavi, continue south on Highway 29 to Yountville and visit shops in Vintage 1870 (40 shops in an historic building formerly a winery/distillery built in—yes—1870). Be sure to leave town by 3:30 or 4:00 to miss most of the traffic.

If you want to have dinner in the valley, stay in Yountville and cross Highway 29 on California Avenue at the south end of Yountville. Just before the entrance to the Veterans Home, turn right into Domaine Chandon. Chandon has an optional tour and excellent sparkling wine. They're usually open till 6 p.m. They also have an outstanding restaurant —étoile. You may get lucky and find they have a table available for dinner.

Or, after your pre-dinner sparkling wine, go back into downtown Yountville and have dinner at one of the many outstanding restaurants in town. (Yountville probably has more good restaurants per capita than any town in California.) By the time dinner is over, you can head home, secure in the knowledge that you've missed the worst of the traffic.

drive out of the valley ahead of the pack of day visitors.

Which part of the valley should you stay in? It really doesn't matter. You're just minutes from wineries no matter where you stay. And the various towns are separated by about a ten-minute drive, so distance isn't much of a problem. Some towns, such as Yountville and Calistoga, offer many rooms right in the downtown area, so you can spend most of your time afoot. But you'll still have to drive to almost all wineries, no matter where you stay.

If you book a B&B room far in advance of your trip, you should be able to stay anywhere you wish. If you're trying for a last-minute reservation, or you're already in the valley and need a room right now, you may have your best luck with one of the large hotels in the city of Napa.

We suggest that each time you visit the valley, you stay in a different town, so that you can get to know one locale well on each trip.

"Overnight"

The Napa Valley Conference and Visitors Bureau would like you to stay overnight because that way you'll leave more money in the valley. We suggest that you'll find it a good idea for your own reasons, too.

By staying at least one night, you'll be able to enjoy a leisurely dinner, stroll around whichever town you're staying in, and go back to your hotel or B&B for a good night's sleep without having to fight the traffic leaving the valley. The next morning you can enjoy breakfast, shop, visit another winery or two, and then

"Midweek Weekend"

Weekends don't have to mean Saturday and Sunday. If your schedule allows, we suggest that you spend two nights in the middle of the week in the Napa Valley. You'll find far fewer visitors, a greater chance of getting a room in one of the more popular inns and, at some hotels and B&Bs, cheaper room rates as well.

Two nights gives you one full day when you can either kick back and totally relax, or fill the day with dining, wine tasting, shopping, even golf or tennis if you wish. If you want to relax, we suggest you book a room at a place that has a swimming pool, so you can lie in the sun with a book and a glass of wine. If you want to fill your day with activities, you might consider a B&B located right in one of the downtown areas, so you can walk in minutes to shops and other entertainments.

Read the various town sections of this book and pick a place that seems to offer what you seek. If you're looking for a full-service spa, as well as shops, restaurants and near-by wineries, Calistoga is the place to stay. St. Helena offers a good variety of shops and restaurants, as well as some of the Napa Valley's oldest and best-known wineries. Yountville is famous for its restaurants, and its many shops include those at the historic Vintage 1870 building.

The city of Napa offers hotels and B&Bs, excellent restaurants, museums, historical buildings and Victorians, and such visitor favorites as Copia and the Opera House. In Napa you'll also find movie theaters and other amenities that only the largest town in the valley can offer.

Wine Bars/Tasting

If you'd like to sample wines from a variety of wineries, but your visiting time is limited, consider *wine bars*. Wine bars offer you the opportunity to taste wines from a number of wineries at a single location.

In the past year, the number of wine tasting bars in the Napa Valley has greatly increased. There is a fee for sampling the wines, but the wine bars are convenient and they also give you a chance to try hard-to-find, limited-production wines.

You'll find the wine bars listed in the section for each town.

The city of Napa itself is home to the most convenient cluster of wine bars that you can find in any wine region in the world. To find out about the Napa WineWalk, see page 243.

Towns and Regions

Towns are listed south to north, starting with the southernmost town of American Canyon. Wineries, resorts and other attractions that are located on the Silverado Trail are listed in the *Silverado Trail* section (page 132), rather than by their respective towns. St. Helena Highway is also known as Highway 29.

Unless otherwise stated, restaurant prices are for dinner entrées only.

Bed and breakfast inns are listed on page 154.

All prices provided for restaurants, lodging, transportation, attractions, wine tastings and all other activities are subject to change at any time.

We debated whether to even *include* prices, since they change so frequently, but decided that they are good as a *relative* measure when comparing restaurants. Just be aware that the prices you encounter will likely be different (almost invariably higher) than those in this book—even if you bought the book the day it was published.

Varietals listed for wineries are also subject to change depending on availability.

American Canyon

American Canyon is Napa County's newest and second-largest city, incorporated in 1992. For those who drive north up Highway 80, it's the "gateway" to the Napa Valley.

Café Rosario's Pizza & Deli
3425 Broadway Street
American Canyon CA 94503
707.643.5464
www.rosariopizza.com
Pizza/Pasta - Entrees $7.95-$10.95

Home style Italian food from the former owners of Belle Arti in Napa.

Cartlidge & Browne
205-B Jim Oswald Way
American Canyon CA 94503
707.552.5199
www.cartlidgeandbrowne.com

American Canyon's only winery, with sales and tasting. Located at the end of Green Island Road one mile off Highway 29. Chardonnay, Merlot, Cabernet Sauvignon, Syrah. Exceptionally low prices. Also produces Manzanita Canyon and Stratford labels.

Fairfield Inn & Suites
3800 Broadway
American Canyon CA 94503
707.643.3800
http://marriott.com/property/propertypage/SFOAC
80 rooms - $130 and up

Operated by Marriott hotels. Complimentary continental breakfast, outdoor swimming pool, exercise room, free Internet access. 600 square foot meeting room accommodating 50 people.

Gaia Napa Valley Hotel

3600 Broadway (Highway 29)
American Canyon CA 94503
707.674.2100
www.gaiahotelnapavalley.com
133 rooms - $130 and up

Fitness center, four meeting rooms, free wireless Internet, pool, spa, business center. A totally "green" hotel that has been awarded LEEDS certification. You'll be amazed at the number of things the hotel has done to cut down on energy and resource use, all without skimping on a luxurious experience for their guests.

Marshall's Farm Honey

159 Lombard Road
American Canyon CA 94503
707.556.8088, 800.624.4637
www.marshallshoney.com

From Napa go south on Highway 29 toward Vallejo. The next road after Green Island Road is Napa Junction. Turn right on Napa Junction, then take the first right onto Lombard Road. You'll see the honey-colored buildings and the little red barn.

Natural and organic gourmet honey from over 650 beehives at 100 locations throughout the San Francisco Bay Area. From wildflower to eucalyptus to lavender to berry to orange blossom. Over 50 delicious varieties, depending on the season.

Napa-Sonoma Wine Country Visitors Center

101 Antonina Drive
American Canyon CA 94503
707.642.0686 800.723.0575 Fax: 707.642.4610

Tourist information, wine tasting, delicatessen, light meals and souvenirs. They can also arrange for last-minute lodging. Tasting bar offers a sample of four wines. Usually they'll include a dessert wine as well.

The Visitors Center is the first wine-related location for visitors coming from the East Bay. They have information on the Sonoma Valley, too, but naturally we think you should visit *our* valley. It's still the place for wine and beauty.

Paintball Jungle

Eucalyptus Drive
American Canyon CA 94503
707.552.2426
www.paintballjungle.com
Admission $20

Open every Saturday and Sunday from 8:30 am to 4:00 pm., weekdays by arrangement for private groups. Admission charge includes goggles and face mask. Gun rentals start at $20/day. Paintballs and CO_2 refills average $20-$40/day.

American Canyon Paintball Jungle is located in a flat, lush Eucalyptus grove just minutes from Discovery Kingdom in Vallejo. Its 50 acres of playing fields include forts, bunkers, a speedball course, a teepee village, and team practice fields. It's considered to be one of the finest paintball playing fields in the country.

Ristorante La Strada

6240 Napa-Vallejo Highway
American Canyon CA 94503
707.226.3027
Northern Italian – Entrees $12.95 - $19.95

On the east side of Highway 29 between American Canyon and Napa. It's owned by the same people who have La Strada in San Pablo, off Highway 80 towards Oakland.

Specialties include veal scaloppini, la strada (veal with eggplant and mozzarella in a light tomato sauce), carciofi (with artichokes, mushrooms and bell peppers), picatta, polo marsala, petrale alla Fiorentina, and gamberi bordolese (sautéed with garlic, rosemary and white wine.)

Carneros

The Carneros Region, with a climate similar to that of Burgundy in France, is a prime area for growing Pinot Noir and Chardonnay grapes.

Grapes have been grown in the Carneros since the 1830s, and the first Carneros winery, Winter Winery, was built in 1870. In the 1870s and 1880s, phylloxera destroyed almost all vineyards in the area, except the Stanly Ranch. In 1929 Beaulieu Vineyard and Louis M. Martini Winery began purchasing Carneros grapes, and in 1942 Martini purchased 200 acres of vineyard on the Stanly Ranch and later began planting Pinot Noir and Chardonnay.

The next key event was in 1960 when Rene di Rosa established Winery Lake Vineyard. The next year Beaulieu purchased 142 acres and planted Pinot Noir and Chardonnay. As the success and fame of di Rosa's grapes spread, more and more wineries purchased Carneros land. In 1985 the Carneros Quality Alliance (www.carneros.com) was formed, and it now has 29 winery members in the Carneros area of both Napa and Sonoma Counties, and over 40 vineyard members.

The Carneros is an uncrowded area with excellent wineries, low rolling hills and superb bicycling roads—if you stay off the highway.

Acacia Winery
2750 Las Amigas Road
Napa CA 94559
707.226.9991
www.acaciawinery.com

From Highway 121/12 turn south on Duhig Road. Follow Duhig for 1.5 miles, then turn left onto Las Amigas Road. Acacia is 100 yards up Las Amigas on the left.

Acacia has been producing wine in the Carneros since 1979. Now part of the Chalone Wine Group, it continues to focus on single vineyard wines. Pinot Noir, Chardonnay.

April in Carneros
800.825.9457
www.carneroswineries.org

Annual open house and festival sponsored by wineries in the Carneros District.

Artesa Winery
1345 Henry Road
Napa CA 94558
707.224.1668 Fax: 707.224.1672
www.artesawinery.com

Go south from Napa to Highway 12/121 and turn west toward Sonoma. Turn right on Old Sonoma Road at Mont St. John Winery. Go one block, then turn left on Dealy Lane, Proceed due west on Dealy Lane, which becomes Henry Road where the road curves beyond Carneros Creek Winery. Turn left into Artesa's driveway. (Not easy, is it? But it's worth the drive.)

In 1872, the Codorniu family of Barcelona created the first *methode champenoise* sparkling wine in Spain. 120 years later they came to the Napa Valley to create premium, distinctly California sparkling wine. They now primarily produce still wine here. The winery, initially named Codorniu Napa, blends into the surrounding landscape and is as beautiful as their wine as delicious. You'll find Chardonnay, Pinot Noir, Merlot, Syrah, Cabernet Sauvignon, Gewürztraminer.

Artesa Winery showcases the work of Napa artist Gordon Huether. (Photo courtesy of the artist.)

The view from the winery towards San Pablo Bay and the lower Carneros is gorgeous. But it's the art that truly sets it apart from other wineries. The stained glass and sculpture (inside and outside) by local—but internationally known—artist Gordon Huether is exquisitely beautiful. We won't attempt to describe it, because we can't do it justice, but we're sure you'll be entranced by it.

Boon Fly Café
4048 Sonoma Highway
Napa CA 94559
707.299.4900
www.thecarnerosinn.com/pj_boonfly.html
Modern Rustic Cuisine - Dinner
Entrees - $16-$19

The Boon Fly was named for a Carneros pioneer who planted orchards and vineyards in the mid-1800s. It's a gathering place for inn guests and locals, particularly since the Carneros Inn where the café is located also has a community post office and general store for people living in the Carneros.

The café offers breakfast, lunch and dinner, with a wine bar focusing on Carneros wines, among others. Don't miss the donuts.

Bouchaine
1075 Buchli Station Road
Napa CA 94559
707.252.9065
www.bouchaine.com

From Highway 121/12 turn south on Duhig Road. Follow Duhig for 1.5 miles, then turn left onto Las Amigas Road. Turn right (south) on Buchli Station Road. Bouchaine is on the right.

Founded in 1981, Bouchaine is the oldest continually operating winery in the Carneros, producing primarily Chardonnays and Pinot Noirs with some Gewürztraminer.

Carneros Creek
1285 Dealy Lane
Napa CA 94559
707.253.9463
www.carneroscreek.com

From Highway 121/12 (Carneros Highway) turn north on Old Sonoma

Road. Take first left onto Dealy Lane, winery is down Dealy Lane on left side.

Founded in 1972, with over 160 acres devoted to Pinot Noir. Owners Francis and Kathleen Mahoney also produce Chardonnay, Syrah, Merlot and Zinfandel.

Carneros Inn

4048 Sonoma Highway
Napa CA 94559
707.299.4900
www.thecarnerosinn.com
86 cottages including 10 suites -
$375 - $1200

A brand-new resort in the Carneros District located on the Carneros Highway (Highways 12/121) a short ways west of Highway 29. Cottages offer between 975 to 1800 sq. ft. of indoor/outdoor space, and include private patio and garden with gas-fired heater, wood-burning fireplace, high-speed Internet connection, bathroom with soaking tub, shower and heated slate floors, and a large-screen flat-panel television with DVD player.

Other features include the inn's private dining room, a full-service spa, swimming pool, bocce ball, croquet, and the Boon Fly, a café and wine bar, as well as over 1,000 sq. ft. of meeting space. The complex also offers 24 homes at prices ranging from $1,000,000 to $1,800,000.

Carneros Wine Alliance

www.carneros.org

Association of growers and wineries in the Carneros appellation.

Di Rosa Art & Nature Preserve

5200 Carneros Highway 12/121
Napa CA 94559
707.226.5991 Fax: 707.255.8934
www.dirosapreserve.org

Drive south of Napa on hwy 29. Turn right onto Carneros Hwy 121/12 toward Sonoma, and continue 2.5 miles. The di Rosa Preserve is on the right, just beyond Domaine Carneros winery.

Rene di Rosa was a trailblazer in developing vineyards in the Carneros region. His Winery Lake Vineyard was legendary for its Chardonnay grapes. He now focuses fulltime on his art collection, over 1000 works created in the greater San Francisco Bay Area during the latter part of the 20th Century. The art varies from stunning to whimsical (such as the late Veronica di Rosa's sheep and cows) to outrageous, and the environment is absolutely beautiful. There's also a gift store.

Reservations are required and tours can accommodate up to 25 people. Hours and days of operation are subject to change. Admission is $12 per person. Wear comfortable clothing because you'll be wandering around in what is also a nature preserve.

Domaine Carneros Winery

1240 Duhig Road
Napa CA 94559
707.257.0101
www.domaine.com

The Chateau for this sparkling wine producer was inspired by Chateau de la Marquetterie, the historic 18th century Champagne residence owned by the principal founder of Domaine Carneros, Champagne Tattinger of Reims, France. Their tour includes a DVD presentation in English, French, Spanish, German and Japanese. Sparkling wines and Pinot Noir.

Domaine Carneros Winery greets visitors along the Carneros Highway

Etude Wines

1250 Cuttings Wharf Road
Napa CA 94559
707.257.5300
www.etudewines.com

Turn south off the Carneros Highway about one mile west of Highway 29.

Tony Soter is consulting winemaker to a number of cult wineries. Now he's opening his own winery facility where he'll continue to produce his own label with its focus on Pinot Noir and Cabernet Sauvignon. It's at the site of the former RMS Brandy distillery.

Farm, The

4048 Sonoma Highway
Napa CA 94559
707.299.4900
www.thecarnerosinn.com
Wine Country - Entrees $20-$32

The Carneros Inn's main public restaurant.

Madonna Estate Winery / Mont St. John

5400 Old Sonoma Road
Napa CA 94559
707.255.8864
www.madonnaestate.com

Madonna Estate is on Old Sonoma Road just west of Highway 12/121 before it meets Highway 29. The Bartolucci family has been growing grapes organically for their estate wines for 80 years, originally in Oakville and now, for the last 30 years, in the Carneros. You'll enjoy all their wines, but keep in mind that their Johannisberg Riesling, Gewürztraminer and Muscat di Canelli are available only at the winery. Also Pinot Grigio, Chardonnay, Dolcetto.

Moore's Landing Bar & Grill

6 Cuttings Wharf Road
Napa CA 94559
707.253.2439
American/Mexican - Entrees $7.25-$12.49
Lunch every day except Monday. Also dinners Friday and Saturday, and brunch Saturday and Sunday from 9 a.m.

At the very end of Cuttings Wharf Road (turn south off Carneros Highway).

A funky right-on-the-Napa-River lunch and (sometimes) dinner spot that's a favorite of locals. Great *tostada ceviche*. Also burgers, sandwiches, enchiladas, burritos. It's particularly popular for weekend brunch on the deck overlooking the river. Pull right up on your boat, if you have one. A hangout for Carneros wine folks.

Brunch on the River—the view from
Moore's Landing

The Napa Valley Marina—you can
sail right into wine country.
(Photo courtesy of Kathryn
Winter)

Napa-Sonoma Marshes Wildlife Area

www.dfg.ca.gov/lands/wa/region3/
napasonomamarshes.html

Over 13,000 acres of saltwater
ponds, tidal marshes, and wetlands
managed by the State of California
Department of Fish and Game. Just
north of San Pablo Bay. This area is
made up of levees and sloughs. Many
waterfowl species and shorebirds
including the California clapper rail
can be found here. Most of the area
is accessible by boat only.

Napa Valley Marina

1200 Milton Road (Off Cuttings
Wharf Road)
Napa CA 94559
707.252.8011
www.napavalleymarina.com

From Napa go south on Highway 29,
turn west on Highway 12/12. Go 1.4
miles and turn left (south) on
Cuttings Wharf Road. Go 1.8 miles
and veer right onto Las Amigas
Road. Go .6 miles and turn left onto
Milton Road. Go another .6 miles to
marina.

Two-hundred deep-water slips,
storage, chandlery, sales. In the
heart of the Carneros wine country,
and just 9 miles up the Napa River
from San Pablo Bay.

Saintsbury

1500 Los Carneros Avenue
Napa CA 94559
707.252.0592
www.saintsbury.com

From Highway 121/12 turn south
onto Los Carneros Avenue, then left
onto Withers Road. Saintsbury is off
Withers Road between Los Carneros
and Cuttings Wharf.
   Richard Ward and David Graves
have been making Pinot Noir and
Chardonnay in the Carneros since
1981. They were convinced the
Carneros could produce excellent
Burgundian wines. Critics who've
tasted their wines agree.

Truchard Vineyards

3234 Old Sonoma Road
Napa CA 94559
707.253.7153
www.truchardvineyards.com

Small family owned vineyard
established in 1974, making its own
wine since 1989. Truchard makes 11

different wines including Cabernet Franc, Roussanne, Tempranillo, Pinot Noir, Chardonnay, Cabernet Sauvignon and Zinfandel. Tours and tasting by appointment only.

Napa

The City of Napa is the county seat and was founded in 1848 by Nathan Coombs. The word "napa" is of Indian derivation and has been translated as "house," "motherland," "fish," or "grizzly bear." The most likely is that it is derived from the Patwin Indian word "napo" meaning "house".

During Gold Rush days, cattle and lumber were mainstays of the local economy. Today the economy is based on wine and tourism. More than 72,000 people live here.

Napa is home to the most convenient cluster of wine bars that you can find in any wine region in the world. To find out about the Napa WineWalk, see page 243).

251TOGO
1420 Third Street, Suite 1
Napa CA 94559
707.251.8646
www.251togo.com

Food delivered from local Napa restaurants directly to your home. Order by phone or online. Napa delivery only.

Adobe House Restaurant
376 Soscol Avenue
Napa CA 94559
707.255.4310
Mexican – Entrees $10.75-$21.95

Napa's oldest and most historic building, the Adobe House was built in 1840 by Don Cayetano Juarez, whose land-grant Rancho Tulocay spread out over 8,800 acres east of the Napa River. It's located at the intersection of Soscol Avenue and the beginning of the Silverado Trail.

Watch your head when moving from room to room. Doorways were lower in the 1840s.

Alexis Baking Company & Café

1517 Third Street
Napa CA 94559
707.258.1827
American with a Wine Country Flair – Entrees (lunch) $9.00-$10.00

The "ABC" is one of Napa's most popular coffee and lunch spots. Highly recommended. For breakfast, try Alexis Handleman's scrambled eggs with potatoes and tomato-basil toast. If you're lucky, she'll feature her grilled vegetable sandwich at lunchtime. Don't miss the unique— and uniquely labeled—bathrooms.

Allegria

See Ristorante Allegria – page 68.

Alpacas of Napa Valley

3233 Dry Creek Road
Napa CA 94558
866.431.8978
707.257.2226
www.alpacasofnapavalley.com

Open seven days a week by appointment only. Visits can include shearing days, Alpaca husbandry and petting Alpacas. Alpaca wool products are available including sweaters, shawls, baby blankets, fiber and yarn, and even an entire Alpaca (or more) if you'd like to breed them.

Alston Park

707.257.9529
On Dry Creek Road on the northeastern edge of town.

Alston Park is a Napa City "open space" park. Parking for the 157-acre park is at the north and south ends of the park off Dry Creek Road. At each lot there are hiker entrances and bicycle and horse gates to allow access to three miles of trail.

Three small picnic areas within the park allow for views of the Napa Valley. Portable restrooms are available at the south park entrance.

American Center for Wine, Food and the Arts

See Copia – page 43.

Andretti Winery

4162 Big Ranch Road
Napa CA 94558
707.255.3524   888.460.8463
www.andrettiwinery.com

Open daily for tasting. Founded in 1996 by famed race car driver Mario Andretti. Cabernet Sauvignon, Merlot, Sangiovese, Chardonnay, Sauvignon Blanc.

Anette's Chocolate & Ice Cream Factory

1321 First Street
Napa CA 94559
707.252.4228
www.anettes.com

Ice cream fountain (they make more than 25 flavors), candy factory, wine-flavored truffles, sugar-free chocolates. They ship UPS almost everywhere. Anette is maintaining a 50-year tradition, and the quality is outstanding. Try Brent's Chocolate Wine and Liqueur Sauces.

Angèle Restaurant

540 Main Street
Napa CA 94559
707.252.8115
www.angelerestaurant.com
French Country - Entrees $12-$19

A French Provençal country farmhouse restaurant and bar run by Claude Rouas and his daughters Bettina and Claudia. Rouas founded the *Auberge du Soleil* inn and restaurant in Rutherford and *Piatti's* in Yountville. Located at the Napa Mill in downtown Napa. Outdoor dining available overlooking the Napa River.

Annaliên

1142 Main Street
Napa CA 94559
707.224.8319
www.restaurantannalien.com
Vietnamese - Entrees $13-$23

Friendly staff and wonderful food. Try the Crispy Rolls—meat or vegetarian—and the Ha Long Bread for appetizers, or the Green Papaya Salad. For entrees, we love the Vietnamese Crepe (Half Moon Banh Xeo) and the Lavender Sea Salt Rack of Lamb. Desserts are as beautiful as they are delicious. If it's on the menu, it's excellent.

Arts Council of Napa Valley

1041 Jefferson Street, Suite 4
Napa, CA 94559
707.257.2117
www.artscouncilnapavalley.org

The Arts Council's mission is to support and provide programs for the literary, visual and performing arts of Napa County. It promotes and supports the artistic community, provides arts education in the schools and holds the annual Open Studios event in the fall, where hundreds of local artists welcome visitors to their studios.

The Arts Council offers an excellent guide to events in the Napa Valley. It's at:

www.nvarts.org

Back Room Wines

974 Franklin Street
Napa CA 94559
707.226.1378 877.322.2576
www.backroomwines.com
Between First and Second Streets in Downtown Napa.

A wine shop and tasting bar. Winetasting by the half-glass or glass, as well as artisan cheeses and charcuterie. Tasting flights of six wines are also available.

BarBersQ

3900 Bel Aire Plaza
Napa CA 94558
707.224.6600
www.barbersq.com

American Heritage - Entrees $8.25 - $34.50

Menu includes pulled pork, grilled oysters, chicken and grass-fed rib-eye steak. Open daily 11 am - 11 pm. Sidewalk dining.

Bay Area Ridge Trail

415.561.2595
www.ridgetrail.org

The Ridge Trail is a 400-mile multiple-use trail connecting parks and preserved open spaces along the ridgelines surrounding California¹s San Francisco Bay.

In Napa County it currently passes through Skyline Wilderness Park heading east to Solano County. The trail segment west to Sonoma County is not yet in place.

Ridge Trail - Napa County Segment

Length is about 4.4 miles with an elevation change of about +900 feet.

Leave the picnic area near the Skyline Wilderness Park entrance and take gravelled Lake Marie Road, which crosses a causeway between two ponds, Lake Louise and Lake Camille. Lake Marie Road bends left (east), and in about 600 feet you turn right (southeast) off it onto Skyline Trail. In a few yards you pass the junction with Buckeye Trail.

Skyline Trail zigzags up a steep hill and soon enters oak and buckeye woods where the trail straightens, levels off a bit, and heads south. Pass the junction with Bayleaf Trail by staying right on Skyline Trail. Soon, pass the spur road which goes to the right through Passini Gate.

Just beyond, you begin climbing to high grasslands. Traverse a steep hillside, pass the skeleton of a house in a small clearing, and continue to follow Skyline Trail on an old, rocky roadbed through oaks and firs. Pass the junction with Chaparral Trail on the left, following a creek on Skyline Trail. Cross to the south side of Marie Creek, draining into Lake Marie below. Soon you reach the locked boundary gate near the southeast corner of the park.

Bay Leaf Restaurant
2025 Monticello Road
Napa CA 94558
707.257.9720
www.bayleafnapa.com
American Cuisine with
French/Italian – Entrees $14 - $32

Drive east on Trancas Street, which becomes Monticello Road. Drive one-tenth mile past the Silverado Country Club/Atlas Peak Road turnoff. Restaurant is on right just past Vichy Avenue.

A restaurant near Silverado Country Club with a focus on top-notch service. Extensive wine list with a large selection of half-bottles (why don't more restaurants do this?). Offers a comfortable bar, outdoor dining when weather permits, and free valet parking. Entrees include pizza, pasta, Beef Wellington, lamb shanks, pork and veal loins. Comfort food with a flair.

Beaded Nomad
1238 First Street
Napa CA 94559
707.258.8004

An incredible selection of beads of all size, shapes, colors and materials. Truly unique! Ready to purchase earrings, necklaces and other jewelry as well.

Big D Burgers
1005 Silverado Trail
Napa CA 94559
707.255.7188
Hamburgers

Popular local place with great burgers, milk shakes, fish and chips, salads, chili and more.

Bistro Don Giovanni
4110 St. Helena Highway (Highway 29)
Napa CA 94558
707.224.3300
www.bistrodongiovanni.com
Italian/French Country - Entrees $13-$24

From Napa take Highway 29 north. After passing the Salvador Avenue traffic light, continue for about 300 yards and turn right into the first driveway. The road turns right but veer left into the restaurant parking lot.

Overlooking vineyards and the hills beyond, Bistro Don Giovanni captures the essence of Italy with all the charm and elegance of the Napa Valley. Excellent menu featuring pizzas, pastas, grilled dishes (try the seared salmon with buttermilk), and exquisite salads (we like the spinach salad with Stilton cheese and fresh beets). We recommend the terrace on a warm wine country evening, surrounded by the gardens that supply many of the herbs and vegetables for your meal.

Bleaux Magnolia

1408 Clay Street
Napa CA 94559
www.bleauxmagnolia.com
707.252.2230
Nouvelle Creole – Entrees $16-$23

Seafood Gumbo, Duck Breast Jambalaya, Cornbread Crusted Catfish, and desserts like beignet and caramel apple bread pudding. New Creole cooking with a California touch.

Bookends Book Store

1014 Coombs (at First Street)
Napa CA 94559
707.224.1077
www.bookends-napa.com

General, children's. Napa Valley books and authors. Napa's oldest bookstore.

Bounty Hunter Rare Wine & Provisions

975 First Street
Napa CA 94559
707.255.0622 800.943.9463
www.bountyhunterwine.com

Mark Pope focuses on rare, limited-production wines, primarily from California but including wines and wine paraphernalia from throughout the world. He's in the historic Semorile Building, constructed in 1888 and located between Main Street and the river. Mark also offers a wine bar and *charcuterie* for tasting and fine snacking.

Bridgeford Flying Services

Napa Valley Airport
Napa CA 94558
(Halfway between Napa and Vallejo)
707.224.0887
www.bfsnapa.com

Tours of Napa Valley, Lake Berryessa, the Golden Gate Bridge and San Francisco Bay, and the Marin and Sonoma Coasts. Cessna Skyhawk (1-3 passengers) or Cessna Centurion (4-5 passengers).

A flying tour of the Napa Valley offers a truly unique and breathtaking perspective of our enchanted valley. You realize just how much of the surrounding area is still in its natural state. It's also the only way to see how the "other half" live (well, maybe less than half). The hills on both sides of the valley are filled with estates and compounds built by the wealthy. Most of these homes are visible only from the air.

Bubbling Well Pet Memorial Park

2462 Atlas Peak Road
Napa CA 94558
707.255.3456
www.bubbling-well.com

It's not exactly a major wine country tourist attraction, but the pet memorial park is open 365 days a year for visitation. The park is located in the hills behind Napa, two miles beyond Silverado Resort. Established in 1971, it is now the final resting place for over 10,000 pets. The park was the star of the unique documentary film *Gates of Heaven*.

Buckhorn Grill

1201 Napa Town Center (near Mervyn's)
Napa CA 94559
707.265.9508
American Grill - Entrees $6-$10

Buckhorn was a weekly hit for years at the summertime Chef's Market in Napa. Now it's permanent. It's a place for a tasty and reasonably priced meal, specializing in tri-tip sandwiches, chicken and salmon. Popular with locals and tourists.

Butter Cream Bakery

2297 Jefferson Street
Napa CA 94558
707.255.6700

Try their "champagne cake." No, it doesn't have champagne in it. But it deserves to accompany a glass of the bubbly. If you can't handle a whole cake, you can buy it by the slice. Lots of other goodies, too, all with Butter Cream's special touch.

Truly a Napa institution and a popular hangout place for breakfast or lunch. There's usually a line of people waiting to select their favorite goodies from a wide variety of delicious pastries, so don't forget to take a number when you walk in.

Caffe Cicero

1245 First Street
Napa CA 94559
707.257.1802
www.caffecicero.com
American – Entrees $8.99-$13.99

Open for breakfast, lunch and dinner until midnight during the week, and until 1 a.m. on Friday and Saturday evenings. Dinner menu includes soups, salads, pastas, sandwiches and burgers. Beer and wine. One of the *very* few late-night places in town so you can stop by after a movie, play, concert or other event. Comfortable décor featuring the old bar from the sadly-departed *Carriage House*. Acoustic music, book and dramatic readings, and other events.

Caldwell Winery/Cave

270 Kreuzer Lane
Napa CA 94559
707.255.1294
www.caldwellvineyard.com

17,000 square foot cave. Tours by appointment, $25/person. Bottle and barrel tastings.

CalWine

1215 Silverado Trail
Napa CA 94559
707.226.7671
www.calwine.com

Napa Valley wines, particularly "cult" wines, available online and at their Napa store.

Celadon

829 Main Street
Napa CA 94559
707.254.9690
www.celadonnapa.com
Wine Country - Entrees $16-$20

An immediate favorite of locals since it opened in 1996, now located at the historic Napa Mill. Owner/chef Greg Cole says his place serves "global comfort food." The 2002 Zagat Survey gave Celadon its Award of Distinction, and the Wine Spectator gave its Award of Excellence. The S.F. Examiner once said Cole was one of the Top 10 Undiscovered Chefs in Northern California. He's not undiscovered any longer, but he's still top.

Cellar Collections

1852 W. Imola Avenue
Napa CA 94559
707.251.9553
www.cellarcollections.com

Stephen Goldberg seeks out hard-to-find wine lots, and consistently sells at below winery prices. His store is located at the southern entrance to Napa on Imola Avenue, which is the street on the northern edge of Napa State Hospital.

Chablis Inn

3360 Solano Avenue
Napa CA 94558
800.443.3490
707.257.1944
www.chablisinn.com
34 rooms - $90-$235

Located just off Highway 29 at the north end of Napa. All rooms recently renovated and some include whirlpool bath or private spa room.

Chamber Music in the Napa Valley

707.252.7122
www.chambermusicnapa.org

Classical pianists, string quartets, solo violinists, opera singers and chamber orchestras in the intimate setting of the Napa Valley Opera House.

Chardonnay Golf Club

2555 Jamieson Canyon Road
(Highway 12 between Highway 29 and Highway I-80)
PO Box 3779
Napa CA 94558
707.257.1900
www.chardonnaygolfclub.com

Twenty-seven holes through 130 acres of Chardonnay and Merlot vineyards, lakes and creeks.

Chateau Hotel and Conference Center

4195 Solano Avenue
Napa CA 94558
707.253.9300 800.253.NAPA
(California only)
www.napavalleychateauhotel.com
115 rooms - $100-$175

At the north end of Napa just off Highway 29. Nine thousand square feet of meeting space.

Christian Brothers Retreat & Conference Center

4401 Redwood Road
Napa CA 94558
707.252.3810
www.christianbrosretreat.com
14 rooms, 2 suites - $115-$170

Surrounded by 500 acres of vineyards and wooded hills. Conference room and dining for up to 100 people. Perfect for individuals, focus groups, budget meetings, seminars, marketing "think tank," team building, retreats or just a company "getaway."

Cinedome 8
825 Pearl Street
Napa CA 94559
707.257.7700
www.cinemark.com

There's nothing unique or interesting about this theater. It's part of a large chain and exists solely to show mainstream movies. Despite its promises to the city the last time it was allowed to expand, it seldom shows art or independent films. The web site has current listings, but you'll first have to search for the Napa theater to find them.

Cole's Chop House
1122 Main Street
Napa, CA 94559
707.224.6328
www.coleschophouse.citysearch.com
Classic steakhouse - Entrees $16-$38

Greg Cole was so successful with his Celadon restaurant that he opened his dream restaurant—a classic American steak house. The menu features 21-day dry-aged prime steaks, certified Angus Beef, formula fed veal, New Zealand lamb and fresh seafood. And a large variety of martinis and other classic cocktails.

Sunset Magazine says the "aged prime steaks are incredible." You will, too.

Copia
The American Center For Wine, Food And The Arts
500 First Street
Napa CA 94558
707.259.1600 (tickets) 707.265.5900 (admin)
www.copia.org

Adults: $12.50 Seniors/Students: $10.00 Children: $7.50 Annual memberships available.

Copia is situated on 12 acres on the banks of the Napa River, a short walk from downtown Napa. The center celebrates America's contributions to wine, food and the arts.

Copia—The American Center for Wine, Food and the Arts.

It includes a 280-seat theater for films and lectures, a café gift shop, an 80-seat demonstration kitchen, a 500-seat concert terrace, a restaurant named after honorary trustee Julia Child (Julia's Kitchen") and 3.5 acres of landscaped edible organic gardens for hands-on learning about soils, farming and viticulture. It offers films, classes, readings, lectures, demonstrations, tastings and workshops.

Another feature at Copia is the *Wine Spectator Tasting Table* with wines from throughout the world.

Visitors can sample from more than 40 wines, changed monthly.

Copia offers a variety of wine education classes with such titles as *The ABCs of Starting a Wine Cellar* and *The Carpenters of Wine: All About Wine Barrels and Cooperage*, as well as Wine Certificate programs in partnership with the Wine and Spirits Education Trust. Over 40 different wine courses are offered, most paired with food. It also offers more than 200 food classes, including both cooking and non-cooking programs.

Visual and performing arts programs include photography, design, music, theater, film, dance, art, performance, literature, history, archaeology and fashion. Copia also offers an artist-in-residence Legacy Program for prominent winemakers, chefs, artists, poets, authors, filmmakers, dancers, nutritionists and scientists.

Copia is the inspiration of winemaker Robert Mondavi and his wife Margrit, and it was he who purchased the land and donated it to the non-profit institution for its new home, along with $20 million to get the project going. Many other individuals and organizations also donated funds. Honorary trustees include chef Alice Waters, good-taste expert Martha Stewart, and wine critic Robert Parker.

Copperfield's Books

3900A Bel Aire Plaza
Hwy. 29 & Trancas Street
Napa CA 94558
707.252.8002
www.copperfields.net

Used, antiquarian, new and bargain books. Free wifi Internet access.

Corley Family Napa Valley

4242 Big Ranch Road
Napa CA 94558
707.253.2802
www.corleyfamilynapavalley.com

The Corley family has been producing limited-edition wines for over 30 years. Their winery is also known as Monticello Vineyards. Try their beautifully soft Corley Proprietary Red, a blend of three wines. It's available only at the winery. Picnic grove available to visitors. Cabernet Sauvignon, Chardonnay, Pinot Noir, Merlot, Zinfandel.

Cuvée Napa

1650 Soscol Avenue
Napa CA 94559
707.224.2330
www.cuveenapa.com
American Modern Comfort Food - Entrees $15-$22

Bib Gourmand rating (good meals at moderate prices) in the Michelin Guide to the San Francisco Bay Area. Located adjacent to the River Terrace Inn. Indoor and outdoor dining. Excellent local wines on tap at very reasonable prices.

Del Dotto Wine Caves and Tasting Room

1055 Atlas Peak Road
Napa, California
707.256.3332
www.deldottovineyards.com

Open daily. Tours and tasting by appointment only. Located near Silverado Country Club in the historic Hedgeside Distillery building, constructed in 1884. Cabernet Sauvignon, Merlot, Cabernet Franc, Sangiovese.

DJ's Growing Place

4074 Big Ranch Road
Napa CA 94558
707.252.6445
www.djsgrowingplace.com

Family-owned and operated nursery.
All plants grown on site to ensure
they're acclimated to local
conditions. Friendly, helpful,
knowledgeable service. We use them.
On Big Ranch Road just north of
Salvador Avenue.

Downtown Joe's

902 Main Street
Napa CA 94559
707.258.2337
www.downtownjoes.com
American - Entrees $8.50-$18

Joe's is a popular lunch, dinner and
evening spot for locals and those
visitors who are lucky enough to find
out about it. It has live music almost
every night and "open mike" nights
on Tuesday. Not the place for a
quiet, intimate dinner, but nice
outdoor dining where you can sit
and look at the river. Great beers
too, brewed right on the spot at Joe's
own microbrewery.

Downtown Trolley

707.255.7631
www.nctpa.net/trolley

There's now a free trolley service
that travels a circuit in Napa,
arriving at each stop every 20
minutes. The trolley, a diesel-
powered replica of an early 1900s
trolley, stops at 14 locations,
including the downtown Napa plaza,
the Napa Town Center, Napa
Premium Outlets, Napa Valley Expo,
Copia, the Wine Train, Fuller Park in
the heart of Old Town and the public
library.

Napa's Downtown Trolley—Free rides
to key places in the city of Napa.
(Photo courtesy of Napa County
Transportation and Planning Agency.)

Each trolley holds about 30 seated
passengers and two wheelchairs. The
trolley also connects to the
city/county bus system for travel to
other areas.

The fact that it's fun to ride is
indicated by the number of local
residents who can be found on the
trolley. You'll like it too, particularly
if you're staying at a hotel or B&B
near one of the stops.

Dreamweavers Theatre

1637 Imola Avenue in the River Park
Shopping Center
Napa CA 94559
707.255.5483
www.dreamweaverstheatre.org

Local non-profit live theater. Small,
comfortable theater with a varied
line-up of shows. Examples from
their 2002 schedule give an idea of
the variety of their plays: *Steambath*,
David Mamet's *Oleanna*, *Getting
Away with Murder*, *Gross
Indecency—The Three Trials of
Oscar Wilde*, *To Kill a Mockingbird*,
Waiting for Godot, *The Man Who
Came to Dinner*, and *Measure for
Measure*.

Eagle Vines Golf Club

580 South Kelly Road
PO Box 2398
Napa CA 94558
707.257.4470
www.eaglevinesgolfclub.com

18-hole, par 72. Open to the public. 7,283 yards - six sets of tees including two ladies'.

Embassy Suites

1075 California Boulevard
Napa CA 94559
707.253.9540 800.433.4600 Fax: 707.253.9202
www.embassynapa.com
205 two-room suites - $144-$294

A large and conveniently located inn just off Highway 29 (take the First Street exit). All 205 units are two-room suites, each with two phone lines with voice mail.

Suites face the indoor, skylighted atrium, the outdoor pool, or the sun-drenched (and swan-inhabited) mill pond. There's also an indoor pool, spa, sauna and steam room. Guests enjoy a complimentary cooked-to-order American breakfast each morning, and an equally complimentary beverage reception each evening—with Napa Valley wine, of course. *Rings Restaurant* in the courtyard serves from an Italian menu, and *Joe's Bar* offers live music and great drinks.

Evans Airport Service

4075 Solano Avenue
Napa CA 94558
707.255.1559
707.944.2025 (upvalley)
www.evanstransportation.com

Scheduled trips to and from San Francisco and Oakland airports, with stop in Vallejo.

Filippi's Pizza Grotto

645 First Street
Napa CA 94559
707.254.9700
www.realcheesepizza.com
Italian - Entrees $6.50-$12

Basic Italian food from a small family-owned chain.

First Presbyterian Church

1333 Third Street
Napa CA 94559
707.224.8693
www.fpcnapa.org

Historic First Presybterian Church. (Photo courtesy of the church.)

A beautiful late-Victorian Gothic church, all of wood, built in 1874, and designed by pioneer architects R. H. Daley and Theodore Eisen. Designated by the state as a historical landmark and on the National Register of Historic Places.

First Squeeze Cafe

1126 First Street
Napa CA 94559
707.224.6762
American

Breakfast/lunch with dinner on weekends. Good vegetarian options.

Foothill Cafe & Rib House
2766 Old Sonoma Road
Napa CA 94558
707.252.6178
www.foothillcafe.com
California - Entrees $15-$22

An out-of-the-way place with tremendous food. Get grilled anything. Owner Jerry Shaffer was formerly a chef at Masa's in San Francisco. The S.F. Chronicle says his place is the equal of any restaurant in the Napa Valley.

Fujiya Restaurant
921 Factory Stores Drive
Napa CA 94559
707.257.0639
Japanese – Entrees $12-$17

Located at the Napa factory outlets, it's our favorite Japanese restaurant in the valley. The sushi is excellent with a wide range of choices served at the sushi bar or at your table. The rest of the menu offers dishes such as tempura, teriyaki and sukiyaki.

Fuller Park
Jefferson Street at Oak Street
707.257.9529

A city park located at the edge of Napa's Old Town. This 10-acre park is a favorite spot for picnics (25 tables and three reservable group sites) and birthday parties.

Located throughout the park are various monuments and plaques commemorating important events. Perhaps the most prominent monument is a watering fountain for horses and small animals. Moved to the park in 1965, the fountain was originally created to stand in the center of the intersection of Polk and Franklin Streets in downtown Napa.

Fumé Bistro & Bar
4050 Byway East
Napa CA 94558
707.257.1999
www.fumebistro.com
American/California - Entrees $15.95-$24

In north Napa, turn east off Highway 29 onto Trower, take the first left and the first left again (just past the John Muir Inn). Continue a short distance along the highway frontage road and you'll see Fumé on the right.

A comfortable neighborhood restaurant with a mouth-watering list of pizzas and pastas that might include Asparagus Ravioli with fresh sage cream sauce and baby cress salad or Rock Shrimp Pizza with braised leeks, sun dried tomatoes, kalamata olives and herb goat cheese. Entrees such as Roasted Sea Bass and Manila Clams and Oven-Roasted Sonoma Organic Chicken.

Genova Delicatessen
1550 Trancas Street
Napa CA 94558
707.253.8686
www.genovadelicatessen.com

A wide selection of cheese, meats and Italian specialties. They'll whip you up a sandwich or an entire picnic basket. If you can't find something here to delight your taste buds, you probably shouldn't have come to the Napa Valley in the first place. Take a number when you walk in, or you may be left watching while everyone else gets their food.

Gillwoods Restaurant

Napa Town Center (next to the
Visitors Center)
Napa CA 94559
707.253.0409
American - Entrees $7.95-$9.75.
Breakfast and lunch only.

One of the nicest places in
downtown Napa for breakfast or
lunch. Excellent comfort food at
reasonable prices. Outdoor tables.
Lots of people passing by. And it's
right next to the Visitors Center.

Grandpa Jacks Farm

707.226.9291
www.grandpajacksfarm.com

Seven-acre farm in Napa producing
heirloom and unusual vegetable
varities, free range eggs, and
occasional surprises like homemade
pies and Thanksgiving turkey.
Weekly box provides average family
of four with all the fresh vegetables
and eggs they can handle. Home
delivery.

Grill at Silverado, The

Silverado Resort
1600 Atlas Peak Road
Napa CA 94558
707.257.5400
www.silveradoresort.com
Wine Country Cuisine - Entrees $12-
$15

At the north end of Napa on
Highway 29 turn east on Trancas
Street. Continue on Trancas and
follow the sign to Lake Berryessa
(Highway 121 - Monticello Road). At
Atlas Peak Road turn left for .8
miles. Turn right at the traffic light
and drive into Silverado Resort.
   Hawaii-born chef Peter Pahk
creates wine country cuisine with an
Asian flair, emphasizing fresh and
sustainable products from local
vendors. Entrees include *Roasted
Fulton Valley Chicken Breast,
Grimaud Farms Muscovy Duck,
Seafood "Hot Pot", Saffron Scented
Fish Broth, Crab, Tuna, Scallops
with Traditional Aioli*, and *Merlot
and Vanilla Braised Lamb Shank*.
   The prices at the grill are
remarkably reasonable for such
outstanding quality and service, and
Chef Pahk is to be commended for
operating a kitchen that appeals to
locals as well as smart visitors. As
Pahk says, "It has been our mission
to create a wonderful restaurant in a
beautiful setting which is welcoming,
affordable, and convenient. Our
average dinner entrée is priced at
$14 and we offer complimentary
valet parking." The Grill overlooks
the golf course and is open for
breakfast, lunch and dinner.

Harms Vineyards and Lavender Fields

3185 Dry Creek Road
Napa CA 94558
707.257.2683
www.harmsvineyardsandlavenderfie
lds.com

Tours by appointment. Certified
organic lavender (actually their
lavender is not only organic, it's
biodynamic, which is even more
stringently controlled.) Open house
one weekend every June.

Hawthorn Inn & Suites

314 Soscol Avenue
Napa CA 94559
707.226.1878 800.527.1133
www.napavalleyinns.com
60 rooms - $149-$199

Located on the east side of Soscol
Avenue as you enter Napa from the

south. Studios and suites. Two phone lines in each room with T-1 Internet connection.

Henry's
823 Main Street
Napa CA 94559
707.257.3008

There aren't many stand-alone bars in the Napa Valley, and even fewer that are worth stepping into. Henry's is one that is. It offers honest drinks for honest prices. At an earlier location it had a back door off an alley where lawyers and judges could pop in unobserved for a quick drink and negotiations. At its current location it has only a front, very visible, door across the street from Veterans' Park, so the legal profession is seldom to be seen. At least during daylight hours.

As a matter of fact, until a few years ago, even Henry's was seldom to be seen. It didn't have a sign out front, so only the regulars knew it existed. But new owners decided they'd like some new, additional customers, and it's now clearly marked.

Henry's doesn't open until late in the afternoon, so if you're looking for action, wait until late in the evening. The later it gets, the younger the crowd is. Of course, if you're just looking for a good drink, any time is fine.

Henry Joseph Gallery
2475 Solano Ave.
Napa CA 94558
707.224.4356

"California style watercolors" by artists such as Vernon Nye, Justin Faivre, Charles Surendorf and Crandell Norton. Also Napa Valley artists such as Roger Blum, Jay Golik, Joanna Matthews and Kristi Rene.

Hess Collection Winery
4411 Redwood Road
Napa CA 94558
707.255.1144
www.hesscollection.com
Open daily for self-guided tour and tasting.

Off Highway 29 in north Napa, turn west on Redwood Road (to the east this road is called Trancas Street). Stay on Redwood Road approximately 6.5 miles to the winery on the left, being careful to turn left over a bridge at the junction of Mount Veeder Road. Look for the sign on the bridge.

A dramatic painting at the Hess Collection. (Photo courtesy of the winery.)

The Hess Collection is both a winery and an art museum. Swiss owner Donald Hess, who now lives in Argentina, has assembled one of the largest modern art collections available for public viewing in California. This remarkable collection complements a winery that produces superb wines. Plus there's an excellent 12-minute audio-visual presentation on the winery. Highly recommended.

Hilton Garden Inn Napa

3585 Solano Avenue
Napa CA 94558
707.252.0444 Fax 707.252.0244
www.hiltongardeninn.com
80 rooms - $109-$379
Located at the north end of Napa
just north of Trancas Street. Solano
is the frontage road on the west side
of Highway 29.

All rooms have two phone lines with
voicemail and high speed Internet
access. Includes the *American Grill*
restaurant and a wine tasting bar.

Humanitas

1081 Round Hill Circle
Napa, CA 94558
707.259.0349
www.humanitaswines.com

All profits go to charities dealing
with hunger, affordable housing and
illiteracy. Funds go to regional
chapters in the communities where
the wine is sold, not to national
headquarters. Chardonnay, Cabernet
Sauvignon and Merlot.

Inn at the Vines

100 Soscol Avenue
Napa CA 94559
707.257.1930 877.846.3729
www.innatthevines.com
68 rooms $102 - $252

Best Western hotel at the south end
of Napa on Soscol Avenue near Napa
State Hospital and Napa Valley
College. Swimming pool, jacuzzi.

Inn at Town Center

First Street
Napa CA 94559
144 rooms

Opening Spring 2008 in downtown
Napa.

In-N-Out Burger

820 Imola Avenue
Napa CA 94559 (Just off Soscol
Avenue)
www.in-n-out.com

Okay, so it has nothing to do with
the Napa Valley or even wine
country. It's just a California
hamburger chain. But if it's possible
to say "healthy fast food", this is the
place. In-N-Out uses 100% pure
beef, hand leafs its lettuce, bakes its
own buns, slices fresh potatoes right
in the store and cooks them in
vegetable oil, uses real cheese, and
puts only real ice cream in the
shakes. The wait is longer than most
fast-food places but that's because
they cook your order on the spot.
They don't use a microwave, heat
lamp or freezer. And their wages and
benefits are the best in the industry.
An In-N-Out burger may not be wine
country cuisine, but it's delicious.

Real fans also know the "secret
menu" such as "protein style"
(hamburger wrapped in lettuce
without the bun), "Animal style"
(bun is grilled with mustard, and
grilled onions, pickles and extra
sauce are added), and "Neapolitan
shake" (a mix of chocolate, vanilla
and strawberry).

Jarvis Conservatory

1711 Main Street
Napa CA 94559
707.255.5445
www.jarvisconservatory.com

An absolutely exquisite theater
devoted to an art form little known
in this country: Spanish opera, called
"zarzuela," something like a Spanish
version of Gilbert & Sullivan.
Situated in the building that once
housed the Joseph Mathews
distillery (and later winery), the

Conservatory offers classes and public performances of zarzuela and other operatic music. If there's a performance happening while you're in the valley (they're usually in June), give it a try.

On the first Saturday of each month, Jarvis hosts "opera night". Vocalists from around the San Francisco Bay Area come to perform. Tickets are $15 and include complimentary tapas, wine and mineral water at intermission. Tickets are available at the door on the day of the event, opening at 6:30 pm for ticket sales. Doors open at 7:30 and singing starts at 8:00.

Jarvis Vineyards
2970 Monticello Road
Napa CA 94558
800.255.5280
www.jarviswines.com

Tasting tours daily by appointment only. Cost is $15 per person. Four miles east of Napa on the road toward Lake Berryessa. The entire winery is located within a stunning 45,000 square feet of caves, with cast bronze doors, fiber optic chandeliers, and an underground stream and waterfall. Cabernet Sauvignon, Cabernet Franc, Merlot, Malbec, Chardonnay, Petit Verdot. Owned by William Jarvis, founder of Jarvis Conservatory.

Jessel Gallery
1019 Atlas Peak Road
Napa CA 94558
707.257.2350
www.jesselgallery.com

On the road to Silverado Country Club. Unique gifts, crafts, books, tools and decorations. Works by Clark Mitchell, Alan Sanborn, Brigitte McReynolds, Mei Yulo and gallery founder Jessel Miller. Jessel also offers Jammin'@Jessel's—music and wine on Monday evenings.

John Muir Inn
1998 Trower Avenue
Napa CA 94558
707.257.7220 800.522.8999
www.johnmuirnapa.com
60 rooms $95 - $210

At the north end of Napa on the northeast corner of Highway 29 and Trower. Convenient to both downtown Napa and upvalley wineries.

Jonesy's Famous Steak House
Napa Valley Airport
2044 Airport Road
Napa CA 94558
707.255.2003
www.jonesyssteakhouse.com
Steakhouse - Entrees: $9.75 - $18.95

Since 1946. Known by pilots all over the country who fly in just for lunch or dinner. Steak, chicken and seafood. A favorite of old-time Napans.

Joy Luck House
1144 Jordane Lane
Napa CA 94559
707.224.8788
Chinese - Entrees $6.95-$10.50

Mandarin, Hunan and Szechuan. Popular restaurant with "less oil, no MSG".

Julia's Kitchen
500 First Street
Napa CA 94558
707.265.5700
www.juliaskitchen.org
California-French - Entrees $18.50-$27.00

Hours vary depending on season and day of the week. Call for current information.

Located at Copia, Julia's Kitchen is named after famed chef and cookbook author Julia Child. Child was also an honorary trustee of, and adviser to, Copia. She not only donated her name, she also donated her collection of copper cookware to the center.

The open kitchen allows 75 guests to watch the chefs—and visiting chefs and cooking teachers—at work while they dine on regional and seasonal foods highlighting produce and herbs from Copia's own gardens. While at Copia, you can tour the three and a half acres of organic gardens. Reservations are recommended.

JV Wine & Spirits
First Street and Silverado Trail
Napa CA 94559
707.253.2624
www.jvwineandspirits.com

The place where Napans go for good prices on wine and spirits. It's just over the river from Copia. The largest wine selection in the Napa Valley, with over 1200 different wines, including more than 250 Cabernets, 320 Chardonnays, 120 Zinfandels and 140 Merlots.

If that's not enough for you, try one of the more than 115 different micro and imported beers. Wine tasting Wednesday through Sunday with a rotation of 45 different wineries.

Kelley's "No Bad Days" Café
976 Pearl Street
Napa CA 94559
707.258.9666
707.258.9667
California – Entrees $9.50-$16.50

Just off Main Street towards the Cinedome Theater. Kelley Novak offers a tasty menu that includes such dinner entrees as grilled ribeye steak with Cabernet sauce, grilled baby back ribs with Hoisin glaze, and sautéed seasonal vegetables with shallots and garden herbs. Appetizers include tiger prawns wrapped in pancetta, beef satay, and panko sautéed oysters. A comfortable local place with excellent food. Corkage $10.

Kennedy Park
On Highway 221 just south of Napa Valley College
707.257.9529 Golf Course:
707.255.4333

J.F. Kennedy Park is a Napa City park that runs along the Napa River. The 350-acre park includes five reservable picnic areas. The park also offers softball, soccer, volleyball, boat launching, hiking, a children's playground, and the 18-hole Napa Golf Course. The Pelusi Recreation building can be reserved for meetings, weddings or private parties.

Kirkland Ranch Winery

1 Kirkland Ranch Road
Napa CA 94559
707.254.9100
www.kirklandranchwinery.com

Open daily for tours and tastings.
On Highway 12 in Jamieson Canyon
between Interstate 80 and Highway
29. Sangiov ese, Gewürztraminer,
Sauvignon Blanc, Merlot, Cabernet
Sauvignon, Syrah, Chardonnay,
Pinot Grigio, Muscat Canelli.

La Gondola Cucina Italiana

1001 Second Street
Napa CA 94559
707.224.0607
Italian - Entrees $12-$18

Pastas, chicken, veal, seafood, pizza.
Traditional Italian food prepared
deliciously. One of our favorites.

Labyrinth at the Methodist Church

Napa First United Methodist Church
625 Randolph Street at Fifth Street
Napa, CA 94559
707.253.1411
www.napaumc.org

A walk-it-yourself replica of the
labyrinth in the famed Chartres
Cathedral.

The labyrinth is patterned after the
original in France's Chartres
Cathedral. Visitors walk along the
path, winding back and forth, until
they reach the center of the design.
Unlike a maze, a labyrinth has a
specific path with no confusing
choices. No one gets lost in a
labyrinth.

Walking the labyrinth is a sacred
act, a moving meditation that can
have profound effects on the walker.

The church's congregation has
designed an outdoor labyrinth with
the help of the Veriditas Project at
Grace Cathedral in San Francisco. It
makes the labyrinth public so that
others can enjoy the peaceful,
healing and self-understanding
effects of working with the labyrinth.

The labyrinth is open for walking
Monday through Friday from 11 a.m.
to 2 p.m. Groups may arrange for
group walks, with or without a
facilitator, between 9-11 a.m. and 2-4
p.m. Suggested donation is
$3/person. For more information,
call the church at the above number.

Laird Family Estate

5055 Solano Avenue
Napa CA 94558
877.297.4902
www.lairdfamilyestate.com

Tours and tastings by appointment.
On the west side of Highway 29 at
the intersection of Oak Knoll
Avenue. The Laird family has been
growing grapes since 1970 and
eventually opened their own winery.
The winery also serves as a "custom
crush" facility for a number of other
Napa Valley wineries. Chardonnay,
Cabernet Sauvignon, Merlot.

Las Palmas Meat - Seafood

1740 Yajome Street
Napa CA 94559
707.253.2036

Excellent quality meats and seafood. The fish is hand-selected every morning in San Francisco.

Lobster Shack

806 Fourth Street
Napa CA 94559
707.258.8200
www.oplobster.com
Seafood - Entrees $3.50 - $26.75

Lobster, lobster rolls, seafood, chowder, fish and chips, sandwiches.

Locos Tex Mex Grill

1040 Main Street
Napa CA 94559
707.251.8058
Tex-Mex - Entrees $7.95-$20.95

Grilled meats, chili and seafood entrees. At the former location of Belle Arti, in back of the building next door to the Opera House.

Mason Cellars

714 First Street
Napa CA 94559
707.255.0658
www.masoncellars.com

Tasting room near the Oxbow Market and Copia. They specialize in Sauvignon Blanc, but also offer Cabernet Sauvignon.

Meritage Resort at Napa

875 Bordeaux Lane
Napa CA 94558
866.370.6272
www.themeritageresort.com
158 rooms - $300+

Located in the Napa Valley Corporate Park.

Also includes 180 timeshare rooms. Guest rooms include 32-inch plasma televisions, wireless Internet connection, and DVD/CD players. Fitness center, wine tasting, local shuttle service. "Siena" restaurant.

Estate Wine Cave has banquet facilities and Spa Terra, the world's only underground spa cave. Eight acres of vineyards. Accomodates meetings of 10 to 1,100 with more than 14,000 square feet of banquet and meeting space, including 10,500 square foot ballroom. Private chapel holds 60 guests.

Monteverdi Spirits

P.O. Box 6079
Napa CA 94581
707.255.5368
www.monticellovineyards.com

Makers of Nocino, a traditional walnut liqueur in Italy and southern Switzerland.

Murals

Throughout Downtown Napa.

Outdoor murals depicting the history of Napa Valley.

The Napa Chamber of Commerce has an ongoing mural project, creating large hand-painted murals on the sides of buildings in downtown Napa. The murals depict various scenes and times in Napa's history. The project was initiated by Leadership Napa Valley and intends to produce at least one dozen murals.

The Napa River in the 1800s. One of the murals in downtown Napa.

Mural #1 - 19th Century Napa River

Location: First and Main Streets
Artists: Steve Della Maggiora and Susan Clifford

The scene selected for this mural is the Napa River circa 1900. The view is from the Third Street Bridge looking south. The two artists, Steve Della Maggiora of Napa and Susan Clifford of St. Helena, have used a realistic style with true colors and hues with a warm summer sky casting glistening shadows onto the river. The colorful history of Napa is exemplified with the many wharfs, mills, wineries, schooners and steamships. It is important to note that no 19th century structure directly related to Napa's maritime commerce still exists.

The schooner "Emma," piloted by Captain George Pinkham, and the sternwheeler "Zinfandel," piloted by Captain N.H. Wulff, are both depicted in the mural. Both men lived in Napa and their original homes still stand and have been designated City Landmarks by the Cultural Heritage Commission. "Emma" (on the left) began serving Napa in the 1870s and could carry up to 70,000 square feet of lumber, 25 tons of flour, 80 tons of wheat, or 60 tons of sand. The "Zinfandel" (in the center) was brought to Napa in June 1889. She could carry 250 tons of cargo, had facilities for 36 passengers, and made three weekly round trips (down one day, back the next) between Napa and San Francisco.

Mural #2 - Famous Napa Valley Residents and Buildings (circa 1907)

Location: First and Randolph Streets
Artist: Mikulas Kravjansk

Credit the 1908 "Napa City and County Portfolio and Directory" and extensive research by the artist for this remarkable reflection of Napa in the year 1907. Prominently featured are Sheriff David Dunlap (with hat), Napa Mayor David Sterling Kyser (moustache and sideburns), Superior Court Judge Henry C. Gesford (with beard), and Justice of the Peace (and later State Senator) Nathan Coombs. Shown on the newspaper page is Lena A. Jackson, school superintendent.

The mural also includes noteworthy buildings of the day, including (left to right) the Goodman Library, Napa County Courthouse, Migliavacca Mansion, and Central School. Prominent industries and styles of the time are also featured.

Napa resident Mikulas (Miky) Kravjansky devoted months of effort to this work of art. The Czechoslovakian-born artist has gained an international following, with his works featured around the world.

Mural #3 - Independence Day in Napa

Location: Pacific Bell Building (East side on Randolph Street, near the Napa Valley Conference and Visitors Bureau in the Napa Town Center) Artist: David Huddleston

A scene depicting the July 4, 1908 Independence Day parade. "Miss Liberty" (Mazie Behrens) rides in a vehicle invented by fellow Napan Lyman Chapman.

Huddleston is an artist and teacher of art whose primary medium is watercolor. He has taught in France, Mexico, Hong Kong and China as well as the United States.

Mural #4 - Hispanic Americans in Napa County

Location: 1127 First Street (across from the plaza in front of Mervyn's) - Artists: Cor Greive and Jose Charles

This mural honors Hispanic Americans in Napa County, including historic (General Mariano Vallejo, who once owned what is now Napa Valley) and contemporary (including Hope Lugo and Tala De Wynter, both local Hispanic community leaders). The mural also includes Mexican-American labor activist Cesar Chavez and Mexican painters Diego Rivera and Frida Kahlo. It's interesting to note that although the farmworkers who tend the vines and pick the grapes are the backbone of the Napa Valley's economy, not one is pictured working in this mural.

Mosaic Mural at Napa Mill

Note: You can also see a beautiful mosaic mural at the Napa Mill (see page 58). It's located in the Riverbend Plaza on the river side of the complex.

Napa County Historical Society

1219 First Street
Napa CA 94559
707.224.1739
www.napahistory.org

Located in the historic Goodman Building in downtown Napa. Books, manuscripts, photographs, maps. Operated by volunteers. Call for hours.

Napa County Landmarks

1030 First Street
Napa CA 94559
707.257.1836
www.napacountylandmarks.org

Napa County Landmarks is a non-profit historic preservation organization. Its headquarters are in the 1916 National Register building above Ristorante Allegria in downtown Napa.

At its headquarters—and at the Napa Valley Conference and Visitors Bureau, and the Napa Valley Museum—the organizations sells a $3 copy of *Historic Walking Tours of Napa*, an illustrated narrative on four different self-guided walks covering a total of nearly 100 historic buildings and sites. It also offers, also for $3, *Architecture Napa*, a guide to the land, buildings and styles of Napa County. Both guides are available through the website as well.

Napa Downtown
www.napadowntown.com

Website for the Napa Downtown merchants association. Click on "Visitors" and then on "Maps" for free downloadable maps for shops and restaurants, parking and the downtown trolley.

Napa Downtown Farmers Market
Copia South Parking Lot
500 First Street
707.252.7142
www.commongreens.com

May through October. Tuesdays 7:30-Noon & Saturdays 8:30-Noon

Napa Fermentation Supplies
575 Third St, Bldg A
Napa CA 94559
707.255.6372
www.napafermentation.com

Located at the Napa Valley Expo fairgrounds. A very popular place for locals—professional and amateur—to get the equipment and supplies they need to make their own wine, beer and olive oil.

Napa Firefighters Museum
1201 Main Street
Napa CA 94558
707.259.0609
www.cityofnapa.org/Departments/Fire/WebPages/Fire/museum.htm
Free Admission. Open Wednesday through Sunday 11 am to 4 pm. On weekends, call first to make sure they're open.

Napa's Firefighter Museum is a unique and popular attraction.

Features an 1859 handpumper, a 1904 horse-drawn steamer, a 1913 Model T Ford, and 1926, 1931 and 1948 engines. Also tools, equipment and uniforms, and badges from all over the world. A great place for kids!

Napa General Store
500 Main Street
Napa CA 94559
707.259.0762
www.napageneralstore.com

A specialty market and cafe with an outside dining terrace overlooking the Napa River. Part of the Napa Mill complex. Also offers pizza, picnic baskets, and a tasting bar. Visitors can choose from a daily selection of four reds and four whites, which are in turn chosen from a rotation of 25-30 varietals.

Napa Golf Course
2295 Streblow Drive
Napa CA 94558
707.255.4333
www.playnapa.com

18-hole, par 72. 6,730 yards Public golf course located in Kennedy Park off Highway 221 at the south end of Napa. Reasonable fees, uncrowded. Discounts for residents of Napa city and county.

Napa Mill

500 Main Street
Napa CA 94559
707.252.9372
www.napamill.com

Napa Mill includes the Napa River Inn and the Hatt Market. The project is located on nearly three acres along the Napa River, on the site of the 1884 Hatt Building. The former feed and grain business and flour mill has been redeveloped into a sixty-five room hotel, restaurants, shops and food markets. A weekend farmers' and craft market is also planned. This is one of the key features of the Napa River development plan and a favorite place for locals as well as visitors.

Napa Premium Outlets

Highway 29 at First Street Exit
Napa CA 94559
707.226.9876
Monday - Saturday 10a.m.-8p.m.
Sundays 10a.m.-6p.m.

Includes Esprit, Jones New York, Calvin Klein, J. Crew, Kenneth Cole, Dansk and Mikasa. Are these factory outlets filled with unique wine country gifts? No. Are they popular with tourists? You bet. That's why we've included them. And, if you get hungry, there's a great local Japanese restaurant, Fujiya (see page 58). It also has an excellent sushi bar. You can also get to the outlets from downtown Napa on the free trolley.

Napa River Adventures

PO Box 10881
Napa CA 94581
707.224.9080
www.napariveradventures.com

Guided tours of the river on a comfortable electric-powered boat. It's also available for weddings and other private charters. Package tours are available combining a boat trip with many other Napa Valley activities.

Napa Riverfront District

www.napariverfront.com

Organization of shops, restaurants and businesses along Main Street. Website offers news of events and other information.

Napa River Inn

500 Main Street
Napa CA 94559
707.251.8500
www.napariverinn.com
66 rooms - $159-$399

New, elegant and a couple of minutes walk from downtown. Rooms right on the Napa River. Restaurants and spa on site as well as shops. In the former Hatt Building, and part of the Napa Mill complex.

Napa River

(Information courtesy of Friends of the Napa River,
www.friendsofthenapariver.org).

The Napa River is one of the largest Central Coast Range Rivers draining 426 sq. miles on its 50 mile journey from Mt. St. Helena to the San Pablo Bay. The last 17 miles of this journey, from Trancas St. in Napa to Vallejo, are an estuary system. In summer, the salinity at Trancas may be 10%, in winter, it is freshwater.

The Napa River and its 47 tributaries serve as a linear wilderness running through the heart of an intensely farmed and partially urbanized valley. At one time, a dense canopy of riparian habitat dominated by cottonwoods and willows lined the river's upper reaches. For the most part, the gallery forest bordering the riparian zone is gone and the remaining vegetation exists only in the channel. Friends of the Napa River is working to restore the riparian habitat.

Wildlife Along the River

The endangered Chinook Salmon and steelheads spawn in the Napa River and in its many tributaries. The steelhead run has been reduced from historical levels of 6000 adults to a few hundred fish. Nonetheless, the river still supports an active recreational fishery. We find bluegill, black bass in the upper river; and striped bass, sturgeon and many non-game species such as the endangered splittail, yellowfin globy and silversides in the lower river.

Bird species dependent on the river include mallards, green-winged teals. mergansers, wood ducks, herons, egrets, kingfishers, rails and grebes as well as the endangered Clapper Rail. Mink muskrat, raccoons, deer, gray fox and bobcat also live in the riparian habitat

River Trails

1. Kennedy Park features a section of the Napa River Trail along the river.
2. At northwest end of Lincoln Bridge near Soscol Avenue go just right of River Pointe to enter the Napa River Trail, which runs along the west bank of the river north to Trancas.
3. At southeast corner of Soscol Avenue and Trancas St. walk in at right of bridge to connect with the Napa River Trail on the west bank of the river.
4. At the California Department of Fish and Game eco-reserve at the Yountville Cross Road. bridge is a beautiful spot to see the river.

Boating

1. Small boats, kayaks and canoes can be put in the river at China Point at First and Soscol streets in downtown Napa.
2. There is a boat launch at John F. Kennedy Park, just south of Napa Valley College.
3. Boat trips can be taken with Napa River Adventures leaving from the Kennedy Park dock.

Napa River Watershed

The area that drains into the Napa River contains 250 miles of streams and covers over 270,000 acres at the north end of the San Francisco/San Pablo Bay. It runs approximately 40 miles north to south and 15 miles east to west at its widest point. About forty thousand acres are vineyards, and 102,000 acres are range and grazing lands. Only 3% of the area is urbanized. Between 1992 and 1997 vineyard land in the watershed expanded approximately 2.1% annually. An additional 17,000 acres had to be replanted in the 1990's due to phylloxera.

Planning officials expect Pope Valley, the hillside areas of American Canyon, Jameson Canyon, and the western side of the Napa Valley to be the primary vineyard expansion areas in the future. They anticipate that over 4,000 acres will be planted in the next 10 years, primarily on hillsides, since there is very little acreage left unplanted on the valley floor.

There are currently 134,500 acres of Napa River watershed land in protected status in public or quasi-public ownership. This includes over 50,000 acres protected through fee title or conservation easement by the Napa County Land Trust. There are nearly 20,000 acres of the watershed under hardened pavement or rooftops, and over 6,500 acres of valley floor wetlands have been drained and filled since the 1800's.

The result is that Steelhead Trout runs that once surpassed 6000 adults have been reduced to several hundred. A Silver Salmon run that once numbered up to 2,000 adults is now extinct. Stream channel and floodplain modification has resulted in the discharge of more water at high velocities, producing increased bank erosion, sedimentation and downstream flooding.

In 1987 the Napa River was listed as "impaired" by the State Water Quality Control Board under the authority of the federal Clean Water Act. As we mentioned early, Friends of the Napa River and other agencies are working hard to restore the river to full health.

Napa River Trail

www.cityofnapa.org/Menu/MnuCo mmunityResources.htm

The City of Napa is also creating its own trail, running along the banks of the Napa River from Trancas Street at the northern end of town to John F. Kennedy Park at the southern end.

Currently, the segment from Trancas Street to Lincoln Avenue is in place, as is the area at Kennedy Park. The downtown restoration and flood control project will result in the completion of the other segments.

Napa Riverfront District

www.napariverfront.com

Organization of shops, restaurants and businesses along Main Street. Website offers news of events and other information.

Napa State Hospital

2100 Napa-Vallejo Highway
Napa CA 94558
707.253.5026
www.dmh.cahwnet.gov/Statehospita ls/Napa/

It's not a tourist spot, but this hospital for the mentally ill has had an important role in Napa's history and economy, and deserves mention. The 500-bed, four-story Gothic hospital building opened in 1875. It had a perimeter of one mile. Its first two clients were San Franciscans. It began on 192 acres purchased for $11,506 from Don Cayetano Juarez, part of the original Rancho Tulocay Mexican Land Grant that Juarez had received from General Mariano Vallejo. Over the years the property expanded to over 2,000 acres.

The land extended from the Napa River to the eastern edge of what is now Skyline Park, providing room for dairy and poultry ranches, orchards, vegetable gardens and farming. Farming ended in the late 1960's and most of the land is now occupied by Kennedy and Skyline Parks and Napa Valley College. The hospital's highest population was in 1960 with over 5,000 patients. The current population is approximately 1,000.

Napa Town & Country Fair

Napa Valley Exposition
575 Third Street
Napa CA 94559
707.253.4900
www.napavalleyexpo.com

The really big fair in Napa County. Held in early August.

Napa-Vallejo Flea Market and Auction

303 South Kelly Road
Napa CA 94559
707.226.8862

On the east side of Highway 29 a short ways north of American Canyon and south of Highway 12. Entrance is on South Kelly Road.

Sundays from 5 am to 5 pm. Over 500 vendors, primarily Hispanic, selling new and used items including collectibles, CDs, food, produce, furniture, and clothing.

Napa Valley Airport

2030 Airport Road
Napa CA 94558
707.253.4300
www.napacountyairport.org

No scheduled commercial flights. Private and corporate aircraft only.

Napa Valley Christmas Tree Farm

2130 Big Ranch Road
Napa CA 94558
707.252.1000

Take Highway 29 north through Napa to Trancas Street. Turn east on Trancas to Big Ranch Road. Turn left (north) and go 1/2 mile north. Farm is on the right. Open: Friday after Thanksgiving until a few days before Christmas. Hours Noon to 4:30 pm, but call first to confirm.

Five acres under night lighting. Douglas Fir. Cut Silvertip, Noble Fir, Fraser Fir and Douglas Fir. Special order trees. Commercial tree service. Certified flame retarding. Flocking available. Picnic area. Free garlands/boughs. School tours available by reservation.

Napa Valley Coffee Roasting Company

948 Main Street
Napa CA 94559
707.224.2233   800.852.5804

Freshly-roasted coffee in downtown Napa. At corner of First and Main. Small but convenient. They have a larger version in St. Helena.

Napa Valley College

2277 Napa-Vallejo Highway
Napa CA 94558
707.253.3000
www.napavalley.edu

Two-year community college. Specialties include nursing, law enforcement and enology. Also has upvalley campus in St. Helena which includes a cooking school (see page 144). Both campuses offer community education programs.

Napa Valley College Theatre

2277 Napa-Vallejo Highway
Napa CA 94558
707.253.3200
www.napavalley.edu
South of Napa on Soscol Avenue just south of Imola.

The Napa Valley College Division of Fine and Performing Arts sponsors approximately 100 events each year: plays, musicals and concerts (choral, jazz, and instrumental), including events for young audiences.

Napa Valley Conference and Visitors Bureau

1310 Napa Town Center
Napa CA 94559
707.226.7459
www.napavalley.org

Hidden in the Napa Town Center deep in the heart of downtown Napa, yet it gets tens of thousands of visitors a year. (Just follow the blue and white "Tourist Information" signs through Napa.) The CVB volunteers are outstanding: helpful, friendly and knowledgeable. Take advantage of their expertise to plan your valley destinations. (Even if you have this book, it can't hurt.)

These people volunteer because they love talking with visitors. And they love the fact that they're wined and dined by the valley's best wineries and restaurants so that they'll have first-hand experience of the area's attractions. Most, but not all, are retired, so they have the time to help you and your fellow visitors enjoy their home.

Napa Valley Country Club

3385 Hagen Road
Napa CA 94558
Golf Shop 707.252.1114. Business Office 707.252.1111
www.napavalleycc.com

Private course. Members and guests only. Reciprocal with other private clubs. Guest Fees - $90, includes cart. 18-holes. 5,285/6,148 yards - par 72. Three tees.

Napa Valley Emporium

1319 First Street
Napa CA 94559
707.253.7177
www.napavalleyemporium.com

A must as you wander through downtown Napa looking for some place to spend money. The most complete selection of Napa Valley-themed gifts and souvenirs in the valley. Art, gifts, clothing, t-shirts. If you don't want something for yourself, bring something back to a loved one.

Napa Valley Equestrian Center

1132 El Centro
Napa CA 94558
707.255.0302
www.napahorses.com

Ten-acre English hunt seat riding facility. Lessons, dressage, boarding, tack shop

Napa Valley Exposition

575 Third Street
Napa CA 94559
707.253.4900
www.napavalleyexpo.com

Expo is home to the annual *Napa Town & Country Fair*, which is held every August and is the biggest fair in Napa County. It's also the site of a large number of community and visitor events, including the *Mustard Festival Marketplace* in March.

Napa Valley Lavender Company

500A Main Street
Napa CA 94558
707.257.8920
www.napa-lavender.com

Located in the Napa Mill. Products from eight different types of lavender plants. Sachets, pillows, clothing, candles, bath salts, soaps and lotions.

Napa Valley Marriott

3425 Solano Avenue
Napa CA 94558
707.253.7433 Fax: 707.258.1320
www.napavalleymarriott.com
272 rooms, five suites - $129-$279

Turn west on Redwood Road, cross the Wine Train tracks and turn right on Solano Avenue. Hotel is on the left.

Two restaurants, and a spa. Heated outdoor pool and water spa. Lighted tennis courts. Fitness center. Summer training home of the Oakland Raiders football team. (They practice at Redwood Middle School just in back of the hotel).

Napa Valley Opera House

1040 Main Street
Napa CA 94559
707.226.7372
www.napavalleyoperahouse.org

The theater was built in 1879, and although never actually used for opera, presented everything from readings by Jack London and performances by John Philip Sousa's band to vaudeville, political rallies and local dance recitals. It closed in 1914 but has now been restored, offering theatrical performances and musical revues since June of 2002.

The reopening of the Napa Valley Opera House after 88 years dramatically added to the entertainment scene in Napa.

The Café Theatre on the ground floor has cabaret-style seating for 180 people, where patrons can enjoy wine and snacks before and after performances. The theatre offers performances of popular, jazz, blues, Latin, world and chamber music, as well as comedy and shows for the family.

The larger Margrit Biever Mondavi Theatre is located upstairs and seats 380 on the main floor and 120 in the balcony. It offers similar entertainment as well as plays, musical theater, opera and dance.

Napa Valley Redwood Inn

3380 Solano Avenue
Napa CA 94558
707.257.6111
www.napavalleyredwoodinn.com
58 rooms - $62-$148

Two-story motel. High-speed Internet access in all rooms. Swimming pool.

Napa Valley Soap Company

1644 Yajome Street
Napa CA 94559
707.257.1151
www.napavalleysoapcompany.com

Handcrafted soaps, lotions, bath gels and shampoos. Call for hours.

Napa Valley Symphony

860 Kaiser Road, Suite E (enter on Enterprise Drive)
Napa, California 94558
707.226.6872
www.napavalleysymphony.org

The Napa Valley has developed an outstanding group of musicians. Most concerts are held in the Lincoln Theater at the Veterans Home in Yountville. There's also an annual free concert by the river at Veterans Park in downtown Napa.

Napa Valley Traditions

1202 Main Street (corner of Pearl)
Napa CA 94559
707.226.2044 Fax: 707.226.2069
www.napatraditions.com

Traditions is a coffee house that also sells (and offers tasting of) food and wine. It specializes in Napa Valley products, including nuts, wine vinegars, olive oils, wine jellies, mustards and, of course, wines. Lots of wine paraphernalia too, such as wine racks, coasters, cork pullers and the like.

Traditions is one of the original coffee hangouts in both Napa and California. It's a quiet and cool place to sip coffee or tea, with a play area for your little ones to occupy themselves while you relax. Traditions is just across the street from the Napa Firefighters Museum

which is also a great place to take kids.

Napa Valley Travelodge

853 Coombs Street
Napa CA 94559
707.226.1871
45 rooms - $119-$159
www.the.travelodge.com/napa09557

Located in the heart of downtown Napa, a short walk from restaurants, shops and Copia.

Napa Valley Wine & Cigar

3780 Bel Aire Plaza
Napa CA 94558
707.253.8696
www.napavalleywineandcigar.com

Located in the same local shopping plaza just of Highway 29 (and Trancas Street) where Trader Joe's is located. A small but excellent wine shop focusing on Napa and Sonoma wines but also offering wines from elsewhere in California and around the world. A particularly good selection of ports and a wide range of cigars.

Napa Valley Wine Train

1275 McKinstry
Napa CA 94559
707.253.2111. 800.427.4124 Fax: 707.253.9264
www.winetrain.com

On-Train Restaurant: Wine Country Cuisine -
$85-$110 prix fixe

From Soscol Avenue turn east on First Street and take the first left onto McKinstry Street. Take the second left into the parking lot of the McKinstry Street Depot.

The Napa Valley Wine Train—
gourmet dining on the rails through
the heart of the wine country. (Photo
courtesy of Napa Valley Wine Train.)

A 36-mile, three-hour fixed-price
brunch, lunch or dinner excursion
that travels year round through the
heart of the Napa Valley.
Meticulously restored 1917 Pullman
dining car, damask linens, bone
china, silver flatware, lead
crystalware. Lounge and wine
tasting cars are resplendent in
polished mahogany, brass and
etched glass.

Wine Emporium stocks over 200
Napa Valley wines for purchase or
shipping. Special "Winemaker
Dinner" trips. There's also a less
expensive "open-air" car—the
"Silverado", and a more expensive
vista dome car. Basic no-food fare is
$40. A la carte lunches are $6.95 to
$16.95.

You can take the brunch, lunch or
dinner runs all the way to St. Helena
and back to Napa, or you can enjoy
the special luncheons that include a
tour of Grgich-Hills Winery in
Rutherford or Domaine Chandon
Winery in Yountville.

The Wine Train is fun, folks. If you
like trains, great food, great service
and/or a great view, take a trip. The
whole thing is done with superb
flair. If you think you'll be hungry
soon, make sure you get the first
seating. The second seating doesn't

happen until one and half hours
later when the train starts its return
trip from St. Helena—although you'll
have hors d'oeuvres and beverages
on the trip upvalley.

Napa Wine Merchants

1146 First Street (corner of Coombs)
Napa CA 94559
707.257.6796
www.napawinemerchants.com

A shared tasting room offering wines
from such wineries as Gustave
Thrace, Benessere, Bacio Divino,
Harrison, Liparita, Rocca, Michael
Scott, Young Ridge, Astrale Terra
and Hendry.

New Technology High School

1746 Yajome Street, Suite A
Napa, CA 94559
707.253.4400
www.newtechhigh.org

A unique high school for 200 junior
and senior students where there are
as many computers as students.
Students develop not only computer
skills but strong individual research
and study skills. All work is *project-
based* and much is done as teams.
Completed work is turned in, usually
as multimedia, on computer.
Students can also study at local high
schools and the community college.

New Tech High is a true pioneer in
digital education, and was created by
a joint effort of the local business
and education communities. It has
received a multi-million dollar grant
from the Bill and Melinda Gates
Foundation to replicate itself in
other parts of the country. While it
isn't open to the public, educators
can arrange a tour by appointment.

The author's daughter attended this school and he was particularly impressed by two non-academic features: The students are treated as adults, and the school is spotless; no graffiti, no trash. There just might be a connection.

N.V. Restaurant & Lounge
1106 First Street
Napa CA 94559
707.265.6400
www.nvrestaurantandlounge.com
Wine Country - Entrees $20 - $27

Chef/owner Peter Halikas, former executive chef at Dean & DeLuca, has opened a new restaurant on the downtown plaza at the former location of Bombay Bistro, next to Mervyn's. Entrees such as beef tenderloin, herb crusted lamb loin, and seared scallops. Outdoor seating.

Organic Abundance
PO Box 3144
Napa CA 94558
707.251.5500
Napa CA
www.organicabundance.com

Regional organic produce delivered weekly or bimonthly to your home in Carneros, Napa, Yountville, Oakville, Rutherford and St. Helena. Call for brochure.

Osprey Seafood Market
1014 Wine Country Avenue
Napa CA 94558
707.252.9120

At the north end of Napa just west of Highway 29. An attractive selection of deliciously fresh seafood. Includes live crab and lobster.

Oxbow Public Market
600 First Street (next to Copia)
Napa CA 94559
www.oxbowpublicmarket.com

Food vendors and small restaurants similar to those at the Ferry Building Marketplace in San Francisco. Plans currently include around 30 tenants, including four mini-restaurants, a bakery, and meat, fish and produce vendors. The Market is being overseen by Steve Carlin, the project manager for the Ferry Building attraction. Scheduled to open in Fall 2007 on the other side of the parking lot from Copia.

Oxbow School
530 Third Street
Napa, CA, USA 94559
707.255.6000
www.oxbowschool.org

This school, a short walk from downtown Napa, was founded by Bay Area resident Ann Hatch, who also founded the Capp Street Project in San Francisco. Her goal was to "give young people meaningful access to living artists and a chance to practice [visual] art at a high level." She was joined in the project by Robert and Margrit Mondavi, who at the same time were also launching the nearby *Copia—The American Center for Wine, Food and the Arts*. The school opened in 1999.

The Oxbow School is open to high school juniors and seniors who come from across the country and abroad for a one-semester residential program. There are no public tours, but occasional guest lectures by visiting artists are free and open to the public.

Palmaz Vineyards
4029 Hagan Road
Napa CA 94556
707.226.5587
www.palmazwinery.com

The winery was built by the co-inventor of the "stent" used for heart patients.The entire winemaking and aging takes place in a wine cave 18 stories deep. The fermentation dome is the world's largest underground reinforced structure. Produces Cabernet Sauvignon, Chardonnay, Johannisberg Riesling and Muscat Canelli.

Pasta Prego
3206 Jefferson Street
Napa CA 94558
707.224.9011
www.pastapregonapa.com
Italian - Entrees $11.95-$18.95

Excellent food in a neighborhood restaurant in a small, non-descript mall. The locals all know about it, and apparently some of them have passed on news of its existence to visitors as well. The usual palette of pastas—lasagna, ravioli, fettuccini—all with delicious sauces, as well as risotto, pizzas, veal piccatta and fish. On our last visit we had Gamberi e Finocchio, sauteed prawns on a bed of leek pancake with fennel, and a sun-dried tomato shrimp and cumin sauce. And that was just for openers.

Pearl
1339 Pearl Street #104
Napa CA 94559
707.224.9161 Fax: 707.255.6825
www.therestaurantpearl.com
California Cuisine - Entrees $9.75 - $18.95

Open for lunch and dinner Tuesday through Saturday. Pearl owners Nickie and Pete Zeller formerly owned the Brown Street Grill in Napa, and Nickie was co-owner of the legendary Diner in Yountville. Pearl is a gem and one of Napa's very best restaurants. The beautiful hex symbol paintings on the walls are all for sale.

Peterson Family Christmas Tree Farm
1120 Darms Lane
Napa CA 94558
707.259.1712

Go north on Highway 29 through Napa. North of Napa, turn left at the signal lights at Oak Knoll Avenue. Immediately turn right on Solano Avenue, which is the frontage road. Continue almost one mile on Solano to Darms Lane and turn left. The farm is a short distance down Darms Lane on the righthand side.

Open Friday after Thanksgiving to approximately December 20th on Fridays, Saturdays and Sundays from 9 am - 5 pm.

3.5 acres of Douglas and White Fir and Norway Spruce. Also walnuts and other assorted goodies.

Piccolino's Italian Café
1385 Napa Town Center
Napa, CA 94559
707.251.0100 Fax: 707.224.1232
Entrance on First Street at Franklin
www.piccolinoscafe.com
Old World Italian - Entrees $10.95-$17.95

A popular Italian restaurant on downtown Napa's main street. Comfortable atmosphere with lots of windows so you can look out on sidewalk and street. Pasta, seafood and meat specials, wine bar with music on Friday and Saturday evenings, Italian night every Wednesday evening with an Italian accordionist. Patio dining available in season. Lunch and dinners seven days a week.

Pilar
807 Main Street
Napa CA 94559
707.253.8203

Pilar Sanchez is the former executive chef of the Wine Spectator restaurant at the Culinary Institute of America at Greystone in St. Helena. She and co-owner Dieder Lender were both previously chefs at Meadowood Resort in St. Helena. Now they have their own place in downtown Napa.

Pizza Azzurro
1400 Second at Franklin
Napa CA 94559
707.255.5552
Pizza – Entrees $8.95-$10.95

Chef/owner Michael Gyetvan offers pizzas, pastas, salads and wine at prices that appeal to locals. But it's not your local pizza joint. Gyetvan is a graduate of the Culinary Institute of America in New York and former *chef de cuisine* at *Tra Vigne* in St. Helena. The place is casual and comfortable, and the food, featuring local produce, is delicious and very popular.

Red Hen Cantina
4175 Solano Avenue
Napa CA 94559
707.255.8125
www.redhencantina.com
Mexican - Entrees $ 9.75-$15.95

For years the Red Hen was located further north of Napa on the west side of Highway 29. It had a great outdoor dining area with a view of vineyards and hills. It's now in Napa at the former location of Pairs Restaurant. It's still got outdoor dining on the deck.

Red Rock Café and Catering
1010 Lincoln Avenue
Napa CA 94558
707.226.2633
American Burger - Entrees $4.50-$14.95

Great hamburgers and onion rings. Tri-tip and barbecued ribs, too. Consistently voted the best hamburger in Napa.

Ristorante Allegria
1026 First Street
Napa CA 94559
707.254.8006
www.ristoranteallegria.com
Northern Italian - Entrees $10.95-$23.95

Northern Italian food with an elegant décor. Located in an historic bank building in Downtown Napa next to the plaza (where the much-despised Clocktower formerly stood). Friends say it has the best tiramisu they've ever tasted.

River City Bar & Grill
505 Lincoln Avenue
Napa CA 94558
707.253.1111
American - Entrees $16-$25
www.rivercitynapa.com

Traditional menu with entrees such as salmon, halibut, chicken, pork chops, lamb and steak. Very pleasant outdoor dining with a view of the Napa River. 3,000 sq. ft. of banquet facilities.

Riverdog Farm

PO Box 42
Guinda CA 95637
916.796.3802
riverdog@yolo.com

A community supported agriculture (CSA) farm that delivers organic produce in Napa, St. Helena and Oakville

River Terrace Inn

1600 Soscol Avenue
Napa CA 94559
866.627.2386
www.riverterraceinn.com
106 guest rooms including 28 suites - $139-$339

An "upscale boutique hotel"on the Napa River. Complimentary high-speed Internet and Wi-Fi access, wine bar with tapas, pool, and all suites have whirlpool/hot tubs. A stop on the Downtown Trolley route and a close walk to the Wine Train station.

Robert Craig Wine Cellars

880 Vallejo Street
Napa CA 94559
707.252.2250
www.robertcraigwine.com
Tasting $5/glass.

From downtown Napa take Main Street north to Vallejo. Turn right and continue two blocks east.

Although his wine is made elsewhere and comes from vineyards in such varied locations as Coombsville, Mt. Veeder, Howell Mountain and the Carneros, Robert Craig has opened a convenient tasting room just minutes from downtown Napa. Stop by to try his wines or phone in advance for a barrel tasting.

Cabernet Sauvignon, Chardonnay, Syrah, Zinfandel.

Rocca Family Vineyards

1130 Main Street
Napa CA 94559
707.257.8467
www.roccawines.com

Although their vineyard is in Yountville, Rocca offers tasting and sales at their tasting room in Napa. By the tasting, glass or bottle. Cabernet Sauvignon, Merlot, Syrah.

Royal Oak

Silverado Resort
1600 Atlas Peak Road
Napa CA 94558
707.257.5400
www.silveradoresort.com
Regional Specialties - Entrees $25-$38

At the north end of Napa on Highway 29 turn east on Trancas Street. Continue on Trancas and follow the sign to Lake Berryessa (Highway 121 - Monticello Road). At Atlas Peak Road turn left for .8 miles. Turn right at the traffic light and drive into Silverado Resort.

Hawaii-born chef Peter Pahk turns out a wide variety of wonderful food featuring everything from *Grilled Kauai White Prawns*, to *Hawaiian Swordfish* to *Triple Cut Baby Lamb Chops* and *Muscovy Duck Breast*. Pahk focuses on local vendors to turn out his outstanding regional dishes. Dinner only. Dress is Resort Casual, one of the few places in the valley that ask you to dress up a little.

Seguin Moreau Napa Cooperage

151 Camino Dorado
Napa CA 94558
707.252.3408
www.seguin-moreau.fr
Small charge for tour. Just off Highway 29 south of Napa. Call for directions.

How many places can you actually watch wine barrels being made? A fascinating part of the wine business that most visitors miss. A wonderful educational experience for kids as they watch skilled coopers plying their art in nearly the same fashion as their ancestors have for hundreds of years. Yes, kids, people still do this. And isn't it neat the way they build a fire inside the barrel to "toast" it?

Shackford's Kitchen Store and More

1350 Main Street
Napa CA 94559
707.226.2132
Open Monday through Saturday, 9:30 a.m. to 5:30 p.m.

Complete collection of cookware and cutlery (they'll sharpen your knives, too), kitchen accessories, baskets and gifts, canning and candymaking tools. This place is absolutely loaded with kitchen stuff. We always walk out with something, generally more than we came in for. It's the kind of place every town used to have. Napa still has one. The staff is friendly and knowledgeable and its prices are competitive with factory outlet stores. What more could you ask?

Siam Thai House

1139 Lincoln Avenue
Napa CA 94558
707.226.7749
www.siamthaihouse.micronpcweb
.com
Thai

Authentic Thai restaurant open for lunch and dinner.

Siena

Meritage Resort
875 Bordeaux Way
Napa CA 94558
707.251.1950
www.themeritageresort.com
Wine Country Tuscan - Entrees $18-$34

Tuscan-themed restaurant that specializes in wine country/Tuscan-food.

Silverado Resort

See Silverado Trail section – page 137.

Skyline Wilderness Park

2210 Imola Avenue
Napa CA
707.252.0481
www.skylinepark.org
Hours: Monday-Thursday 9 a.m. to dark Friday-Sunday 8 a.m. to dark

Skyline Park is an 850-acre wilderness area, totally operated by volunteers. It has over 25 miles of trails for hiking, biking and equestrian use. (If you're put off by the occasional horse droppings, keep in mind that it was the horse people that saved the park.)

The two-and-a-half mile main trail leads to Lake Marie at the eastern end. There's also an alternate route along the ridge trail that is a much better workout, but is not for those out of shape. From this trail on a clear day you can see San Francisco Bay, Mr. Tamalpais and Mr. Diablo. Beautiful.

Skyline also offers picnic and barbecue areas, an RV park, and tent camping. Daily visitor's fee is $4.00 per vehicle, RV camping is $14.00, and tent sites are $8.00. The best place to hike in Napa.

Small World
932 Coombs Street
Napa CA 94559
707.224.7743
Mediterranean/Middle Eastern

Just off First Street. Falafel, gyros, shwarma, salads, smoothies. Delicious food at very reasonable prices.

Squeeze Inn
3383 Solano Avenue
Napa CA 94558
Hamburgers

Next to Vallerga's off Redwood Road. Legendary (in its home of Sacramento) burger joint. People claim it's the best burger (try it with the cheese skirt) they've ever had—anywhere. Also tacos and sandwiches.

Stave Wine Lounge
1149 First Street
Napa CA 94559
707.259.5411
www.stavewinelounge.com

Wine bar with automatic wine dispensers. Buy a card, then use it to pour yourself one of the many available wines from small Napa Valley producers and elsewhere. The dispensers automatically give you a one-ounce taste. You can also buy a bottle of any of the tasting wines, and take it home or sit back and enjoy it in Stave's comfortable surroundings.

Thirty-two wines available for tasting, including eight international wines. Cost per ounce tasting ranges from $1.10 to $9.00. By the bottle from $10 - $100. Local wineries include Venge, Igneous, Macauley, Punk dog, Parallel, Trespass and Terraces. Free wi-fi. [Accepts "Taste Napa Downtown" card]

Suppertime
2977 Solano Avenue
Napa CA 94558
707.224.3097
www.suppertimeinnapa.com
American - Entrees $6.50-$10.50

Full take-out meals. Lunch Mon-Fri, Dinner Mon-Sat. Or you can eat there and even enjoy Irish music on Friday nights.

Sweeney's Sport Store
River Park Shopping Center
1537 Imola Avenue West
Napa CA 94559
707.255.5544

Open 7 days a week. Sweeney's is fishing center for tackle and information. Free flycasting classes every Saturday morning at 9 a.m.

Stonehedge Winery
1004 Clinton Street
Napa CA 94559
707.256.4444
www.stonehedgewinery.com

The winery's upvalley but the tasting room is in Napa. Cabernet Sauvignon, Merlot, Pinot Noir, Syrah, Petite Sirah, Zinfandel, Chardonnay and Sauvignon Blanc.

Sweetie Pies

520 Main Street
Napa CA 94559
707.257.8817
www.sweetiepies.com

A bakery located at the Hatt Mill that offers light lunches, coffee, breads and individual desserts as well as specialty cakes, breakfast pastries and cookies. Also offers wine and beer. Open seven days a week.

Taco Trucks

Along Soscol Avenue between First Street and Lincoln Avenue
Mexican - $1.25 and up

In the afternoon and early evening you'll find trucks with kitchens and serving windows parked along both sides of Soscol Avenue. These independently-owned mobile restaurants cook and sell Mexican food such as tacos, quesadillas and burritos. Customers sit on the grass along the sidewalk, eat in their cars or take their meals home. It's tasty, home-made fast food at a very reasonable price.

Trader Joe's

3654 Bel Aire Plaza
Napa CA 94558
www.traderjoes.com

Located just off Trancas Street at Highway 29. Turn east on Trancas and take the first left into the shopping center.

A chain of nearly 200 stores located throughout the United States. Trader Joe's offers food (fresh and packaged —much of it organic and/or vegetarian) and beverages, including spirits and wines. Their selection includes specialty and imported items, and prices on everything are exceptionally low. Trader Joe's has built a fanatic following of customers, and the public clamor (including letters to the editor) for a TJ's in the Napa Valley took on near-cargo cult dimensions. The pleas were successful.

Trancas Steak House

999 Trancas Street
Napa CA 94558
707.258.9990
www.trancassteakhouse.com
American - Entrees: $11.95-$25.95

Steak house open for lunch and dinner. Outdoor dining. Bar open till 2 am.

Tulocay Cemetery

411 Coombsville Road
Napa CA 94558
707.252.4727
www.tulocaycemetery.org
Open 8 a.m. to sundown

Napa's historic cemetery, 50 acres established on land deeded in 1858 by Don Cayetano Juarez from his 8,800-acre Rancho Tulocay. Juarez was himself buried there in 1883. Another inhabitant of the cemetery is Lilburn Williams Boggs, who was born in Kentucky in 1796, married Daniel Boone's granddaughter, and was governor of Missouri from 1836 to 1840.

Also interred there are Nathan Coombs, who founded the city of Napa in 1848, and Mary Ellen Pleasant, known as the "mother of the civil rights movement in California" and (to her intense dislike) as "Mammy Pleasant." (For more on Pleasant, see our Napa Valley Trivia section on page 232).

Tuscany

1005 First Street (corner of Main)
Napa CA 94558
707.258.1000
Northern Italian - Entrees: $10-$30

A very popular place with great ambiance. At the corner of First and Main in downtown Napa. Open windows so you can watch the passers-by.

Ubuntu Restaurant and Yoga Studio

1140 Main Street
Napa CA 94559
707.251.5656
www.ubuntunapa.com
Contemporary Garden Fresh – Entrees $15-$25

Vegetables and fruit grown from within 150 miles, with many from the restaurant's own local organic garden. Dairy products and eggs with vegan options, but no meat.

Ubuntu is a Zulu word for "humanity for others". The restaurant will serve breakfast, lunch and dinner.

Patio dining, demonstration kitchen and large community table. The yoga studio is on the level above. Opening late summer 2007.

Uptown Theater

1350 Third St.
Napa CA 94559
707.256.0150
www.napauptown.com

Not yet reopened. The theater originally opened in 1937. Over the years it was divided into two theaters and eventually into four. In the 1980s and 1990s, several different owners tried to compete with the chain-owned multiplex in town by focusing on independent and art films.

When renovation is completed, the Uptown will hold 1000 people in one big-screen theater furnished with plush French-made theater seats. Murals on walls and ceiling are being painstakingly restored, and an authentically restored marquee is now in place outside the theater. The goal is to present high quality live entertainment as well as special movies and satellite broadcasts. Other possible events include a Napa Valley film festival and ongoing arts and lecture series.

Uva Trattoria Italiana

1040 Clinton
Napa CA 94558
707.255.6646
Northern Italian - Entrees: $6-$16.50
www.uvatrattoria.com

A comfortable and tasty northern Italian restaurant. A very short walk from downtown Napa's main street. Half portions of pasta are available, which is a great idea that we'd like to see other restaurants offer.

Vallerga's Market

3385 Solano Avenue
Napa CA 94558
707.253.2621
www.vallergas.com

An excellent supermarket with outstanding gourmet foods and Napa Valley food products, perfect for picnic lunches. Just off Highway 29 at Redwood Road towards the north end of Napa.

Villa Corona
3614 Bel Aire Plaza
Napa CA 94558
707.257.8685
Mexican – Entrees $3.95-$10.25

Our favorite Mexican restaurant. A small place in a shopping center (the same one where Trader Joe's is located) that's a little hard to find, but worth the effort. They're at the southeast corner, off the alley. A few tables inside, and more outside overlooking the parking. People go there for the food, not the ambiance.

Great Mexican cooking with everything from chile rellenos, burritos and chimichangas to enchiladas, flautas, and the T's— tacos, tamales and tostadas. Beer is available but if you're going to eat outside, tell them and they'll pour it in a paper cup. They don't take checks, but cash and plastic work fine. Closed Mondays. They also have a location in St. Helena.

Villa Romano
1011 Soscol Ferry Road
Napa CA 94558
707.252.4533
www.villaromanorestaurant.com
Northern Italian – Entrees $15-$21

Located near the divide of Highway 29 and Highway 121 south of Napa. At the traffic light at the divide, make an immediate left onto Soscol Ferry Road, which is the southern extension of Soscol Road. See the web site for a map.

The two-story restaurant was built as a stagecoach stop in 1855. It offers an extensive selection of appetizers, salads and pastas, and entrees such as Scallopine, Osso Bucco and *Misto Griglio*—grilled King Salmon, prawns and Ahi tuna served over linguini. A comfortable place for dining by candlelight and fireplace.

Vintage Sweet Shoppe
3261 Browns Valley Road
530 Main Street
Napa CA 94558
707.226.3933
www.vintagesweetshoppe.com

Family candy-making business with shops at the Napa Mill and in Browns Valley in West Napa. 200 different hand-made chocolate confections, including truffles and their unique chocolate-dipped wine bottles.

Vintner's Collective
1245 Main Street
Napa CA 94559
707.255.7150 Fax: 707.255.7159
www.vintnerscollective.com

A co-op tasting room representing a number of Napa Valley boutique wineries. This is the only place in the valley you can sample these excellent wines. Wineries include D Cubed Cellars, Elan Vineyards, Frazier Winery, Judd's Hill, Mason Cellars, Melka Wines, Mi Sueño Cellars, Patz & Hall, Strata Vineyards and Vinoce Vineyards. The Collective also offers additional "guest wineries" on Saturdays.

Westin Verasa Napa Residences
1141 First Street
Napa CA 94559
800.509.8090
www.westinnaparesidences.com
160 rooms

Luxury condo-hotel scheduled to open in the next two years. 10,000 square feet of conference space.

Separate restaurant fronting on Soscol Avenue.

Westwood Hills Park

On Browns Valley Road, about one mile west of Highway 29
707.257.9529

Westwood Hills Park is a heavily-wooded Napa City park. The park provides three miles of trails through beautiful groves of oak trees and grassy meadows, and affords expansive views of the city. The park includes benches and picnic tables near the parking lot and along the trails.

The non-profit Napa Valley Naturalists operate the Carolyn Parr Nature Museum near the parking lot at the park. The Center's exhibits depict the plants and animals found in Napa County's five different habitats. There's also a children's nature library, "hands-on" corner of skins, nests and bones, and an extensive nature reference library. The Center is open year-round on Saturdays and Sundays from 1-4 pm. During the summer it is open Tuesday-Sunday at the same hours.

Whole Foods

3682 Bel Aire Plaza
Napa CA 94558
www.wholefoods.com

Opening early 2008 in the Bel Aire Shopping Center. First location in Napa County for the popular organic foods chain.

Wine and Crafts Faire

Downtown Napa
707.257.0322

Wine tasting, crafts, food, entertaining. Held in September, it's the big street fair of the year in the city of Napa.

Wine Valley Lodge

200 South Coombs Street
Napa CA 94558
707.224.7911
www.winevalleylodge.com
55 rooms $99 - $165

One-story motel at the south end of Napa a few minutes' drive from downtown. Frommer's travel guide says: "Dollar for dollar, the Wine Valley Lodge offers the most for your vacation budget in the entire wine country." If Elvis Presley, Marilyn Monroe and Rock Hudson could stay here, why not you?

Wineries of Napa Valley

1285 Napa Town Center
Napa CA 94559
707.253.9450   800.328.7815
www.napavintages.com

Open daily with sales, tasting and concierge services located right next to the Visitors Center in downtown Napa. Wines from a number of wineries.

Zaré

5091 Solano Avenue
Napa CA 94558
707.257.3318
www.zarenapa.com
Contemporary Mediterranean -
Entrees $19-$26

Namesake restaurant of chef Hoss Zaré. Entrees such as Seared Sea Scallops, Herb-Crusted Grilled Salmon, and Lamb Sirloin. Outdoor seating available. No corkage fee for up to two bottles. Very comfortable atmosphere, excellent food. The lamb is fantastic.

Zinsvalley Restaurant

3253 Browns Valley Road
Napa CA 94558
707.224.0695
www.zinsvalley.com
American/California - Entrees
$13.50-$25.95

From downtown Napa take First Street west over Highway 29, go 1.3 miles and turn left into the Browns Valley Shopping Center.

Out of the way and unknown to most tourists, Zinsvalley is a favorite of the people in the area. Friendly service, excellent food, and a relaxing creekside patio for dining. No corkage fee.

ZuZu

829 Main Street
Napa CA 94559
707.224.8555
www.zuzunapa.com
Spanish Tapas - Plates: $3-$8 each.

Located across the street from Veterans' Park and the Napa River, ZuZu has been packing them in since the day it opened. It didn't hurt that the *San Francisco Chronicle* gave ZuZu the greatest raves we've ever seen in their restaurant reviews. Zuzu doesn't take reservations, so be prepared to wait. Its menu focuses on Spanish "tapas," those delicious little mini-dishes prepared both cold (*tapas frias*) and warm (*tapas calientes*). Enjoy them with a glass of sherry.

Our personal favorites are the Mexican corn soup and the Flat-Iron Steak, but we're always pleased no matter what we order. Excellent, friendly service, a lively atmosphere, and wonderfully tasty food. In fact, we get more excited about the food each time we go there. It's delicious.

Yountville

In 1831, George Yount, the first American settler in the Napa Valley, came to the area now called Yountville. He received an 11,000-acre Mexican Land grant and built the first structures in the area, a Kentucky blockhouse and mill. Even more importantly, he planted the first grapevines in the Napa Valley.

In 1855 Yount hired a surveyor to lay out a town site and named it "Sebastopol", ignoring the fact that a town in neighboring Sonoma County already had that same. In 1865, two years after death, the town was renamed in his honor. His grave can be found in Pioneer Cemetery, next to Yountville Park at the north end of town.

When Yountville incorporated, it wanted to be called a "village." The State of California didn't allow for villages, so Yountville had to refer to itself as a town. It still feels like a village, with a population of approximately 3,500, which includes 1,100 residents of the Veterans Home of California.

Yountville is a walking town filled with excellent shops, restaurants, and lodging. Spend some time here. You'll enjoy it. Oh, yes, and it does happen to have a whole bunch of really good restaurants.

Ad Hoc

6476 Washington Street
Yountville CA 94599
707.944.2487
www.adhocrestaurant.com
Comfort Food - $45 prix fixe

Yet another Thomas Keller restaurant (*French Laundry, Bouchon*). Since its existence has always intended to be fleeting, Keller tentatively considered calling it "Brigadoon", after the Broadway musical's Scottish village that appeared briefly once every 100 years.

Keller has stated that he might open a hamburger joint called *Burgers and Bottles*, inspired by one of his favorite places, In-n-Out Burger (see page 50), possibly replacing Ad Hoc.

Four-course (includes salad course, protein with vegetables, cheese course and dessert) prix fixe menu that changes daily. It's on the site of the former Wine Garden and the legendary, and sadly departed, Diner. Open 5 pm - 9:30 pm, closed Tuesdays and Wednesdays. Corkage $10. Call for the day's menu.

Antique Fair
6512 Washington Street
Yountville CA 94599
707.944.8440
www.antiquefair.com

French furnishings and art, European art.

Bardessono Inn & Spa
Yountville, CA 94599
62 rooms

Located in downtown Yountville. To open in 2008.

Barrel Cellar
Vintage 1870
6525 Washington Street
Yountville CA 94599
707.944.8057
www.thebarrelcellar.com

Specializing in Napa Valley wine accessories and gifts.

Bell Wine Cellars
6200 Washington Street
Yountville CA 94599
707.944.1673
www.bellwine.com

Open daily for tasting by appointment. Cabernet Sauvignon, Viognier, Chardonnay, Merlot and Shiraz.

Bistro Jeanty
6510 Washington Street
Yountville CA 94599
707.944.0103
www.bistrojeanty.com
French Bistro - Entrees $15-$25

One star in the Michelin Guide to the San Francisco Bay Area. Chef Philippe Jeanty, former long-time chef at Domaine Chandon, has created an authentic French bistro. A very popular place. Open till 10:30 p.m.

Blue Heron Gallery
Vintage 1870 6525 Washington St.
Yountville CA 94599
707.944.2044

The artwork of a dozen local artists. Welded sculpture, watercolor, oil, acrylic, pastel and prints. A focus on painted Napa Valley landscapes and florals. Also includes a wide variety of artwork from pounded metal masks and small wire sculpture to handmade dolls and jewelry.

Bouchon
6534 Washington Street
Yountville CA 94599
707.944.8037
www.bouchonbistro.com
French Bistro - Entrees $15-$25

One star in the Michelin Guide to the San Francisco Bay Area. A traditional French bistro owned by Thomas Keller. Keller also owns the renowned French Laundry (see page 79) just down the street.

Bouchon Bakery
6528 Washington Street
Yountville CA 94599
707.944.2253 (BAKE)
www.bouchonbakery.com

Adjacent to Bouchon restaurant and also owned by Keller. Supplies breads and pastries to both Bouchon and French Laundry restaurants, as well as to the public. One of our favorites (we have many) is their namesake Chocolate Bouchon.

Brix
7377 St. Helena Highway
Yountville, CA 94599
707.944.2749 Fax: 707.944.8320
www.brix.com
Wine Country - Entrees $16-$32

One of the Napa Valley's nicest restaurants, with excellent food and service and a very comfortable atmosphere. Outside dining overlooking the vineyard and hills. One of our favorites.

Burgers and Bottles
See Ad Hoc – page 76.

Cliff Lede Vineyards
1473 Yountville Cross Road
Yountville CA 94599
707.944.8642 800.428.2259
www.cliffledevineyards.com

Tour and tasting by appointment only. Formerly S. Anderson Vineyard.

Compadres Bar & Grill
6539 Washington Street
PO Box 3186
Yountville CA 94599
707.944.2406 Fax: 707.944.8407
California-Mexican - Entrees $10-$19
Located between Vintage 1870 and the Vintage Inn. Hours: Monday through Friday from 11 a.m., Saturday and Sunday from 9 a.m.

Indoor and outdoor seating. Reservations not required. Award-winning Cal-Mex cuisine, with traditional and not-so-traditional favorites complemented by an array of grilled items, including *fajitas*, *carnitas* and *pollo borracho*, as well as fresh fish Vera Cruz style. Very casual, great for families and large parties. Sample from their "Wall of Fire"—over 50 hot sauces, or try one of the 50 tequilas at the bar. No corkage fee, but who cares when the margaritas are so good?

Cosentino Winery
7415 St. Helena Highway
Yountville CA 94599
707.944.1220
www.cosentinowinery.com

Open daily for tasting. Located just north of Mustard's Grill. More than 30 wines, including Cabernet Sauvignon, Cabernet Franc, Pinot Noir, Zinfandel, Merlot, Meritage, Port, Sauvignon Blanc, Chardonnay, Viognier, Semillon, Gewürztraminer, Pinot Grigio.

Domaine Chandon Winery—The étoile Restaurant

1 California Drive
Yountville CA 94599
707.944.2280
www.chandon.com
French-inspired California - Entrees
$18-$29
West side of Highway 29 (at
Yountville). Take the Veterans Home
exit. Cross railroad track and turn
right into Domaine Chandon.

Domaine Chandon is owned by Moët
et Chandon, and its sparkling wines
are superb. It also offers an excellent
tour, giving you a chance to see how
sparkling wine is made, which is a
quite different process from the
"still" wines made in most other
Napa Valley wineries (although
Chandon is starting to produce some
still wines).

Domaine Chandon's restaurant is
one of the most outstanding in the
valley. The food, presentation,
service and views are superb. Unless
you're very lucky, you'll need
reservations well in advance.

French Laundry Restaurant

6640 Washington
Yountville CA 94599
707.944.2380
www.frenchlaundry.com
French Laundryish - $240 prix fixe

Reservations are made 60 days in
advance, but once in a while they
actually get a cancellation and the
vacancy could be yours. Reservations
got even harder when Chef Thomas
Keller was named the top chef in
America by the James Beard
Foundation. And then: Thee stars
(The highest rating and the only one
in the Bay Area) in the Michelin
Guide to the San Francisco Bay Area.

The *New York Times* called the
Laundry the "most exciting
restaurant in the United States." In
2002 Keller was named the first-ever
World Master of Culinary Arts,
competing against top chefs from all
over the world. And to top it off,
Restaurant magazine in the U.K.,
after a poll of 300 chefs and food
critics around the world, has several
times declared the Laundry the "best
restaurant in the world".

The French Laundry is considered by
many to be the finest restaurant in
the (at least) United States.

The French Laundry is a fixed-price
restaurant, and that price most
recently was $240.

George Yount Blockhouse

Location: NE corner of Cook Rd and
Yount Mill Rd, 1 mile north of town.

Site of the log block-house
constructed in 1836 by George
Calvert Yount, pioneer settler in
Napa County. Nearby was his adobe
house, built in 1837, and across the
bridge were his grist and saw mills,
erected before 1845. Born in North
Carolina in 1794, Yount was a
trapper, rancher, and miller. He
became grantee of the Rancho
Caymus and La Jota. He died in
Yountville in 1865.

Goosecross Cellars

119 State Lane (off Yountville Cross
Road)
Yountville CA 94599
707.944.1986   800.276.9210
www.goosecross.com

Open daily by appointment. Small
family-owned winery producing
Chardonnay, Sauvignon Blanc,
Merlot, Syrah, Zinfandel, Cabernet
Sauvignon, Viognier. You can even
pick up some of their Chardonnay
smoked wild Alaska salmon.

Goosecross also offers an excellent
"Wine Crash Course", a 90-minute
wine class held every Saturday
morning September through
November. In this free class you'll
learn about tasting techniques, the
structure and components of wine,
winemaking styles, wine jargon,
serving and storing wine and much
more. We took the class and enjoyed
it a lot. Contact the winery for
reservations.

Gordon's Café and Wine Bar

6770 Washington Street
Yountville, CA 94599
707.944.8246
California - Entrees $6.55-$11.95
Friday night *Prix fixe* 3-course
dinner $45

A local hangout for breakfast and
lunch. Delicious, organic, fresh,
locally grown foods. Dinners served
every Friday evening.

Grave of George C. Yount

Location: George C. Yount Pioneer
Cemetery, Lincoln and Jackson
Streets at the north end of town.

George Calvert Yount (1794-1865)
was the first United States citizen to
be ceded a Spanish land grant in
Napa Valley (1836). He encouraged
American pioneers to establish
ranches in the area, so it was well
populated even before the gold rush.

Groezinger Wine Merchants

16484 Washington Street, Suite E
Yountville CA 94599
800.356.3970
www.groezingers.com

In the heart of Yountville. A retail
wine shop with a focus on wines
from boutique, small production
California wineries.

Havens Wine Cellars

2055 Hoffman Lane
Yountville CA 94558
707.945.0921
www.havenswine.com

Producing award-winning wines
since 1984. Their Carneros Syrah is
exceptional. They're the only winery
in the valley to produce an Albariño,
grown from that unique white grape
originally from Spain and Portugal.
Tastings and tours are by
appointment, and the winery is open
for retail sales throughout the week.
Also Merlot, Syrah, Bourriquot,
Cabernet Franc.

Hurley's Restaurant and Bar

6518 Washington Street
Yountville CA 94599
707.944.2345
www.hurleysrestaurant.com
Wine Country - Entrees $12-$23

Bob Hurley is one of Yountville's
favorite chefs—and that's saying a lot
in this town with so many
outstanding restaurants. Formerly at
the Napa Valley Grille, he now has

his own place across the street from Vintage 1870. Hurley serves fresh seasonal wine country food with a Mediterranean flair. Fun and casual with outdoor dining in the patio.

Inn at the French Laundry
Webber and Washington Streets
Yountville, CA 94599
20 rooms

Renowned architect Antoine Predock is designing Thomas Keller's country inn that will be an extension to his French Laundry restaurant. Predock describes it as "20 idiosyncratic rooms - each with a mirror outdoor room, combine with dining/lounging spaces, spa, and gardens to create a continuous fabric of walls". Possible opening is 2008.

Jessup Cellars
6740 Washington Street
Yountville CA 94599
707.944.8523
www.jessupcellars.com

Although their winery is on Mt. Veeder on the west side of the valley, Jessup has a tasting room in Yountville at the north end of town. They pour Cabernet Sauvignon, Merlot, Zinfandel, Zinfandel Port and Cabernet Sauvignon Port.

Lincoln Theater
Veterans Home of California
Yountville CA 94599
707.944.1300 866.944.9199
www.lincolntheater.org

The Lincoln Theater has a seating capacity of 1,200, the largest in the valley. It is the home of the Napa Valley Symphony and many other events.

Magical Moonshine Puppet Theater
PO Box 2296
Yountville CA 94599
707.257.8007
www.magicalmoonshine.org

This is another Napa Valley treasure. Unfortunately, performances are only held sporadically. Fortunately for locals, they're frequent enough to be a favorite, and held at locations throughout the valley. A wonderful experience for kids, no matter what their age.

Mustard's Grill
7399 St. Helena Highway (Highway 29)
Yountville CA 94599
707.944.2424
www.mustardsgrill.com
Wine Country - Entrees $10-$27

One of the most popular restaurants in the Napa Valley and one of the pioneers of California Cuisine. And one of the best. If you try the Mongolian pork chops, you might end up asking for them every time. However, if it's within your price range, try the filet mignon; it's pure manna from heaven and simply melts in your mouth. Mustard's prides itself on its outrageously comprehensive wine list (nearly 400 wines at last count) and the highly professional staff is well educated and able to advise you on an appropriate wine for your meal. Mustard's is truly a dining experience.

Napa River Ecological Reserve
East of Yountville on the north side of Yountville Cross Road between Highway 29 and the Silverado Trail.

The 73-acre habitat of riparian forest and meadows is a remnant of the riparian habitat that once existed all along the Napa River. The land is managed by the California Department of Fish and Game.

On both sides of the river are large meadows, which are sometimes flooded in winter. The meadows are a favorite place for deer to browse and a home to California quail and many species of finches and sparrows, including Lincoln's sparrow.

The interior forested area is a haven for birds, including breeding, wintering and migrating species. It is the most southerly point in Napa County where yellow-breasted chats breed. Wood ducks nest near the river, and varied thrushes and red-breasted sapsuckers winter here.

Willow flycatchers and several western warbler species settle in for temporary feeding on their migration routes. Acorn woodpeckers, scrub jays, white-breasted nuthatches, Anna's hummingbirds, and dozens of other species live here year-round. A total of 146 bird species have been sighted in the reserve, with 67 species known to nest here.

Other birds that can be seen here include cormorants, herons and egrets, Canada geese, golden eagles, falcons, great horned owls, and woodpeckers.

The reserve is also home to at least 40 different species of butterflies, including swallowtails, whites, sulphurs, coppers, hairstreaks, blues, brushfoots and skippers.

(Thanks to the Napa-Solano Audubon Society for the above information.)

Napa Valley Grille

6795 Washington Street (in Washington Square)
Yountville CA 94599
707.944.8686 Fax: 707.944.2870
Banquets: 707.944.8506
www.napavalleygrille.com
Wine Country - Entrees: $12.95-$25.95

The Grille, just off Highway 29 and Madison, is one of Yountville's and the valley's favorite places. Seasonal, ingredient-driven wine country cuisine with an emphasis on hard-to-find California wines. Outdoor dining with a great view of vineyards and hills, and a wide variety of seating choices, including a number of private dining rooms. Best of Award of Excellence 1997-2001 from Wine Spectator magazine. Highly recommended.

Napa Valley Lavender Company

PO Box 2509
Yountville CA 94599
707.257.8920
www.napa-lavender.com

Products from eight different types of lavender plants. Sachets, pillows, clothing, candles, bath salts, soaps and lotions.

Napa Valley Lodge

2230 Madison Street
Yountville, CA 94599
707.944.2468 800.368.2468
www.napavalleylodge.com
55 rooms - $282-$595

Guest rooms and conference facilities at the north end of Yountville. Just across the street from Yountville Park and a comfortable walk to all shops and restaurants in town.

Napa Valley Museum

55 Presidents Circle (in the Veterans Home)
Yountville CA 94599
707.944.0500
www.napavalleymuseum.org
Open Wednesday - Monday from
10am to 5 pm. Adults $4.50,
Students/Seniors $3.50, Ages 7-17
$2.50, Children under 4 free.

Take Yountville-Veterans Home exit off Highway 29, turn west onto California Drive. Follow the tree-lined drive to the stop sign and turn right.

The museum is devoted to the land, the people, and the art of the Napa Valley. A special permanent interactive exhibit is entitled: *California Wine: The Science of an Art.*

Napa Valley Railway Inn

6523 Washington Street
Yountville CA 94599
707.944.2000
www.napavalleyrailwayinn.com
9 rooms - $110-$210

Rooms are in converted railroad cars sitting on original track from the Napa Valley Railroad in the heart of Yountville. Guests have complimentary use of the nearby Yountville Fitness Center. No phones, no smoking.

Pacific Blues

6525 Washington Street (Vintage 1870)
Yountville CA 94599
707.944.4455
www.pacificbluescafe.com
American - Entrees $9.00-$15.00

Open daily for breakfast, lunch and dinner. Blues, burgers and barbequed oysters. Great list of local wines and on-tap beers. Dining on the deck or inside. A local favorite.

Ranch Market Too!

6498 Washington Street
Yountville CA 94599
707.944.2662.
Open 6 a.m. to 10 p.m. daily.
Delicatessen closes at 8 p.m.

Yountville's "supermarket." Not haute cuisine, but a great place to pick up a deli sandwich. Call ahead with your order to save time.

RASgalleries

6540 Washington Street
Yountville CA 94599
707.944.9211
www.rasgalleries.com

One-of-a-kind works in glass by Jerry Cebe, Richard Silver, John Lotton and others in a collection of vases, perfume vials and sculpture.

Redd

6480 Washington
Yountville CA 94599
707.944.2222
www.reddnapavalley.com
Contemporary Napa Cuisine -
Entrees $20-$29

Redd's chef is Richard Reddington, formerly at Auberge du Soleil in Rutherford, Masa's in San Francisco and at Spago in Beverly Hills. Special tasting menus of five to nine courses at $60-$95. At the former location of Piatti's.

Robert Sinskey Vineyards

6320 Silverado Trail
Yountville CA 94599
707.944.9090
800.869.2030
www.robertsinskey.com

Open daily for tastings; tours by appointment. Sinskey is farming its vineyards organically, and also using the even stricter methods of *biodynamics*. Pinot Noir, Chardonnay, Merlot, Cabernet Sauvignon, Cabernet Franc.

V Wine Cellar

6525 Washington Street
Yountville CA 94599
707.531.7053
www.vwinecellar.com

Wine shop located in the back of Vintage 1870. International and California wines, including wineries producing as little as 100 cases. A selection of more than 3,000 wines. Cigars too.

Veranda Club Spa

Washington Square
Yountville CA 94599
707.944.1906 Fax: 707.944.0766
www.verandaclubspa.com

Proprietor Wil Anderson has practiced and taught in Germany and Switzerland, and is a specialist in a variety of massage techniques, including the esoteric and remarkably effective deep body massage called *Chua Ka*.

This mini-day spa has no lodging, but it does offer massage, facials, body treatments and total fitness programs. It's one of those intimate little places that make the Napa Valley so special, and it's very popular with locals who want the personal attention that larger spas can't provide. If you're staying at one of the inns or B&Bs in Yountville, you can walk here in minutes. Spoil yourself. After all, you're on vacation.

Veterans Home of California, Yountville

Yountville CA 94599
On California Drive west of Highway 29
707.944.4600
www.cdva.ca.gov/homes/yountville.asp

The Veterans Home of California, Yountville opened in 1884. It's open to anyone from California who served in the military and currently has over 1400 residents—and a waiting list. The grounds are open to the public; feel free to wander around. You also might want to visit the home's museum near the entrance.

The Napa Valley Museum is also located on the Vet's Home grounds. The Napa Valley Symphony performs in the home's Lincoln Hall, and Fourth of July fireworks are held here every year. In fact, this is probably the most popular place in the valley for fireworks.

Villagio Inn & Spa

6481 Washington Street
Yountville CA 94599
707.944.8877 800.351.1133
www.villagio.com
112 rooms - $210-$950

From the same group that owns Vintage Inn. Nicely designed complex of buildings, vineyards, gardens, fountains and waterways. A very complete spa offering just about every kind of body care you can think of. It doesn't have its own restaurant, but Yountville's many restaurants are just a minute or two away.

Vintage Inn

6541 Washington Street
Yountville CA 94599
707.944.1112
www.vintageinn.com
80 rooms - $210-$485

A beautifully designed (by the same architect who did the spectacular *Ventana Inn* at Big Sur) and landscaped inn in the heart of Yountville. This used to be an old-growth vineyard with gnarly old vines just across the street from an earlier home of the writer of this book. If the vineyard had to go—and there was no way of preventing it—there could be no better development to replace it than the Vintage Inn. An excellent place to stay and relax.

Vintage 1870

6525 Washington Street
Yountville CA 94599
707.944.2451 Fax: 707.944.2453
www.vintage1870.com
Hours: daily 10 am to 5:30 pm

Listed in the National Registry of Historic Places, Vintage 1870 was built as distillery and winery by Gottlieb Groezinger in 1870. Today it offers more than 30 specialty shops, restaurants and a picnic garden. Vintage 1870 is probably the most popular place for tourists to shop in the entire Napa Valley.

Vintage 1870 Wine Cellar

6525 Washington Street (in Vintage 1870)
Yountville Ca 94599
707.944.9070 800.946.3487
www.vintagewinecellar.com

A wine shop offering more than 800 wines with a tasting bar offering 12-15 wines each day.

Vintner's Golf Club

7901 Solano Avenue
Yountville, CA 94599
707.944.1992
www.vintnersgolfclub.com

9-hole, par 34. 4,258/5,573 yards. Three sets of tees. Located just off Highway 29 at the Veterans Home.

Volakis Gallery

6730 Washington Street
Yountville CA 94599
707.945.1125
www.volakisgallery.com

Focus on black and white photography, sculpture, and mixed media work that incorporates sculptural and/or photographic processes.

Yountville Appellation

www.yountvillewines.com

Association of more than 20 wineries and more than 60 growers in the Yountville Appellation.

Yountville Farmers Market

Compadres Parking Lot (next to Vintage 1870)
Yountville CA
707.252.7142
Wednesday 4 p.m.-8 p.m.
May through October
www.commongreens.com

Yountville Inn

6462 Washington Street
Yountville CA 94599
707.944.5600 808.972.2293
www.yountvilleinn.com
41 rooms - $150-$325

A new, nicely appointed inn at the south entrance to Yountville. A short walk to all Yountville shops and restaurants.

Yountville Park
On Washington Street at the north end of Yountville just across the street from the Napa Valley Lodge.

A very popular place for picnics and one of the best parks around for kids, boasting a unique assortment of play equipment. Across the street from the park is Pioneer Cemetery and the grave of George Yount, first settler in the valley and the founder of Yountville. When Yount first saw the valley in 1831, he said: "In such a place I would like to live and die." He did both, dying in 1865.

Events

Bastille Day Celebration
Domaine Chandon
Yountville 94599
707.944.2280
Held every July 14

Farmer's Market
Parking lot of Compadre's
Restaurant
6539 Washington Street
707.944.0904
Wednesdays, June - September, 4 - 8 p.m.

Festival Of Lights
Town of Yountville
707.944.0904
December
Beautiful Christmas display, music, entertainment.

Fourth of July Fireworks
Veterans Home
Yountville
707.944.4600
The biggest fireworks display in the valley.

Napa Valley Symphony
2407 California Boulevard
Napa CA 94558
707.226.6872
www.napavalleysymphony.org

The Napa Valley has developed an outstanding group of musicians. Although the symphony's office is in Napa, most concerts are held in the Lincoln Theater at the Veterans Home in Yountville. There's also an annual free concert by the river at Veterans Park in downtown Napa.

Oakville

An unincorporated area with a great little post office. Famous for its grocery store and surrounding wineries.

Cardinale Winery

7585 St. Helena Highway
Oakville CA 94562
707.944.2807
www.cardinale.com

Tours and tastings by appointment only. Originally the site of Pepi Winery, now owned by Kendall-Jackson and producing wines from their estate vineyards on the valley floor, as well as from the slopes of Mt. Veeder and Howell Mountain.

Carmelite House of Prayer

PO Box 347
Oakville CA 94562
707.944.2454
www.ocdwest.org/oakville.html

Founded in 1955 by spiritual descendants of the friars who accompanied Spanish explorer Sebastian Vizcaino's to this area of California in 1603. Vizcaino expedition. It offers retreats and spiritual direction. Visitors are welcome at daily masses.

Far Niente Winery

P.O. Box 327
Oakville CA 94562
707.944.2861
www.farniente.com

Far Niente was founded in 1885 by John Benson, a Gold Rush arrival in California and uncle of the famed painter Winslow Homer. The building was designed by Hamden McIntyre, the architect for Greystone, the former Christian Brothers Winery in St. Helena now occupied by the Culinary Institute of America. Far Niente closed during prohibition, was restored in 1979 by Gil Nickel, and is now on the National Register of Historic Places.

The winery has 13 acres of landscaped gardens and 40,000 square feet of wine caves. It also houses an extensive collection of automobiles and vintage BMW motorcycles, including a 1966 Ferrari 500 Superfast, a 1935 Bentley 3.5 liter Sports Saloon, and a 1951 Ferrari 340 America. The winery produces award-winning Chardonnay and Cabernet Sauvignon. Tours are now available by appointment.

Napa Cellars

7481 St. Helena Highway
Oakville CA 94562
707.944.2565 800.535.6400
www.napacellars.com

Open daily for tasting. Chardonnay, Merlot, Zinfandel, Late Harvest Zinfandel, Syrah, Cabernet Sauvignon.

Napa Wine Company

PO Box 434 7840 St. Helena Highway
Oakville CA 94562
707.944.1710 800.848.9630
www.napawinecompany.com

Tastings by appointment of wines from more than 15 different wineries, all custom crushed at these same facilities. Tastings include Napa Wine Company's own brands, all made from organic grapes, as well wines from Crocker & Starr, Del Bondio, Downing Family Vineyards, Fife, Joel Gott, La Sirena, Lamborn,

Larkmead, Larraine, Madrigal, Mason, Marilyn Merlot, Pahlmeyer, Napa Wine Company, Oakford, Pavi, Michael Pozzan, Showket, Tria and Vinum.

Nickel and Nickel

8164 St. Helena Highway
Oakville CA 94562
707.944.0693
www.nickelandnickel.com

Tours and tastings by appointment only. Founded by Gil Nickel, the late owner of Far Niente Winery, and his nephew Erik. 100% varietal, single-vineyard wines. Chardonnay, Cabernet Sauvignon, Merlot and Zinfandel.

Oakville Grocery

7856 Saint Helena Highway (Highway 29)
Oakville CA 94562
707.944.8802 Fax: 707.9044.1844
www.oakvillegrocery.com

The Grocery's building opened as a general store in 1880 and it is listed in the National Registry of Historic Places.

The Oakville Grocery—not your neighborhood stop and shop.

The Grocery has been featured on national TV shows and in major food and wine publications as one of the best specialty food stores in the country. Grocery, charcuterie, fresh foods, cheese, olives, gift baskets, wines, espresso, baked goods, sandwiches, box lunches, picnics to go and they'll ship anywhere.

Oakville Winegrowers

www.oakvillewinegrowers.com

Association of nearly 40 wineries and more than 20 growers in the Oakville appellation.

Opus One Winery

7900 St. Helena Highway
Oakville CA 94562
707.944.9442
www.opusonewinery.com

Tours and tastings by appointment only. Founded in 1979, Opus One is a joint venture between Robert Mondavi and Baroness Philippine de Rothschild.

Robert Mondavi Winery

7801 St. Helena Highway (Highway 29)
Oakville CA 94562
888.766.6328
www.robertmondaviwinery.com

The place that rekindled the Napa Valley wine industry. Opened in 1967, it was only the second winery built in the valley after Prohibition (that weird "experiment" when Americans decided they didn't want to let themselves drink alcohol). Founder Robert Mondavi has a well deserved reputation as a wine-making icon, and his public relations efforts benefited every winery and person in the valley.

Visitors to Mondavi can find beautiful Spanish-mission style architecture, excellent tours, wonderful wines, frequent art shows and the winery's famous annual *Mondavi Summer Music Festival.*

Robert Mondavi Winery—the catalyst that changed the wine industry in the Napa Valley. (Photo courtesy of the winery.)

If you've never before visited the valley, this is a must stop. Even if you're a frequent visitor, you'll want to stop by again and again. Don't miss the beautiful Beniamino Bufano statue of St. Francis at the main entrance. Fumé Blanc, Chardonnay, Pinot Noir, Merlot, Cabernet Sauvignon, Zinfandel, Cabernet Franc.

Beniamino Bufano's St. Francis. (Photo courtesy of Robert Mondavi Winery.)

Robert Mondavi Summer Festival

Robert Mondavi Winery
Oakville CA 94562
707.226.1395
www.robertmondaviwinery.com/su mmerfest.asp

Margrit Biever Mondavi, vice president of cultural affairs at the Robert Mondavi Winery and wife of the founder, has made this her pet project since 1969. Concerts are open-air, held on the winery's main lawn, and take place in June, July and August. Most concerts begin at 7 p.m., with gates open for picnicking.

A past entertainment lineup gives an idea of the outstanding quality of the performers: New Orleans' Preservation Hall Jazz Band, Cesaria Evora, Buena Vista Social Club, Dan Fogelberg, and Dave Koz.

Wine and cheese tasting are offered at intermission. 2001 tickets ranged from $42-$75, depending on the performer. While children are allowed, we've seldom seen any there.

It's an elegantly casual affair, with most attending in jeans and shorts but some finely dressed. Picnic baskets brought by guests range from French bread and cheese to elegantly prepared meals served with fine china and crystal. It's great fun and outstanding entertainment.

Tickets, which go on sale the end of April, go fast. They're available at the winery and all BASS outlets. A sign at the front of the winery, easily visible from Highway 29, shows the season's schedule and ticket availability.

Silver Oak Cellars

915 Oakville Cross Road
Oakville CA 94562
800.273.8809
www.silveroak.com
On the Oakville Cross Road between
Highway 29 and the Silverado Trail.
Open for tastings Monday through
Saturday. Tours by appointment.

Founded in 1971 and producing
only a very highly regarded Cabernet
Sauvignon.

Turnbull Wine Cellars

8210 St. Helena Highway
Oakville CA 94562
800.887.6285
www.turnbullwines.com
Tours and tastings by appointment
only. Focuses on Cabernet
Sauvignon, but also produces
Merlot, Sangiovese, Zinfandel, Syrah
and Sauvignon Blanc.

Rutherford

Another unincorporated town best
known for its two major wineries on
Highway 29 - Beaulieu and Rubicon
Estate (formerly Niebaum-Coppola,
and even earlier Inglenook).

Alpha Omega Winery

1155 Mee Lane
St. Helena CA 94574
707.963.9999
www.alphaomegawinery.com

Formerly the location of Esquisse
Winery.

Beaulieu Vineyard

1960 St. Helena Highway (Highway
29)
Rutherford CA 94573
707.967.5200 800.373.5896
www.bv-wine.com

For many locals and wine
aficionados, Napa Valley wineries
can be divided into two categories:
Beaulieu Vineyard, and all the
others. BV was winning awards
worldwide when most other current
Napa Valley vineyards were still
planted with prunes. The winery was
founded in 1900 by Georges de
Latour and survived Prohibition by
producing sacramental wines. BV's
wines have been served by every
president of the United States since
Franklin Roosevelt.

A beautiful visitor's center offers
outstanding complimentary wines
and tours by friendly, very
knowledgeable guides.

The redwood vats and aging areas
smell like a winery is supposed to
smell—musky, winey, and absolutely
enticing. A must for your first visit to

the valley. And a great "let's just stop in for a glass or two" for repeat visits. BV offers at least 14 different varietals.

Old and majestic redwood vats at Beaulieu Vineyards. (Photo courtesy of the winery.)

Frog's Leap Winery
8815 Conn Creek Road
Rutherford CA 94573
707.963.4704   800.959.4704
www.frogsleap.com

Tours and tastings by appointment only, Monday through Saturday.

The Red Barn was originally built in 1884 as Adamson Winery and renovated in 1994 by Frog's Leap. The winery's name comes from its earlier location at what used to be a commercial frog farm, and founder John Williams' connection with Stag's Leap Wine Cellars. The winery's motto is "Time's Fun When You're Having Flies."
Organically and biodynamically grown grapes. Sauvignon Blanc, Cabernet Sauvignon, Merlot, Zinfandel, Chardonnay, Syrah, Leapfrögmilch (Riesling/Chardonnay).

Grgich Hills Cellar
1829 St. Helena Highway (Hwy 29)
Rutherford CA 94573
707.963.2784
www.grgich.com
Tours by appointment

Miljenko "Mike" Grgich made the Chateau Montelena Chardonnay that won the legendary Paris tasting in 1976. His wines have gotten even better since then. Mike's also involved in establishing a winery in his native Croatia. Chardonnay, Fumé Blanc, Zinfandel, Cabernet Sauvignon.

Home Winemakers Classic
Held at St. Supéry Winery
8440 St. Helena Highway
Rutherford CA 94573
www.homewine.com

The Home Winemakers Classic is an annual tasting and judging of award-winning home wines by Napa Valley enologists and viticulturists, with music, silent auction of vintage wines, raffle and food. Held every July, it is an extremely popular event for residents and the local wine community.

La Toque
1140 Rutherford Cross Road
Rutherford CA 94573
707.963.9770
www.latoque.com
Wine Country French - $98 Prix-fixe

One star in the Michelin Guide to the San Francisco Bay Area. A fixed-price French restaurant at the

Rancho Caymus Inn with a high reputation.

Wine Spectator magazine called it the "quintessential wine country restaurant" and one of the top 20 in the United States. It's a place where you'll spend the entire evening, and love every minute of it. Jackets preferred for gentlemen.

Napa Valley Grapevine Wreath Company

PO Box 67
Rutherford CA 94573
707.963.8893 Fax: 707.963.3325
Open 10:30 to 5:30 daily except Tuesday.

Every year after harvest, the Wood Family collects pruned cuttings from Cabernet Sauvignon grapevines and weaves them into wreaths, baskets and other useful and decorative shapes. They're a favorite with visitors and can be found at their store on the Rutherford Cross Road just off the Silverado Trail.

Peju Province

8466 St. Helena Highway
Rutherford CA 94573
707.963.3600   800.446.7358
www.peju.com

Open daily for tours and tastings. Chardonnay, Sauvignon Blanc, Cabernet Sauvignon, Cabernet Franc, Merlot, Syrah, Late Harvest Chardonnay. Pinot Noir and more.

Provenance Vineyards

PO Box 668
Rutherford CA 94573
707.968.3633
www.provenancevineyards.com

Open daily for tastings. Cabernet Sauvignon and Merlot. Winemaker and general manager Tom Rinaldi

was winemaker at Duckhorn Vineyards for 22 years.

Rancho Caymus Inn

1140 Rutherford Cross Road
Rutherford, CA 94573
707.963.1777 800.845.1777
www.ranchocaymus.com
26 rooms - $205-$375

Spanish California-style inn whose owners also own Flora Springs Winery. Rooms feature spacious hand-carved walnut beds, wrought iron lamps and distinctive handmade furnishings. Ceiling beams are 100-year-old oak, while the timbers that make up the room's surroundings are black walnut, fir, and redwood. Each suite offers soft wool rugs, hand dyed and woven by the Salazaca and Otavalon Indians of Ecuador. Sink basins are unique hand-thrown stoneware. The excellent *La Toque* restaurant is located here.

Round Pond

PO Box 556
Rutherford CA 94573
877.963.9364
www.roundpond.com

Tours and tasting by appointment. Estate-grown olives from eight different varietals are hand-harvested and pressed in a traditional stone mill to produce a variety of premium olive oils.

Also a winery, it now produces Cabernet Sauvignon, Nebbiolo, and soon Sauvignon Blanc.

Rubicon Estate

1991 St. Helena Highway
Rutherford CA 94573
707.968.1100   800.782.4266
www.rubiconestate.com

$25 admission charge includes tasting, access to the chateau, wine library and centennial museum, and valet parking. a variety of tours are available at extra charge.

In 1995, owner Francis Ford Coppola (director of *The Godfather* and *Apocalypse Now*) and his wife Eleanor expanded their wine estate with purchase of the former Inglenook Winery, which dates back to its founding by Captain Gustave Niebaum in 1879. They originally called it Niebaum-Coppola Winery, later changing the name to the present Rubicon Estate.

The chateau and grounds include a museum of wine and film. A visit gives you both excellent wine and the opportunity to see Oscars won by Coppola, a Tucker automobile from his movie *Tucker*, the boat from *Apocalypse Now*, photos and other memorabilia. Cabernet Sauvignon, Zinfandel, Merlot, Syrah, Cabernet Franc.

Rutherford Dust Society

www.rutherforddust.org

Thirty wineries and 50 growers belong to the Rutherford appellation association.

Rutherford Gardens

1796 South St. Helena Highway
St. Helena 94574
877.627.2645
www.longmeadowranch.com
Open Thursday through Sunday when produce is available.

Located on the east side of Highway 29 across the street from Grgich-Hills Cellar, just north of Rutherford.

The property has been producing vegetables at least since the 1930s. This 5.8-acre property was recently acquired by Long Meadow Ranch, renowned for its organic produce and other foods, including olive oil, wines and Scottish Highland cattle. The roadside stand currently offers a wide variety of heirloom tomatoes, sunflowers, basil, melons, figs and sweet corn. In the fall, visitors can pick a potential jack-o'-lantern from over 2.5 acres of pumpkins.

Rutherford Grill

1180 Rutherford Road
Rutherford CA 94573
707.963.1792
American Grill - Entrees $9-$26

A lively, but often very noisy place. Excellent and varied menu suitable for both kids and adults. And with all the noise, nobody's going to care about a little kid noise. Right next to Beaulieu Vineyard, so you can sip great wine before lunch or after. Outdoor dining. No corkage fee.

Sawyer Cellars

8350 St. Helena Highway
Rutherford CA 94573
707.963.1980
www.sawyercellars.com

Open daily for tours and tasting. Tram tours of the vineyard May through November.   Cabernet Sauvignon, Sauvignon Blanc, Merlot and Meritage.

Sequoia Grove Vineyards

8338 South St. Helena Highway
Rutherford CA 94573
707.944.2945 800.851.7841
www.sequoiagrove.com

Open daily for tours and tasting.
Cabernet Sauvignon and
Chardonnay, including the Allen
Family Wines available only at the
winery.

St. Helena Olive Oil Company

PO Box 389 8576
St. Helena Highway
Rutherford CA 94573
800.939.9880
www.sholiveoil.com

Located at the corner of Highway 29
and Rutherford Cross Road, the
store sells extra virgin olive oil,
vinegars and a variety of other foods
and kitchen/culinary paraphernalia.
They also offer a wine-tasting bar
where visitors can sample wines
made by little-known Napa Valley
wineries with small production
volumes. Also a store in downtown
St. Helena.

St. Supéry Vineyard & Winery

8440 St. Helena Highway
Rutherford CA 94573
707.963.4507 800.942.0809
www.stsupery.com
Open daily for tours and tasting.
Located on east side of Highway 29
between Oakville and Rutherford

Self-guided tours are available
anytime, free of charge. The tasting
fee includes a lifetime tasting pass
per guest and a tasting of daily wine
features. Additionally, reserve
tasting of library and small
production wines is available for an
additional charge. Cabernet
Sauvignon, Merlot, Sauvignon Blanc,
Chardonnay, Cabernet Franc, Syrah,
Moscato, Meritage, Semillon.

Tours include the display
vineyard, where you can wander
among the vines, taste the grapes (in
season), see how different trellising
systems work and take photographs.
Meticulously designed exhibits
explain the making of fine wines
from soil to bottle. The guided tours
end with a conducted tasting of St.
Supéry Wines.

A highlight of the tour is
SmellaVision, which includes two
exhibits, one for Sauvignon Blanc (a
white wine) and one for Cabernet
Sauvignon (a red). Each stand
displays four bottles of the specific
varietal so you can see that even
within a Sauvignon Blanc or
Cabernet Sauvignon there are often
great variations in color, clarity and
appearance.

The "smell" part of the exhibits
comes into play when you push any
one of the four levers at each stand,
put your nose over a long plexiglass
"sniffer tube" and get a whiff of one
of the many aromas that are often
used in describing these wines. At
the wine tasting that follows the
tour, you're ready to search for these
aromas in a real glass of wine.

St. Helena

Founded in 1853 and the high-profile center of the Napa Valley wine industry. This is still a small town with less than 6,000 people. The main street of St. Helena is, coincidentally, called Main Street. (It's also Highway 29 and the St. Helena Highway.) Main Street is loaded with enough boutiques to sink a boatload of yuppies. Enjoy yourself. It's small town America with a designer's touch.

A Dozen Vintners
3000 St. Helena Highway (at Lodi Lane)
707.967.0666
www.adozenvintners.com

Winetasting, sales and delicatessen with outdoor tables overlooking vineyards. The tasting bar features such Napa Valley wines as Adams Ridge, Destino, Eagle and Rose, Fife, Howell Mountain, Livingston-Moffett, Reverie, and Von Strasser.

Armadillo's
1304 Main Street
St. Helena CA 94574
707.963.8082
Mexican

Art on Main
1359 Main Street
St. Helena CA 94574
707.963.3350

Original art, some by Napa Valley artists.

A Dozen Vintners
3000 St. Helena Highway (at Lodi Lane)
707.967.0666
www.adozenvintners.com

Winetasting, sales and delicatessen with outdoor tables overlooking vineyards. The tasting bar features such Napa Valley wines as Adams Ridge, Domaine Charbay, Destino, Eagle and Rose, Fife, Howell Mountain, Koves-Newlan, Lamborn Family, Livingston, Reverie, Spelletich, and Von Strasser.

Auction Napa Valley
PO Box 141
St. Helena CA 94574
707.963.3388
www.napavinters.com

Auction Napa Valley (formerly called Napa Valley Wine Auction) has been held every year since 1981. It is the world's largest wine charity event, with all of the auction's proceeds staying within Napa County.

During that time, the auction's sponsor, the Napa Valley Vintners Association, has donated more than $45 million to Napa County hospitals, clinics, youth and housing organizations.

Azteca Market
789 Main Street
St. Helena CA 94574
707.963.4963
Mexican

Mexican market with tacos, tamales, burritos, quesadillas and more to go.

Bale Grist Mill State Historic Park

3369 North Saint Helena Highway
(Highway 29)
St. Helena, CA 94574
707.963.2236
Three miles north of St. Helena
Hours 10 a.m. to 5 p.m.
www.parks.ca.gov/default.asp?page
_id=482

Open throughout the year. Built in 1846, the mill has been restored to operating condition, complete with its 36-foot wooden waterwheel and big millstones. On weekends, you can watch the mill in action, grinding grain to produce stone ground flour.

You can even buy flour to take home for your own baking. A fun and educational experience for the kids—and parents, too.

Ballentine Vineyards and Winery

2820 North St Helena Highway
St. Helena CA 94574
707.963.7919
www.ballentinevineyards.com

Open Wednesday through Saturday for tasting. The present winery was founded in 1995 but the Ballentine Winery goes back to 1933 and owners Van and Betty Ballentine's grapegrowing roots in the Napa Valley go back to the early 1900s. Zinfandel, Merlot, Syrah.

Beringer Vineyards

1000 Pratt Avenue
St. Helena CA 94574
707.963.4812
www.beringer.com

Built in 1876, the winery has been operating continuously ever since. It is now owned by Foster's Group, known for Australia's Foster's Beer. The famous "Rhine House" contains the visitors' center. This classic Napa Valley winery is a good place to stop for photographs.

The historic Rhine House—symbol of Beringer Vineyards. (Photo courtesy of the winery.)

The winery has been offering tours since 1934, so they've got it down right. The $5 tour includes tasting and a trip inside their hand-dug wine caves. The gardens are so beautiful that they're worth the trip on their own. Beringer produces more than 14 different varietals.

Cameo Cinema

1340 Main Street
St. Helena CA 94574
707.963.9779
www.cameocinema.com

A beautifully renovated single-screen movie theater located in downtown St. Helena. Currently it's the only place in the valley to see quality new release films.

Cantinetta at Tra Vigne
1050 Charter Oak Avenue
St. Helena, CA 94574
707.963.8888
www.travignerestaurant.com

Great deli. You can eat in the courtyard or take your food and have a sandwich somewhere else in the valley.

The Cantinetta Wine Bar offers more than 100 wines by the two or five-ounce glass. glass. Hard-to-find cult wines are available for tasting at considerably higher prices.

C. C. Blue Sushi Bar & Restaurant
1148 Main Street
St. Helena CA 94574
707.967.9100
www.ccbluesushi.com
Sushi and more - $7-$17

St. Helena's first sushi bar.   Also tempura, teriyaki and more.

Chajo Fine Art Furnishings
929 Main St. (across from Tra Vigne)
St. Helena CA 94574
707.257.3676
www.chajo.com

One of a kind furniture from Cook & Edie. Also the work of Robert Gouthier, turned wood artist; Dan Cox, wildlife photographer; and David Coddaire, functional metal sculptor.

Charbay Winery and Distillery
Spring Mountain Road
St. Helena CA 94574
800.634.7845
www.charbay.com

Charbay is owned by the Karakasevic family, whose master distillers have been making distilled spirits for thirteen generations. Miles Karakasevic and his son Marko oversee the very limited production at Charbay, while Miles' wife Susan handles marketing and daughter Lara runs the tasting room.

Visits are by appointment only, and the tasting charge is $50 per person, which can be applied to purchases. State law prohibits tasting of spirits at the winery, but you can taste and purchase their Cabernets, ports (classical and white) and Charbay dessert wine during your visit.

Charbay produces limited release wines and fortified wines at its Napa Valley facility, and spirits at its other facility in Mendocino County. Charbay spirits include fresh fruit vodkas (Meyer Lemon, Key Lime, Blood Orange and Ruby Red Grapefruit), a clear vodka that will produce a truly memorable martini, a black walnut liqueur, an apple brandy, a pastis and an extremely limited amount of absolutely amazing, and expensive, whiskey.

Wines include a special port (blended from Cabernet and Sirah, and five unique brandies); a white port of Chardonnay, Sauvignon and brandy; their dessert wine; and a number of Cabernet Sauvignons.

Charles Krug Winery

2800 St. Helena Highway
St. Helena CA 94574
707.967.2201
www.charleskrug.com

Open daily for tasting and tours. Founded in 1861, Krug is the oldest operating winery in the Napa Valley. It's the long-time location of a number of musical and theatrical events. The owners, the Peter Mondavi family (Peter's brother, Robert, founded Robert Mondavi Winery), have over 800 acres of grapes in the Napa Valley. Cabernet Sauvignon, Merlot, Sangiovese, Chardonnay, Zinfandel, Pinot Noir, Sauvignon Blanc.

Cindy's Backstreet Kitchen

1327 Railroad Avenue
St. Helena CA 94574
707.963.1200
www.cindysbackstreetkitchen.com
Classic Home Cooking – Entrees
$12.95-$19.95

One block off Main Street between Hunt and Adams in the old Miramonte Hotel, built as a railroad hotel in the late 1800s. Owned by Cindy Pawlcyn, whose restaurants include the extremely popular *Mustard's Grill* just north of Yountville. This restaurant offers "Cindy's Cuisine"; fun, rustic variations on classic home cooking. Main entrees include Spring Chicken Vegetable Pie, Sunday Glazed Pork, Wood Oven Duck, and Kitchen Curry Lamb Shank. Wine list focuses on Napa Valley wines while the bar specializes in Kentucky Bourbon, Mexican Tequila and Mezcal.

Cook

1310 Main Street
St. Helena CA 94574
707.963.7088
www.cooksthelena.com
Northern Italian/California

Bib Gourmand rating (good meals at moderate prices) in the Michelin Guide to the San Francisco Bay Area. A neighborhood restaurant run by St. Helena natives Jude and Michael Wilmoth. Jude was previously with Tra Vigne and Napa Valley Grille.

Corison Winery

987 St. Helena Highway
St. Helena CA 94574
707.963.0826
www.corison.com

Tours and tastings by appointment. Cathy Corison produces a limited amount of highly-regarded Cabernet Sauvignon.

Culinary Institute of America at Greystone

2555 Main Street
St. Helena, CA 94574
707.967.1100
www.ciachef.edu/greystone

A majestic building that's a favorite for photographers. Formerly Christian Brothers Winery.

Literally filled with kitchens, as well the outstanding Wine Spectator Restaurant (see page 110), demonstration theaters and the Spice Island Marketplace shop. The West Coast branch of the renowned New York State cooking school, referred to by locals as the "CIA."

The historic Greystone. Now the West Coast home of the Culinary Institute of America. (Photo courtesy of CIA).

Cooking demonstrations are open to the public daily; $12.50 charge. For reservations call 707.967.2328. These are a great bargain and we highly recommend them. We've gone to many of them ourselves and found them very enjoyable and useful. You'll be able to take the recipe they give you, go home and replicate the same dish you saw created at the demonstration.

Greystone also displays a famous collection of over 1,500 corkscrews, gathered over a period of 40 years by former Christian Brothers cellarmaster Brother Timothy.

For a special experience, try Greystone's *A Very Special Afternoon in the Napa Valley*, held Monday through Thursday. The $25 charge includes a cooking demo, glass of wine and *Today's Temptations* (spectacular culinary tastings) in the restaurant. It also includes shopping time and a free Napa Valley food gift in Greystone's food and kitchenware shop which features over 2,000 cookbooks.

Dean and DeLuca

607 South St. Helena Highway
St. Helena CA 94574
707.967.9980

The famous New York delicatessen is also in the Napa Valley. It's not a coincidence that the owner also lives in the valley. A vast selection of deli foods, cheeses, kitchenware, and a multitude of jars and cans of exotic foods, sauces, condiments and other goodies. And, of course, wines.

Eagle and Rose Residence Inn

1431 Railroad Avenue
St. Helena CA 94574
707.963.1532
www.eagleandroseinn.com

Victorian style hotel for short term or extended stays. Kitchenettes, private baths and covered parking. Short walking distance to restaurants and shops.

El Bonita Motel

195 Main Street.
St. Helena, CA 94574
707.963.3216
www.elbonita.com
41 rooms - $89-$279

El Bonita looks like an art-deco motel, but it's much, much more. It's a charming, comfortable, and reasonably priced place to stay, with 2.5-acres of beautifully landscaped gardens. It's where St. Helena residents suggest that their friends stay when they come to the valley.

Flora Springs Tasting Room

677 St. Helena Highway
St. Helena CA 94574
707.967.8032
www.florasprings.com

While the actual winery is on nearby Zinfandel Lane, the Komes-Garvey family has a convenient tasting room on Highway 29 at the south end of

St. Helena, right next to Dean and Deluca. The wines are excellent and very highly regarded. The tasting room selection includes all current vintages as well as some special wines available only here. Cabernet Sauvignon, Merlot, Chardonnay, Pinot Grigio, Sangiovese.

Folie à Deux

7481 St. Helena Highway
Oakville, CA 94562
707.944.2565 800.535.6400
www.folieadeux.com

Open daily for tasting; tours by appointment. Founded in 1981 by Larry and Evelyn Dizmang, psychiatric medicine professionals whose colleagues suggested the name. It means "two people sharing the same delusional idea". The fantasy, however, was a success. It's now owned by Trinchero Family Estates. Zinfandel, Cabernet Sauvignon, Chardonnay, Sauvignon Blanc, Sangiovese.

Franciscan Oakville Estate

1178 Galleron Road
(Highway 29 at Galleron one mile north of Rutherford)
St. Helena, CA 94574
707.963.7111 800.529.9463
www.franciscan.com

Tasting fee refundable with purchase. Franciscan has been making wine in the valley for over 25 years. Its dramatically renovated visitor center also offers special tastings at an additional charge. They include *Mastering Magnificat - The art of blending* (blend your own Bordeaux-style wine); *Riedel Vinum Glass Tasting*, where you can experience the difference that fine glassware makes in the enjoyment of wine; and *Personality of Pinot*, which lets you sample various clones of Pinot Noir. Chardonnay, Cabernet Sauvignon, Merlot, Zinfandel, Meritage.

Freemark Abbey

3022 St. Helena Highway North
St. Helena CA 94574
800.963.9698
www.freemarkabbey.com

Open daily for tasting; tours by appointment. Freemark Abbey was founded in 1939 by three men, portions of whose names were combined to create the winery name. The winery, and the site, had been home to two previous wineries. From 1898 to the onset of Prohibition in 1919 it had been Lombarda Cellars. Originally it had been Tychson Cellars, founded in 1886 by Josephine Marlin Tychson, the first woman to build and operate a winery in California. Cabernet Sauvignon, Merlot, Viognier, Chardonnay, White Riesling, late harvest Johannisberg Riesling.

Gillwood's Restaurant

1313 Main Street
St. Helena CA 94574
707.963.1788
www.gillwoodscafe.com
American - Entrees $7.95-$9.75

Popular local hangout with a community table where solo diners can have mealtime company.

Giugni & Son Grocery Company

1227 Main Street
St. Helena CA 94574
707.963.3421
Sandwiches $4.25-$4.75

Cheapest, best, and biggest sandwiches in town. An institution for years.

Go Fish Grill

641 Main Street
St. Helena CA 94574
707.963.0700
www.gofishrestaurant.net
West Coast-style fish and sushi –
Entrees $14-$27

Another restaurant from Cindy Pawlcyn, who also operates Cindy's Backstreet Kitchen in St. Helena and Mustard's Grill in Yountville. Sushi and sake bar, far bar, fish flown in daily and an on-site organic garden. Choose how you want your fish cooked, or let the chef decide. Patio seating.

Green Valley Café

1310 Main Street
St. Helena CA 94574
707.963.7088
www.greenvalleycafe.com
Italian – Entrees $10-$18

A neighborhood Italian restaurant with excellent food and reasonable prices. Great hamburgers, too.

Hall

401 St. Helena Highway South
St. Helena CA 94574
707.967.2620
www.hallwines.com

Open daily for tasting. On the former site of Edgewood Estate and the even earlier St. Helena Co-Op. Cabernet Sauvignon.

Harvest Inn

1 Main Street
St. Helena CA 94574
707.963.9463 800.950.8466
www.harvestinn.com
74 suites, rooms and cottages -
$240-$675

An English Tudor-style country inn on eight beautifully landscaped acres. Most of the guestrooms have brick fireplaces and private terraces. Two outdoor pools and whirlpool spas, and adjacent jogging and bike trails.

Heitz Cellars

Sales/Tasting Room
436 St. Helena Highway South
St. Helena CA 94574
www.heitzcellar.com

Winery
500 Taplin Road
St. Helena CA 94574
707.963.3542

The sales room on Highway 29 is open daily for tasting. Tours of the winery are by appointment. Founded in 1961 by Joe and Alice Heitz, who produced one of the very first "cult" wines—"Martha's Vineyard"—long before the term "cult wine" was every coined. Cabernet Sauvignon, Chardonnay, Grignolino, Zinfandel, Rosé, Port.

Hotel St. Helena

1309 Main St.
St. Helena CA 94574
707.963.4388
www.hotelsthelena.com
18 rooms - $165-$375

Historic building built in 1881. Downtown. Antique doll collection.

I. Wolk Gallery

1354 Main St.
St. Helena CA 94574
707.963.8800
www.iwolkgallery.com

Contemporary paintings, works on paper, photography and sculpture. Emphasis is on representational imagery including landscapes, still life and figurative subjects.

Inn at Southbridge

1020 Main St.
St. Helena CA 94574
707.967.9400
www.innatsouthbridge.com
20 rooms - $275-$535

Vaulted ceilings, fireplaces, health spa. Near restaurants and shops.

Louis M. Martini Winery

254 South St. Helena Highway
(Highway 29)
St. Helena CA 94574
707.963.2736 800.321.9463
www.louismartini.com

Open daily for tours and complimentary tasting; charge for reserve wines.

In operation since 1933, it was the oldest family-owned winery in the valley until it was purchased by Gallo in fall of 2002. (Well, Gallo is family-owned too, but it's hardly a warm and fuzzy little wine operation.) Great tour guides. Nice picnic facilities. Cult wineries come and go, but Martini stands out as a fine winery that dependably turns out excellent wines at fair prices. A favorite of ours. Martini produces more than 20 different varietals.

Main Street Books

1315 Main Street
St. Helena CA 94574
707.963.1338

New, used and special order. Liza and her bookstore have a special place in the hearts of St. Helena bibliophiles of all ages.

Market Restaurant

1347 Main Street
St. Helena CA 94574
707.963.3799
www.marketsthelena.com
American Neighborhood – Entrees
$7-$12.50

Something rare in the valley. A restaurant that focuses on locals and offers reasonable prices. Especially remarkable when you consider the owners were previously connected with highly-rated (and expensive) restaurants *Gary Danko* and *Jardinière* in San Francisco.

Some of the tables in the bar area are communal—for those who'd like to dine with friends they haven't met yet—and the restaurant has also taken pains to keep the noise level down without losing a lively energy.

Wine by the glass from $5. $15 corkage. Entrees include fried chicken, pork chop, meat loaf, catfish, chicken pot pie, and pulled slow roasted pork sandwich. If this food doesn't comfort you, nothing will.

Markham Vineyards

2812 North St. Helena Highway
St. Helena CA 94574
707.963.5292
www.markhamvineyards.com

Open daily for tasting. Tours by appointment only for trade and corporate groups. Originally founded in 1874 as Laurent Winery, reborn in 1977 as Markham. Merlot, Cabernet Sauvignon, Sauvignon Blanc, Chardonnay.

Martini House

1245 Spring Street at Oak
(Just off Highway 29, also known as Main Street)
St Helena, CA 94574
707.963.2233 Fax: 707.967.9237
www.martinihouse.com
Wine Country - Entrees $17-$28

Pat Kuleto, who designed and owns top restaurants in San Francisco (*Boulevard*, *Farallon*, and *Jardinière*), teamed up with Todd Humphries, formerly at Campton Place in San Francisco and the Wine Spectator restaurant at the Culinary Institute of America in St. Helena, to open Martini House. The comfortable and beautifully decorated restaurant was an immediate hit. A percentage of corkage fees goes to local non-profit organizations, particularly to provide housing for migrant farmworkers.

The restaurant is in the former home of the late Walter Martini, opera singer and bootlegger. Two floors of indoor seating and outdoor garden seating around a 75-year-old fountain and under a vine-covered arbor. Wine selections from the world's great appellations, with an extensive collection of Napa Valley wines.

Meadowood Resort

See Silverado Trail section – page 134.

Merryvale Wineyards

1000 Main St. (Highway 29)
St. Helena CA 94574
707.963.777 800.326.6069
www.merryvale.com
Winery is south of the bridge leading into the heart of downtown St. Helena and within walking distance from town.

A highlight of the Merryvale tour is the barrel room.

In addition to its normal tours and tasting, Merryvale offers *Saturday Morning Seminars* that focus on wine and its essential components: sugar, alcohol, acid and tannin. Merryvale wines are tasted in conjunction with these basic ingredients to demonstrate how they blend together to create balance in wines. But, more important, you'll have a chance to map your own palate and find out about your likes and dislikes. You'll find this an entertaining and educational experience.

Seminars are held from 10:30 a.m. until noon every Saturday. The fee is $10.00 per person. Reservations are required. Cabernet Sauvignon, Sauvignon Blanc, Chardonnay, Pinot Noir, Merlot, Muscat de Frontignan.

Milat Vineyards

1091 St. Helena Highway
St. Helena CA 94574
707.963.0758 800.54.MILAT
www.milat.com

Open daily for tasting. All wines are
estate grown. Guest rooms available
on winery property. Zinfandel,
Cabernet Sauvignon, Merlot,
Chardonnay, Chenin Blanc.

Model Bakery

1357 Main St.
St. Helena CA 94574
707.963.8192
www.themodelbakery.com

An excellent bakery offering
breakfast pastries, coffee, breads,
cookies, sandwiches, wonderful
soups, salads and pizza. Did we
forget anything? It's all delicious.
And the prices are reasonable.

Napa Valley Coffee Roasting Company

1400 Oak Avenue
St. Helena CA 94574
707.963.4491, 800.852.5805 Fax:
707.963.1183

There's one of these in Napa, too,
but this one has lots more room and
outdoor seating. Great atmosphere.
Close to many of the Main Street
shops such as Vanderbilt and
Company, this is the place to start
your morning of shopping in St.
Helena.

Napa Valley Olive Oil Manufacturing Company

835 Charter Oak Avenue
St. Helena CA 94574
707.963.4173

A favorite of locals and visitors.
Quite out of the way, so you're
unlikely to stumble on it unless
someone gives you a hint. Great
cheese and other Italian goodies.
And tremendous (and economical)
olive oil by the jug, made by the
owners.

Napa Valley Wine Hardware

659 Main St.
St. Helena CA 94574
707.967.5503 866.611.WINE

The best source in the valley for wine
racks, and wine storage equipment.
Also lots of wine books and
accessories.

Napa Valley Wine Library

St. Helena Public Library
1492 Library Lane
St. Helena CA 94574
707.963.5145
www.napawinelibrary.org

A vast collection of magazines,
books, interviews, clippings and
other materials devoted to enology,
viticulture and wine lore, with a
focus on the Napa Valley.

Nimbus Arts

St. Helena Marketplace, Suite 1B
St. Helena CA 94574
707.963.5278
www.nimbusarts.org

Art classes and workshops for all
ages.

Pennyweight

1337 Main St.
St. Helena CA 94574
707.963.3198

Wonderful selection of stationery
products and writing instruments.
The only place in the valley where
you can buy the legendary Moleskine

notebook used by Van Gogh,
Cezanne and Picasso. (Well, not
their *own* copies. But you can have
your very own.)

Pizzeria Tra Vigne

1016 Main Street
St. Helena CA 94574
707.967.9999

At the Inn at Southbridge just north
of Charter Oak Street. Tasty pizzas at
reasonable prices.

Prager Ports and Wines

1281 Lewelling
St. Helena CA 94574
707.963.7678
www.pragerport.com
Between Sutter Home Winery and
Harvest Inn. Tasting fee redeemable
toward wine purchase.

A small, family-owned winery whose
ports and wines are sold only at the
winery. Prager also has a two-suite B
& B, one suite over the winery, the
other in the vineyards.

Press

587 St. Helena Highway South
St. Helena CA 94574
707.967.0550
www.presssthelena.com
Wine Country Steakhouse - Entrees
$23-$48

Next to Dean & DeLuca and co-
owned by the delicatessen's owner
Leslie Rudd—who also owns Rudd
Winery—Press is on the site of the
former, and legendary, family-
favorite The Spot. The pizza, burgers
and hot dogs have been replaced by
big food with big wines.

Press serves prime dry-aged beef,
whole roasted chicken, and other
naturally raised birds, leg of baby
lamb, wild fish, heritage pork and

hand-fed veal, all prepared on the
kitchen's centerpiece, a custom
wood-burning grill and rotisserie.
Many of the dishes are carved
tableside and serve two or more.

Wines are specially chosen to
complement the seasonal foods and
showcase the Napa Valley terroir.
The list includes a large selection of
wines by the glass.

Raymond Vineyard & Cellar

849 Zinfandel Lane
St. Helena CA 94574
800.525.2659
www.raymondwine.com

Open daily for tasting; tours by
appointment. Founded in 1971 by
the Raymond Family. The father,
Roy Sr., had entered the wine
industry as a cellar worker at
Beringer Brothers Winery in 1933.
The woman he eventually married,
Martha Jane Beringer, was the
granddaughter and grandniece of the
founders of that winery. The family
is now on its fifth generation as
Napa Valley winemakers. Sauvignon
Blanc, Chardonnay, Cabernet
Sauvignon, Merlot, Zinfandel.

River House Books

1234 Adams Street
St. Helena CA 94574
707.963.1165 Fax: 707.963.1187
www.riverhousebooksnapavalley.co
m

Located next door to the Napa Valley
Roasting Company. Offers a large
selection of general books as well as
Napa Valley titles.

Salvestrin Estate Vineyard & Winery

397 Main Street
St. Helena CA 94574
707.963.5105
www.salvestrinwineco.com

Tours and tastings by appointment. The family has been growing grapes in the Napa Valley for 70 years. Guest rooms available at the family bed and breakfast inn on the property. Cabernet Sauvignon, Sangiovese.

Silverado Brewing Company

3020-A North St. Helena Hwy
St. Helena CA 94574
707.967.9876
www.silveradobrewingcompany.com
Wine Country Brew Pub - Entrees
$11-$14

Ales, beer, stout, root beer and cream soda, all made on the premises. Plus a great selection of food, from oysters, mussels and calamari to burgers, steaks, sausage and fish. And live entertainment on the weekends. Casual and popular with great food. No corkage fee.

Silverado Museum

PO Box 409 1490 Library Lane
St. Helena CA 94574
707.963.3757 Fax: 707.963.0917
Housed in a wing of the St. Helena Public Library. Open daily except Monday and holidays from noon to 4 p.m. Free admission.

Devoted to Robert Louis Stevenson, the author of such classics as *Treasure Island, Dr. Jekyll and Mr. Hyde* and *A Child's Garden of Verses.*In 1880, Stevenson spent his honeymoon in an abandoned bunkhouse at the old Silverado Mine on the slope of Mount St. Helena.

The Silverado Squatters is his account of his stay there. The museum works at all levels, for eager six-year-olds as well as bibliophiles and scholars. Includes original letters, manuscripts, first and variant editions, paintings, sculptures, photographs and memorabilia.

St. Clement Vineyards

2867 St. Helena Highway
St. Helena CA 94574
707.963.7221 800.331.8266
www.stclement.com

Open daily for tasting; tours by appointment. Tasting room is in a 19th Century Victorian. Owned by Australia's Foster's Brewing Company. Sauvignon Blanc, Merlot, Petite Sirah, Cabernet Sauvignon, Chardonnay.

St. Helena Farmers Market

PO Box 70
St. Helena CA 94574
707.486.2662
www.sthelenafarmersmkt.org

Held in Crane Park Fridays 7:30 a.m.- Noon, May through October.

St. Helena Marketplace

Highway 29 North, 2 miles past St. Helena
707.963.7282 Daily 10 am - 6 pm
www.sthelenamarketplace.com

Includes Donna Karan, Brooks Brothers, and Jones New York.

St. Helena Olive Oil Company

1351 Main Street
St. Helena CA 94574
800.939.9880
www.sholiveoil.com

Located in downtown St. Helena (as well as in Rutherford) the store sells extra virgin olive oil, vinegars and a variety of other foods and kitchen/culinary paraphernalia.

St. Helena Wine Center

1321 Main Street
St. Helena Ca 94574
707.963.1313 800.331.1311
www.shwc.com

Located in an historic stone building that was formerly a bank (the vault is definitely more interesting now than when it had just money in it). Offers a large selection of Napa Valley and other California wines, as well as an outstanding selection of ports and spirits.

St. Helena Wine Merchants

699 S. Helena Highway
St. Helena CA 94574
707.963.7888 800.729.9463
www.sthelenawinemerchants.com

Located on the west side of Highway 29 just south of Dean and Deluca and St. Helena

Wine shop specializing in hard-to-find, allocated and small production Napa Valley wines. Hundreds of wines from California and elsewhere.

Spirits In Stone

St. Helena Premium Outlets, Suite 2D
3111 Saint Helena Highway
St. Helena CA 94574

707.963.7000 800.974.6629
www.spiritsinstone.com

Contemporary Zimbabwe Shona Sculpture. Newsweek says, "Perhaps the most important new art form to emerge from Africa in this century." The gallery's brochure says, "Sculpting with simple tools, the self-taught artists carve stones that illumine with more than 200 color variations. A diverse body of work with dynamic, spiritual themes." We say, "This stuff is absolutely beautiful." Go see it!

Spring Mountain Vineyard

2805 Spring Mountain Road. St. Helena
707.967.4188
www.springmtn.com

Tours (by appointment only and there is a charge) of the 1885 estate include winery, vineyards, gardens, caves and tasting in the Miravalle Victorian, a familiar sight for fans of the former TV series *Falconcrest*. The winery produces Sauvignon Blanc, Syrah, Cabernet Sauvignon.

Stony Hill Vineyard

3331 North St. Helena Highway, St. Helena
707.963.2636
www.stonyhillvineyard.com

The first still-in-operation winery built after Prohibition in the Napa Valley, opening in 1952. Visits by appointment only. Stony Hill was the first "cult" winery in the valley and its wines are available only to the members of their small mailing list. The winery produces Chardonnay, White Riesling and Gewürztraminer.

Sunshine Foods

1115 Main St.
St. Helena CA 94574
707.963.7070

It's hard to find a plain old, down-home grocery store in the Napa Valley, although maybe that's not such a bad thing. Sunshine was one once, but no longer. Now it offers a fantastic selection of gourmet (the word isn't overworked here) foods and deli products. You'll find everything you need for a picnic. It's located on the west side of Main Street (Highway 29) at the south end of the business district.

Sutter Home Winery/ Trinchero Family Estates

277 St. Helena Highway South
(Highway 29)
St. Helena CA 94574
707.963.3104
www.sutterhome.com
Open daily for complimentary tasting.

At south end of St. Helena on west side of Highway 29 (across from Louis Martini Winery). Approximately 3.5 miles north of Rutherford.
    The House of White Zin. Originally a small family winery, their invention of White Zinfandel made them a fortune. If you've ever enjoyed a glass of White Zin, you owe it to yourself to stop by Sutter Home, have another and thank the Trinchero (it's pronounced with a hard sound—"Trin-ker'-o") Family for all their work.
    Yes, there is a "Red Zin," and has been for many years In fact, that's what true Zinfandel is. Zinfandel is not a white grape, it's red. (Of course red wines actually come from black grapes and real white wines come

from green grapes, but that's another story.) White Zinfandel is made by removing the wine from contact with the grape skins very early in the fermentation process, so that very little color is extracted. The result is a whitish wine that's usually served cold and is definitely very popular. Sutter Home produces more than 13 different varietals.

Tasting on Main

1142 Main Street
St. Helena CA 94574
707.967.1042
www.tastingonmain.com

Open daily. Tasting bar in downtown St. Helena offering tastes from a variety of Napa Valley wineries including Schweiger Vineyards, Kelham Vineyards, Robert Keenan Winery, Saddleback Cellars, Venge Family Reserve, Ehlers Grove, Oakville Ranch, Richard Partridge and Broman Cellars.

Taylor's Refresher

933 Main St. (Highway 29)
St. Helena CA 94574
707.963.3486
www.taylorsrefresher.com
American - Burgers/Sandwiches $4-$9
Open 11 am to 9 pm, seven days a week.

Sure it's just a walk-up hamburger joint. But how many hamburger joints do you know that serve premium Napa Valley wines, or have a corkage fee if you want to bring your own wine? Plus, the hamburgers and shakes are delicious, and they've got great microbrews. Oh, yeah, and a legendary ahi sandwich. A favorite spot for locals—and, yes, you'll probably spot a winemaker or two here at lunchtime. Taylor's also has a branch at the San Francisco Ferry Building and will be opening another at Oxbow Market (see page 66) in Napa.

Terra

1345 Railroad Avenue St. Helena CA 94574
707.963.8931
www.terrarestaurant.com
Wine Country - Entrees $18.50-$29

One star in the Michelin Guide to the San Francisco Bay Area. A Napa Valley institution. Husband-and-wife team Hiro Sone and Lissa Doumani founded Terra in 1988. A heritage of Japanese, French and California cuisine adds up to an outstanding selection of dishes. Try appetizers such as Fricasse of Miyagi Oysters and Chanterelle in Chardonnay Cream Sauce, or entrees like Grilled Lamb T-bones with Potato Ricotta Gnocchi.

Tra Vigne Restaurant

1050 Charter Oak Avenue
St. Helena CA 94574
707.963.4444
www.travignerestaurant.com
Wine Country Italian - Entrees $14.50-$32.95

Many consider this one of the best restaurants in the Napa Valley. No one denies that it's right up there among the very finest. It's a great place in which to hang out, munching on the marinated olives they serve at the bar.

Tra Vigne also has its Cantinetta, (see page 97) a gourmet deli with pastries, breads, pastas, and wine bar.

V. Sattui Winery

1111 White Lane
St. Helena CA 94574
707.963.7774 Fax: 707.963.4324
www.vsattui.com
Open daily for self-guided tours and complimentary tasting.

Just 1 1/2 miles south of St. Helena along the east side of Highway 29 across from the Beacon gas station. To avoid a parking ticket, park in the winery parking lot, not on White Lane.

Some wineries used to mumble about Sattui being a retail shop rather than a winery (overlooking how many things they sell in their own retail shops). The reality is that Darryl Sattui does a very good job at both winemaking and retailing. Visitors love it. The award-winning wine is excellent and complimentary. (And it's not available anywhere but the winery.)

The gourmet deli offers over 200 different cheeses. And visitors can enjoy lunch in the two-acre shaded picnic area. Highly recommended. Sattui produces more than 15 different wines.

Villa Corona

1138 Main Street
St. Helena CA 94574
707.963.7812
Mexican

Sister to the popular restaurant in Napa.

White Barn

2727 Sulphur Springs Avenue
St. Helena CA 94574
707.251.8715

Locals and visitors enjoy theatrical and musical performances throughout the year in an 75-seat theater that was originally a carriage house built in 1872. All proceeds go to charity. A labor of love for founder/artistic director Nancy Garden and her family.

White Sulphur Springs Retreat & Conference Center

3100 White Sulphur Springs Road
St. Helena CA 94574
707.963.8588 Fax 707.963.2890
www.whitesulphursprings.com
Rooms and cottages – full-time retreat center for the Hoffman Institute Foundation.

The only reservations now being accepted at White Sulphur Springs are for participants of the Hoffman Process or one of the other Hoffman Institute programs.

In St. Helena, turn west on Spring St. at the Exxon gas station. Go 3 miles to end of road.

White Sulphur Springs was California's first hot springs resort. Its natural beauty has been retained since the resort was founded in 1852. Nestled in a canyon just west of St. Helena, this 45-acre resort offers seclusion and tranquillity. Hiking trails lead through mature redwoods, madrone and fir trees, over meandering creeks and around cascading waterfalls.

Whitehall Lane Winery

1563 St. Helena Highway
St Helena CA 94574
707.963.9454 800.963.9454
www.whitehalllane.com

Open daily for tasting. Founded in 1979, owned today by the Leonardini family. Cabernet Sauvignon, Merlot, Sauvignon Blanc, Chardonnay.

Wine Spectator Greystone Restaurant

2555 Main Street
St. Helena, CA 94574
(located at the Culinary Institute of America)
707.967.1010 Fax: 707.967.2375
www.ciachef.edu/greystone/spectator
Wine Country Mediterranean - Entrees $19-$32

Open for lunch and dinner. Greystone's terraced gardens of herbs, vegetables, and flowers provide the perfect introduction to the vibrant colors, enticing aromas and bustling activity of the Wine Spectator Greystone Restaurant. Local, seasonal ingredients are the inspiration for the cuisine, which features California's bounty from the land and sea.

Wine Valley Restaurant

1146 Main Street
St. Helena, CA 94574
707.963.3371
www.winevalleyrestaurant.com
Italian

Moderately priced meals from the chef formerly at the very popular Green Valley Cafe.

Woodhouse Chocolate

1367 Main Street
St. Helena, CA 94574
707.963.8413
www.woodhousechocolate.com

Family-owned chocolatemakers. Some chocolates can be shipped but seasonal creations are available only at the store.

Calistoga

Calistoga was developed in the 1860s and its name is reputed to have been accidentally coined by town founder Sam Brannan. Brannan apparently intended to refer to it as the "Saratoga of California", the *Saratoga* referring to the well-known spa area in New York State. Brannan, having had a few drinks, instead came out with the "Calistoga of Sarafornia". Calistoga it stayed.

Brannan's fortunes didn't get any better. He had to sell most of the resort in 1875 and he died penniless in 1889. A sad end for California's first millionaire.

Calistoga is the place for spas, and it's the only town in the Napa Valley with any real nightlife—despite the fact that it has only one-tenth the population of the city of Napa. People walk along the sidewalks; wander in and out of bars, restaurants and shops; smile at each other; and, in general, have a great time. After all, after lying in mud, soaking in bubbling mineral water and getting massaged throughout the day, you'd be pretty mellow, too.

All Seasons Bistro, Wine Bar and Wine Shop

1400 Lincoln Avenue
Calistoga CA 94515
Restaurant: 707.942.9111 Wine Shop: 707.942.6828 800.804.9463
www.allseasonswineshop.com

California Bistro - Entrees $18-$35

Established in 1983, it was one of the first great restaurants in the valley. Great vegetarian fare and desserts. A favorite with locals as well as visitors. Wine bar offers wines of the world with a focus on Napa Valley and Northern California, and a daily selection of 10-20 wines.

American Indian Trading Company

1407 Lincoln Avenue
Calistoga CA 94515
707.942.9330 877.735.7755
www.spiritfeather.com

An outstanding selection of authentic Native American art, including jewelry, beadwork, drums, pipes, knives, pottery, dolls, bows, quivers, tomahawks, lances, rattles, prayer staff wands, chokers, kachinas, dolls, and more. Tribes represented include Sioux, Navajo, Choctaw, Cherokee, Lakota, Yavapai, Hopi, Zuni, and Navajo.

BarVino

1457 Lincoln Avenue (in the Mount View Hotel)
Calistoga CA 94515
707.942.9900
www.bar-vino.com

Small plates tapas style.

Bosko's Trattoria

1364 Lincoln Avenue
Calistoga CA 94515
707.942.9088
www.boskos.com
Pasta - $8.95-$14.50

Located in a building constructed in 1883 from rock quarried in the valley. Pizza, too.

Bothé-Napa Valley State Park

3801 North Saint Helena Highway (Highway 29)
Calistoga CA 94515
707.942.4575
www.napanet.net/~bothe

See more extensive information on page 175.

Over 10 miles of excellent trails. Picnic grounds and 50 campsites. Includes one campsite for hikers/bikers and another designed for disabled visitors. Outdoor swimming pool. A wonderful place for all ages. Open year round. We consider it the loveliest public place to hike in the entire valley. For reservations, call 1.800.444.PARK.

Guided horseback tours are available at Bothé through Triple Creek Horse Outfit (page 173).

Brannan's

1374 Lincoln Avenue
Calistoga CA 94515
707.942.2233
www.brannansgrill.com
New American - Entrees $16-$28

Located in a renovated 1906 building in the heart of downtown Calistoga. Menu includes Lamb Shank, Roasted Sonoma Chicken, and Pistachio Crusted Mahi-Mahi. Offers seating by the window so you can watch fellow visitors stroll the sidewalks.

Buster's Original Southern Barbecue & Bakery

1207 Foothill Boulevard
Calistoga CA 94515
707.942.5605
Barbecue - $6.50-$9.50

Charles Davis moved to Calistoga in 1999 and he's been turning out authentic barbecue at the intersection of Highway 29 and Lincoln Avenue ever since. Sandwiches, dinners, soda fountain.

Calistoga Creamery & Bakery

1353 Lincoln Avenue
Calistoga CA 94515
707.942.0777
www.calistogacreamerybakery.com

Wonderful European pastries, cakes and cookies, as well as gourmet ice creams.

Calistoga Depot

1458 Lincoln Avenue
Calistoga CA 94515

Built in 1868, it's the second oldest railroad depot in California. Train service is long gone, but the depot offers six renovated rail cars with shops and historical exhibits, including a restaurant and the Calistoga Chamber of Commerce.

Calistoga Farmers' Market

1546 Lincoln Avenue
Calistoga CA 94515
Saturdays 8:30 a.m. - Noon

Vegetables, seasonal fruits, Asian vegetables, plants and more.

Calistoga Inn

1250 Lincoln Avenue
Calistoga, CA 94515
707.942.4101
www.calistogainn.com

18 rooms - $75-$100Turn-of-the-century inn with comfortable rooms and no minimum nightly stay. European-style shared bath accommodations. Each room has sink and mirror; down the hall are shared men's and women's facilities with restrooms and showers. Continental breakfast included. Recommended by *The New York Times* and *Wine Spectator*.

Calistoga Inn Restaurant

1250 Lincoln Avenue
Calistoga, CA 94515
707.942.4101
www.calistogainn.com
California Cuisine - Entrees $14.50-
$21.50

Another long-time favorite of locals
and visitors. Great English-style pub.
Live, local musicians on the
weekends and dynamite buffalo
wings. It also has its own excellent
microbrewery, the Napa Valley
Brewing Company. Large and
attractive patio dining along the
Napa River. One of our very favorite
outdoor dining places in the valley.
Corkage $10.

Calistoga Mineral Water Company

865 Silverado Trail North
Calistoga CA 94515
707.942.6295
www.calistogawater.com

One of the country's most famous
bottled water companies, it has been
owned by Perrier for years. Visitors
are very welcome. During your visit
you'll enjoy a water tasting with lots
of different flavors. Due to
government regulations the
company can't advertise its water as
healthful, but the reality is they've
got lots of testimonials and people
have been drinking (and bathing in)
Calistoga's water for more than a
hundred years as a health tonic.

Calistoga Pack Goats

4762 Petrified Forest Road
Calistoga, CA 94515
707.942.5504
Email: goatwalk@aol.com

Two-hour hikes on Napa Valley
trails. Goats carry your food and
water. You get to stroll along
unencumbered.

Calistoga Pottery

1001 Foothill Boulevard
Calistoga CA 94515
707.942.0216
www.calistogapottery.com

Handcrafted dinner and serving
pieces.

Calistoga Ranch

www.calistogaranch.com
200 rooms - $400 - $650

Auberge Resorts, which also owns
Auberge du Soleil in Rutherford, has
built a new "private residential
resort" 157 acres east of the
Silverado Trail and south of
Calistoga. It includes 27 "owner
lodges" and 47 guest lodges, for a
total of 200 rooms. It also offers spa
services, and a restaurant and
lounge.

Calistoga Roastery

1631 Lincoln Avenue
Calistoga CA 94515
707.942.5757
www.calistogaroastery.com

A friendly local hangout with
pastries and great coffee.

Calistoga Village Inn & Spa

1880 Lincoln Avenue
Calistoga, Ca 94515
707.942.0991
www.greatspa.com
$69 - $159

Rooms, some with whirlpool tubs,
and a full spa located on Calistoga's
main street. Three mineral-water
pools for spa and overnight guests.

Calistoga Wine Stop
1458 Lincoln Avenue #2
Calistoga CA 94515
800.648.4521
calistogawinestp@aol.com

Located in an old railroad car in the middle of the Calistoga Depot. A wide selection of wines, specializing in California labels with a focus on Napa and Sonoma counties.

Castello di Amorosa
4045 North Saint Helena Hwy
Calistoga, CA 94515
800.286.7212
www.castellodiamorosa.com

A spectacular Italian castle owned by Darryl Sattui, who also owns the popular V. Sattui Winery at the south end of St. Helena. Castle has 107 rooms, seven levels (four below ground), a moat (dry) with drawbridge, and a dungeon with assorted instruments of torture including a top-of-the-line model iron maiden. Charge for tasting and additional charge for tour. Appointment necessary for tour.

Ca'Toga Galleria d'Arte
1206 Cedar Street
Calistoga CA 94515
707.942.3900
www.catoga.com

Unique works of art from Carlo Marchiori, including ceiling murals, porcelain, ceramics, watercolor, paintings, tiles, stone plaques, sculpture, furniture, accessories, book, cards and posters. Open daily except Tuesday and Wednesday.

Chateau Montelena
1429 Tubbs Lane
Calistoga CA 94515
707.942.5105
www.chateaumontelena.com

Two miles north of Lincoln Avenue (Calistoga's main street).

Chateau Montelena is one of the two Napa Valley wineries that won top honors in the historic Paris wine tasting in 1976. Montelena won for its 1973 Chardonnay. The winery was founded in 1882 and reborn in 1972. Excellent wines in a beautiful setting. Chardonnay, Cabernet Sauvignon, Riesling.

Checkers
1414 Lincoln Avenue
Calistoga CA 94515
707.942.9300
Pizza – $8.95 and up

Thin-crust pizza, calzones, pasta ($7-$14), sandwiches ($7.95-$8.95) and salads ($6.50-$11). Popular place with the same owners as Brannan's and the Flat Iron Grill.

Clos Pegase Winery
1060 Dunaweal Lane
Calistoga CA 904515
707.942.4981
www.clospegase.com
Open daily for tours and tasting.

SEVEN miles north of St. Helena to Dunaweal Lane and turn right. 1/2 mile to winery on the left

Clos Pegase is named after Pegasus, the winged horse of Greek mythology. According to legend, the birth of both wine and art occurred when Pegasus' hooves unleashed the sacred Spring of the Muses.

Clos Pegase Winery, designed by famed architect Michael Graves (Photo courtesy of the winery.)

After holding an international competition, the winery chose renowned architect Michael Graves, to build a "temple to wine." The architecture is absolutely stunning. It's a rather amazing place for a picnic, which you can do in the company of a 300-year-old oak tree and adjacent Merlot vineyard.

Chardonnay, Merlot, Cabernet Sauvignon, Pinot Noir, Sauvignon Blanc, Cabernet Franc, Zinfandel.

Copperfield's Books

1330 Lincoln Avenue
Calistoga CA 94515
707.942.1616
www.copperfields.net

General, children's, children's Spanish, literature, cooking, story hour, used, rare, new and bargain books.

Enoteca Wine Shop

1348-B Lincoln Avenue
Calistoga CA 94515
707.942.1117

A wide selection of wines from all over the world, ranging from under $10 to over $2,000 in price. Owner Margaux Singleton has assembled cult wines, foreign favorites, reasonably-priced U.S., South African and Australian wines, as well as ports, sherries, sparkling and dessert wines. The interior of the shop has been painted in *tromp l'oeil* style by Carlo Marchiori, Calistoga resident and owner of Villa Ca'Toga, to look like the interior of an underground wine cellar.

Flat Iron Grill

1440 Lincoln Avenue
Calistoga CA 94515
707.942.1220
www.flatirongrill.com
American Grill - Entrees $11-$20

Very comfortable and beautifully decorated, right on Calistoga's main street. A very basic and delicious menu designed for the meat-eater. Steaks, salmon, chicken, ribs and pasta. Their New York Steak special is just $150.95 and includes a bottle of 1998 Opus One. (You can skip the wine and pay only $19.95.)

Frank Family Vineyards

1091 Larkmead Lane
Calistoga CA 94515
800.574.9463
www.frankfamilyvineyards.com

A popular and friendly place producing Cabernet Sauvignon, Chardonnay, Sangiovese and Zinfandel. They also produce a sparkling wine which they, unlike any other winery in California, refer to as "champagne."

Golden Haven Spa Hot Springs Resort

1713 Lake Street
Calistoga CA 94515
707.942.6793
www.goldenhaven.com
29 rooms - $65-$175

Off the beaten path, this inexpensive motel is located three blocks from Calistoga's main street. Open to the public 9 a.m. to 9 p.m A favorite for mud baths, whirlpools, blanket wraps, mineral baths, massage, foot reflexology, swimming pool and hot mineral pool. It's not as fancy as the others, but the prices are reasonable, and it's one of the few places in Calistoga where a couple can enjoy a mud bath together. We like it a lot.

Graeser Winery
255 Petrified Forest Road
Calistoga CA 94515
707.942.4437
www.graeserwinery.com

Open daily for tasting. Cabernet Sauvignon, Cabernet Franc, Merlot. All from vineyards on Diamond Mountain. A beautiful setting one mile above Calistoga.

Hans Fahden Vineyards
5300 Mountain Home Ranch Road
Calistoga CA 94515
707.942.6760
www.hansfahden.com

Open daily for tasting. Driving from Calistoga, the winery is located shortly before the Petrified Forest. It's at 1200 feet elevation. This beautiful property has been in the Fahden family since 1912. Hiking, picnicking among the water gardens. Fly-fishing and wine cave events by appointment.   Estate-grown Cabernet Sauvignon. Also produces vinegar (intentionally).

Hurd Beeswax Candles
1255 Lincoln Avenue
Calistoga CA 94515
707.963.7211 800.977.7211
www.hurdbeeswaxcandles.com

This was a little ways north of St. Helena for 37 years, now it's in downtown Calistoga. A wonderful place for gifts for friends, family and even yourself. Candles in all sizes, styles, colors and shapes. Custom candles, too. Handmade pure beeswax candles made weekdays. Don't miss the demonstration beehive. (Don't worry—it's behind glass.)

Hydro Bar and Grill
1403 Lincoln Avenue
Calistoga CA 94515
707.942.9777
American Grill - Entrees $9.95-$18.95

Burgers, steaks, ribs and chicken. Pizza, too. Great bar and large selection of draft beers. Traditional jazz and swing Wednesday and Sunday evenings. Definitely one of the liveliest places in the valley and a good place to meet people. Comfortable décor, friendly service. One of our very favorite places in Calistoga—or even the valley.

Indian Springs Resort
1712 Lincoln Avenue
Calistoga CA 94515
707.942.4913
www.indianspringscalistoga.com
16 bungalows and 2 houses - $215-$500

The oldest continuously operating thermal pool and spa facility in California. Now includes the former Nancy's Hot Springs. Situated on three thermal geysers and 16 acres of ancient volcanic ash. The 1913 bath house has been restored to pristine condition. Ceiling fans circulate the air, thermal geysers warm the volcanic ash in the mud baths and sterilize the mud after each use, gentle music is piped throughout the treatment rooms, and mineral water fragrant with fresh citrus and cucumber is provided by the well trained and solicitous staff throughout the treatment.

Mud baths, mineral baths, massages, Remy Laure facial and body polish treatments. Large mineral pool. Lodging available in bungalows.

Kitani Sushi
1631 Lincoln Avenue
Calistoga CA 94515
707 942 6857

A sushi restaurant also offering traditional baked and steamed items, including tempura.

Lee Youngman Galleries
1316 Lincoln Avenue
Calistoga CA 94515
707.942.0585
www.leeyoungmangalleries.com

Lodge at Calistoga, The
1865 Lincoln Avenue
Calistoga CA 94515
707.942.9400
www.thelodgeatcalistoga.com

Boutique hotel with 55 rooms - $100-$260

Amenities include geothermal hot springs mineral pool and hot tub, and sauna and steam rooms.

Mayacamas Ranch Conference Center, Group Retreat and Resort
3975 Mountain Home Ranch Road
Calistoga, CA 94515
707.942.5127
www.mayacamasranch.com
26 rooms - $150-$240

On 80 acres in the beautiful Mayacmas Mountains, five miles from Calistoga and 1.25 hours from San Francisco. Mayacamas Ranch is an ideal setting for groups that want to get away from the city to a rustic, yet sophisticated, facility. Groups with 50 or more people can rent the ranch for their exclusive use for overnight visits, meetings, workshops, conferences and other events. Or several smaller groups may occupy separate sections of the ranch at the same time, accessing their own conference room and lodging.

Decorated throughout in a colorful hacienda style, the ranch has one 2,000-sq. ft conference room and two mid-size conference rooms, as well as many outdoor venues for activities. The ranch is a full-service facility complete with gourmet chef and professional kitchen, indoor and outdoor dining rooms and AV systems.

Recreational facilities include horseback riding, hilltop pool and spa, massage/spa treatments, hiking trails, a small lake with canoes and fishing, and gardens. The ranch also has a large, grassy meadow area with awesome mountain views perfect for group activities, weddings, parties and picnics.

Miguel's Bar & Grill
1437 Lincoln Avenue
Calistoga CA 94515
707.942.6868
American/Mexican - Entrees $7-$19.95

American and Mexican comfort food at family-friendly prices.

Mt. St. Helena Golf Course

P.O. Box 344
Calistoga CA 94515
707.942.9966
www.napacountyfairgrounds.com

9-holes, par 34. Men - 2,759 yards.
Women - par 35 - 2,650 yards.
Public course located at Napa
County Fairgrounds.

Mount View Hotel & Spa

1457 Lincoln Avenue
Calistoga CA 94515
707.942.5789 800.772.8838 Fax:
707.942.9165
www.mountviewspa.com
20 rooms, 9 suites, 3 cottages $145 -
$225

An inviting health spa featuring a
pool, natural mineral water,
whirlpool tub, poolside dining,
Swedish massage, sports massage,
shiatsu massage, reflexology,
whirlpool baths, body wraps (herbal,
mud, seaweed, and valerian) and
facials.

Mountain Home Ranch

3400 Mountain Home Ranch Road
Calistoga, CA 94515
707.942.6616 707.942.9091 (fax)
www.mountainhomeranch.com
23 rooms - $45-$132

A family resort ten minutes from
Calistoga run by the same family
since the turn of the century. 350
acres with two swimming pools,
horseshoes, ping-pong, pool table,
tennis court, volleyball, basketball,
hiking trails, a lake for fishing and
swimming, stream, picnic area,
barbeque pit, and natural warm
mineral springs. No phones or
televisions in the rooms, but plenty
of books and board games. Quiet and
secluded, but only ten minutes from

the spas. All prices include full
breakfast.

Lodge rooms; cabins with kitchen,
fireplace and bathroom; and rustic
cabins with beds, toilet, basin and
shared showers.

Napa County Fairgrounds

1435 Oak Street PO Box 344
Calistoga CA 94515
707.942.5111
www.napacountyfairgrounds.com

Site of the Napa County Fair held
every July. Also has a 9-hole golf
course, automobile racetrack and
conference/meeting facilities.

Napa Valley Ovens

1355 Lincoln Ave.
Calistoga CA 94515
707.942.0777

A local bakery with real bread,
hearty and crusty. Pastries as well.
Open 7 a.m. to 3 p.m.

Nicola's Delicatessen & Pizzeria

1359 Lincoln Avenue
Calistoga CA 94515
707.942.6272
Delicatessen - Sandwiches $3.70-
$6.50, Pizza - $5.95 and up

Also burgers, salads and breakfasts.
All soups, sauces, salads, cookies,
cinnamon rolls and muffins are
homemade. Ten beers on tap. A
popular place that's been there for
years.

Oat Hill Mine Trail

The trail is an old wagon road that
originally went to mercury mines.
The trailhead is at the intersection of
Highway 29 and Silverado Trail,
about one-half mile north of

Calistoga. Park alongside either road or on Lake Street, but not in the small dirt lot at the trailhead. The trail begins at the metal gate.

The trail is a strenuous hike, rising 1,900 feet over nearly five miles. Best time to visit is spring. Make sure you bring water.

Old Faithful Geyser Of California

1299 Tubbs Lane
Calistoga CA 94515
707.942.6463 Fax: 707.942.6898
www.oldfaithfulgeyser.com
Open daily at 9 a.m. Charge for admission

Every 40 minutes—woooosh! (Photo courtesy of "Old Faithful of Calistoga.")

One of only three "Old Faithful" geysers in the world, erupting approximately every 40 minutes and shooting water 60 feet into the air.

Geothermal exhibit hall, gift shop, picnic area and self-guided geothermal tour. Private moonlight parties for 20 or more by reservation only.

Petrified Forest

4100 Petrified Forest Road
Calistoga CA 94515
707.942.6667
www.petrifiedforest.org

Open daily 10a.m.- 6p.m .(Winter: 10 a.m.- 5 p.m.) Six miles west of Calistoga. Charge for admission

A fascinating and educational example of the powers of nature and the vastness of time. Huge petrified trees scattered throughout the grounds as well as a museum and gift shop. Excellent for older kids.

Robert Louis Stevenson State Park

3801 North St. Helena Highway
Calistoga CA 94515
707.942.4575
www.parks.ca.gov/default.asp?page_id=472

Drive north from Calistoga on Highway 29 almost eight miles until you see signs for the park. Park in lots on either side of the road. The trailhead is on the west side.

Open during daylight hours. Five mile hiking trail to the top of Mount St. Helena. It's a strenuous hike with an elevation gain of 2,100 feet. The park itself is some 5,000 acres, all undeveloped.

Bring your own drinking water for the long, sometimes very hot, climb up the mountain. Best time to visit is spring or fall, when it's not too hot or not too wet. View from the summit includes the nearby geyser country and, weather permitting, distant mountains such as Lassen, Shasta and the Sierra Nevada. No restrooms.

Famous writer Stevenson, who wrote such classics as *Treasure Island* and *A Child's Garden of Verses*, honeymooned here in an abandoned bunkhouse in 1880. His story *The Silverado Squatters* describes his stay. The Silverado Museum in St. Helena (see page 106)

has an extensive collection of Stevenson memorabilia.

Sam Brannan Cottage,

1311 Washington Street
Calistoga CA 94515

Sam Brannan arrived in Napa Valley in the late 1850s with the dream of making it the "Saratoga of California." In 1866 cottages were built and palm trees planted in preparation for the grand opening of the resort. This is the only cottage still standing.

Schramsberg Vineyards

1400 Schramsberg Road
Calistoga CA 94515
707.942.6668   800.877.3623
www.schramsberg.com

Tours and tastings by appointment only. $20 per person. Designated a California historical landmark. Founded in 1862 by Jacob Schram with caves dug by Chinese laborers at the turn of the century. Robert Louis Stevenson visited the winery in 1880 and devoted a chapter of his book "Silverado Squatters" to Schramsberg and its wines. Schram's original gardens were restored by Jack and Jamie Davies, who purchased the then-abandoned winery in 1965.

Jack Davies was a pioneer in preserving agricultural land in the Napa Valley and the winery's Querencia Brut Rosé was created to honor his efforts and generate funds to continue preserving the valley. Sparkling wines from Chardonnay, Pinot Noir and Pinot Meunier, made using the Méthod Champenoise.

Sharpsteen Museum

1311 Washington Street
Calistoga CA 94515
707.942.5911
www.sharpsteen-museum.org
One block west of Lincoln Ave. on Washington St.
Hours: 10 a.m. - 4 p.m., April - October, and Noon - 4 p.m., November - March. Free admission.

Sweeping dioramas, fascinating artifacts and unusual exhibits in a museum created by Ben Sharpsteen, Walt Disney Studio animator and Oscar-winning producer.

Exhibits include a 32-foot-long diorama depicting 1860s life at the opulent resort that gave Calistoga —"the Saratoga of the Pacific"—its name. An elaborately furnished "Sam Brannan" cottage from the lavish Victorian spa resort. A restored stagecoach that encountered many a bandit on its mountain journeys. A working model of an 1871 train. Vintage car memorabilia. A Native American exhibit. A Robert Louis Stevenson exhibit and bronze sculpture.

Solage Calistoga

Calistoga, CA 94515
www.solagecalistoga.com
89 rooms - $275-$850

From Solage Hotels, the owners of Auberge du Soleil and Calistoga Ranch. Amenities at Solage include restaurant, in-room dining, fitness center, spa and gboutique, pool and hot tub, children's pool, bocce courts, mud bar and bathhouse, complimentary bikes and continental breakfast.

Sterling Vineyards and Sky Tram

1111 Dunaweal Lane
Calistoga CA 94515
707.942.3344
www.sterlingvyds.com
North of St. Helena turn east on Dunaweal Lane. Sky tram charge includes tasting (for adults).

The SkyTram takes visitors to the Sterling Vineyards winery at the top of the hill.

A beautiful Mykonos-style winery, sparkling white on top of a hill just south of Calistoga. Travel the Sky Tram to the winery where you can take a leisurely self-paced tour. Gorgeous views of the valley below.

Cabernet Sauvignon, Merlot, Chardonnay, Sauvignon Blanc, Pinot Noir.

Treasures of Tibet

1458 Lincoln Avenue Suite 4
Calistoga CA 94515
707.942.8287

Books, clothing, music and other items from Tibet and India.

Villa Ca'toga

3061 Myrtledale Road
Calistoga CA 94515
707.942.3900
www.catoga.com

A Palladian villa, created by artist Carlo Marchiori, that serves as his residence and workshop. A large salon and six other rooms are completely decorated in *trompe l'oeil* frescoes.

The garden and grounds include pools, statues, fountains, Roman ruins and 18th century follies. One tour weekly, every Saturday at 11 a.m. from May through October. Charge for tour.

Just one of the sights that await visitors at artist Carlo Marchiori's Villa Ca'toga. (Photo courtesy of Villa Ca'toga.)

The Ca'toga Galleria D'Arte (see page 114) in downtown Calistoga sells Marchiori's art and other works.

Von Strasser Winery
1510 Diamond Mountain Road
Calistoga CA 94515
707.942.0930
www.vonstrasser.com

Tours and tastings by appointment only. Only wines from the Diamond Mountain appellation. Cabernet Sauvignon, Zinfandel, Chardonnay.

Wappo Bar & Bistro
1226 Washington St,
Calistoga, CA 94515
707.942.4712 Fax 707.942.4741
www.wappobar.com
Globally inspired - Entrees $12-22

A unique and sophisticated blend of regional cuisines of the world. Warm copper topped tables and wine bar with a redwood interior, this neighborhood bistro with its relaxed and casual ambience is a favorite among locals, winemakers and food enthusiasts. In the warmer months, a table under the grapevine-covered arbor next to the fountain is a must. There's also a private dining room for large parties and special events.

Dr. Wilkinson's Hot Springs
1507 Lincoln Avenue
Calistoga CA 94515
707.942.4102
www.drwilkinson.com
Rooms and cottages - $109-$189
Located at the corner of Lincoln and Fairway in the heart of Calistoga.

Mud baths, message, mineral baths, facelifts, salt glow scrubs, Terra-Thalasso body treatment and cerofango treatments (a unique application of mud, clay, botanicals and paraffin to the hands and feet). Indoor and outdoor pools, comfortable lodging.

For more than 50 years, Wilkinson's has offered visitors the soothing, invigorating magic of his mud treatments. Lodging available.

Wine Garage
1020 Foothill Boulevard #C
Calistoga CA 94515
707.942.5332
www.winegarage.net

A very personalized wine shop. Owner Todd Miller drives and tastes his way throughout the wine regions of California, seeking great buys from small wineries with limited distribution. No wine is more than $25 and many are less than $10.

Calistoga Spas

What happens in a spa? Why would someone pay to get slimed? Ah, but it's far more than that.

Your Typical Spa Experience

What follows is typical, but each spa has its own physical layout, amenities and treatment order.

If you planned ahead, you already made an appointment before you left home for the Napa Valley. If not, try to do it as soon as you arrive in the valley. If that's not possible, just show up and hope they have an opening.

When you arrive at the front desk, you'll choose your various treatments from an extensive menu of options: baths, wraps, facials, scrubs, massages. Wraps, facials and scrubs can involve many different herbs and scents, all designed to make your skin cleaner and healthier; remove toxins and dead cells from your body; and invigorate your skin, your body and your psyche. Each spa has its own particular formulas.

Mud baths are always optional, and not every spa has them, but if they're available we recommend that you try one.

Once you've picked your choices, you'll be assigned to a room, usually a private one. A few spas are set up so that you and your partner can take mud baths and mineral baths together.

You will disrobe, wrap yourself in a towel, and then be led into another room. There you'll shower and walk over to a mud bath. There are separate rooms for men and women.

Mud Bath

The bath is (usually) a rectangular cement tub filled with dark mud. It's not your average mud, but a mixture of clay or local volcanic ash, imported peat moss and local hot springs water. The purpose of the mud is to remove toxins from your body, relax your muscles and joints, and cleanse and invigorate your skin.

Mud for two. (Photo courtesy of Golden Haven Spa.)

You sit on the edge of the tub, swing your legs into the tub, and then kind of scoot the rest of you over until you're all in. Lie down on your back in the mud, wiggle down as much as possible, then use your hands and arms to pile mud on top of yourself, until as much of you as possible is covered. If you can't get it all, don't worry. The bath attendant will cover the rest of you until only your head is uncovered.

You'll then lie there for 10-12 minutes and soak. Nothing else is expected of you. From time to time an attendant will come by, wipe the sweat off your forehead with a cool washcloth, and give you a glass of cold water to drink (through a straw.)

When the time is up, your attendant will tell you to get out. Do it slowly. Actually, you have no choice. You can't do it quickly anyhow. Hold onto the sides of the tub with your hands, then use the strength of your hands and arms to lift your rear up and swing it over to the side of the tub. Then shove, scrape and wipe as much of the mud off your body as you can back into the tub.

When you're done (don't worry, everyone still has lots of mud on them) go back into the shower and wash off the rest of the stuff. Yes, it does stick into all those cracks and crevices, so do a pretty thorough job. Once you've showered, it's time for the mineral bath

Whirlpool Mineral Bath

This bath often takes place in the same room as the mud bath. If not, you'll be led to the right location. There you'll remove your towel, get into the tub and relax for 10-15 minutes while whirlpool jets blow streams of air and bubbles in the warm water, and you soak peacefully. One spa we like even has a rubber ducky for you to play with. If you have the energy for it, you can always take a sip from the ever-present glass of cold water.

After the mud comes the bubbly water. (Photo courtesy of Golden Haven Spa.)

Blanket Wrap

Your attendant will reappear and tell you that it is time for the blanket wrap. You'll get out of the mineral bath, dry off a little, then head to the wrap room. Here you'll lie down on a comfortable bed on your back, be wrapped in blankets, and again have your forehead wiped and another glass of cold water.

Once again, your only job is to lie there, rest, and slowly cool off from the heat acquired in the mud and mineral baths. It's a good place for a short nap.

After another 10 to 15 minutes, you're once again beckoned from your reverie and led off, most likely to yet another room.

Massage

At most spas, you can choose between a half-hour or full-hour massage, or sometimes even one lasting an hour and a half. A shorter massage will cover your back, neck and shoulders. A long massage will very thoroughly cover everything from nose to toes.

Styles of massage vary, and you can request the kind you like. They range from gentle Esalen-type massage—which is pure, gentle pleasure—up to the much more vigorous Swedish massage, which frequently feels a lot better after you've gotten it than it does during.

During your massage only the area of your body that is being worked on will be exposed. The rest will be discreetly covered with a sheet. If you want to specify a male or female massage therapist, make sure you do it when you book the appointment.

At the end of your massage, you'll be allowed to lie there (many people fall asleep after or even during the massage) until you're ready to get up. You'll probably have carried your belongings along with you, so eventually you can get dressed and go back out into the world, a very different person than when you entered the spa.

Spas With Lodging

Calistoga Oasis Spa
1300 Washington St.
Calistoga, CA 94515
707.942.2122 800.404.4772
www.oasisspa.com
Located on the grounds of the Roman Spa Resort Hotel
60 rooms - $82-$230
Mineral pools

Calistoga Spa Hot Springs
1006 Washington Street
Calistoga, CA 94515
707.942.6269
www.calistogaspa.com
Mineral pools, swimming pool

Calistoga Village Inn & Spa
1880 Lincoln Avenue
Calistoga, Ca 94515
707.942.0991
www.greatspa.com

$69 - $159

Rooms, some with whirlpool tubs, and a full spa located on Calistoga's main street. Three mineral-water pools for spa and overnight guests.

Dr. Wilkinson's Hot Springs

1507 Lincoln Avenue
Calistoga CA 94515
707.942.4102
www.drwilkinson.com
Rooms and cottages - $109-$199
Located at the corner of Lincoln and Fairway in the heart of Calistoga.

Mud baths, massage, mineral baths, facelifts, salt glow scrubs, Terra-Thalasso body treatment and cerofango treatments (a unique application of mud, clay, botanicals and paraffin to the hands and feet). Indoor and outdoor pools, comfortable lodging.

For nearly 50 years, Dr. Wilkinson and his family have offered visitors the soothing, invigorating magic of his mud treatments. Some people say just mentioning Doc's name can relieve stress and relax the soul. Lodging available.

Golden Haven Spa Hot Springs Resort
1713 Lake Street
Calistoga CA 94515
707.942.6793
www.goldenhaven.com
29 rooms - $65-$175

Off the beaten path, this inexpensive motel is located three blocks from Calistoga's main street. Open to the public 9 a.m. to 9 p.m A favorite for mud baths, whirlpools, blanket wraps, mineral baths, massage, foot reflexology, swimming pool and hot mineral pool. It's not as fancy as the others, but the prices are reasonable, and it's one of the few places in Calistoga where a couple can enjoy a mud bath together. We like it a lot. Free wifi Internet access.

Indian Springs Resort

1712 Lincoln Avenue
Calistoga CA 94515
707.942.4913
www.indianspringscalistoga.com
16 bungalows and 2 houses - $215-$500

The oldest continuously operating thermal pool and spa facility in California. Known for more than 80 years as Pacheteau's, Indian Springs now includes the former Nance's Hot Springs. Situated on three thermal geysers and 16 acres of ancient volcanic ash. The 1913 bath house has been restored to pristine condition. Ceiling fans circulate the air, thermal geysers warm the volcanic ash in the mud baths and sterilize the mud after each use, gentle music is piped throughout the treatment rooms, and mineral water fragrant with fresh citrus and cucumber is provided by the well trained and solicitous staff throughout the treatment.

Mud baths, mineral baths, massages, Remy Laure facial and body polish treatments. Large mineral pool. Lodging available in bungalows.

Mount View Spa

1457 Lincoln Ave
Calistoga CA 94515
707.942.5789
www.mountviewspa.com
20 rooms, 9 suites, 3 cottages - $145-$225

Swimming pool

Roman Spa Hot Springs

1300 Washington St.
Calistoga CA 94515
800.404.4772
www.romanspahotsprings.com
60 rooms - $82-$230
Mineral pools.

Silver Rose Inn

351 Rosedale Rd.
Calistoga CA 94515
707.942.9581 800.995.9381
www.silverrose.com
20 rooms - $165-$300
Swimming pools

Spas Without Lodging

Cedar Street Spa

1107 Cedar St.
Calistoga CA 94515
707.942.2947
www.cedarstreetspa.com

Lavender Hill Spa

1015 Foothill Boulevard
Calistoga, CA. 94515
707.942.4495 800.528.4772
www.lavenderhillspa.com

Lincoln Avenue Spa

1339 Lincoln Avenue
Calistoga CA 94515
707.942.5296
www.lincolnavenuespa.com

Angwin

Nestled at the top of Howell Mountain overlooking the Napa Valley is the quiet college community of Angwin.

Angwin Airport
One Angwin Avenue
Angwin CA 94508
707.965.6219 Fax 707.965.6685
www.puc.edu/angwinairport

Angwin Airport (Virgil O. Parrett Field) is owned by Pacific Union College. The college operates the airport, and a small fleet of aircraft, to train new pilots for missionary work in isolated parts of the globe. The runway length is 3,200 feet. Tie down, gasoline, oil and mechanical services are available.

Burgess Cellars
1108 Deer Park Road   PO Box 282
St. Helena CA 94574
800.752.9463 Fax 707.963.8774
www.burgesscellars.com

Open daily by appointment only, Burgess is located just a few minutes down the hill from Angwin. You'll see the sign on the left side of the road as you drive up Deer Park Road from the Silverado Trail.

The winery and adjacent vineyards were originally started in the 1880's, and owner Tom Burgess has been operating here for 30 years. He makes excellent wines, and the view from the winery is spectacular. Bring your camera. Chardonnay, Zinfandel, Syrah, Merlot, Cabernet Sauvignon.

Elmshaven
125 Glass Mountain Lane
St. Helena CA 94574
707.963.9039
www.elmshaven.org

Elmshaven is a Victorian home built in 1885, and now registered as a National Historic Landmark. From 1900 to 1915 it was the home of Ellen G. White, author and spiritual leader of the Seventh-Day Adventists. It is open for visitors Sunday through Thursday 10 a.m. to 5 p.m., Friday from 10 a.m. to 1 p.m., and Saturday from 2 p.m. to 6 p.m. Closed Thanksgiving and Christmas.

Pacific Union College
Angwin CA 94508
800.862.7080. Fax: 707.965.6390
www.pcu.edu

With a student body of 1,500 and a student-teacher ratio of 13:1, this Seventh Day Adventist college is rated one of the top liberal arts colleges in the West. Example: It's one of the top 10 schools in the nation whose graduates are accepted into medical school. PUC's 200-acre campus is surrounded by 1,800 acres of agricultural and forested land—a great hiking area.

Pope Valley

A gorgeous area that 95% of our visitors don't even know exists, let alone take time to visit it. Yet it offers beautiful drives and a number of excellent wineries and other attractions. Since visits to most of the wineries in this area are by appointment only, we recommend that you call first.

Aetna Springs Cellars
7227 Pope Valley Road
Pope Valley CA 94574
707.965.2675
www.aetnaspringscellars.com

A family-owned winery producing small amounts of ultra-premium Cabernet Sauvignon, Merlot and Chardonnay. By appointment.

Aetna Springs Golf Course
1600 Aetna Springs Road
Pope Valley CA 94574
707.965.2115
www.aetnasprings.com

A nine-hole public course built in the late 1800s. (For more information, see our Golf section on page 170.)

Eagle and Rose Winery
1844 Pope Canyon Road
Pope Valley, CA 94567
707.965.9463
www.eagleandrose.com

Family owned winery producing Syrah, Merlot, Cabernet Sauvignon, Sangiovese and Sauvignon Blanc. By appointment. Winery grounds include a 3,700-foot paved lighted private airstrip. Call in advance for landing permission.

Litto's Hubcap Ranch
6654 Pope Valley Road
Pope Valley CA 94574

One of California's exceptional twentieth century folk art environments. Over a period of 30 years, Emanuele "Litto" Damonte (1892-1985), with the help of his neighbors, collected more than 2,000 hubcaps. All around Hubcap Ranch are constructions and arrangements of hubcaps, bottles and pulltops that proclaim that "Litto, the Pope Valley Hubcap King," was here.

Pope Valley Winery
6613 Pope Valley Road
Pope Valley CA 94574
707.965.1246
www.popevalleywinery.com

Originally built 100 years ago. Historic blacksmith shop. Picnicking. Merlot, Zinfandel, Chardonnay, Sangiovese, Chenin Blanc, Late Harvest Chenin Blanc.

Chiles Valley

The Chiles Valley District is a separate wine appellation, located in the hills east of Napa Valley at an average of 1,000 feet above sea level.

Brown Estate Vineyards
707.963.2435
www.brownestate.com

Family-owned winery producing Zinfandel, Chardonnay, Cabernet Sauvignon. Tasting by appointment only.

Catacula Lake Winery

4105 Chiles Pope Valley Road
St. Helena CA 94574
707.965.1104
www.cataculalake.com

Owned by the Keith family. Tours and tasting by appointment. Produces Sauvignon Blanc, Zinfandel, Petite Sirah and Cabernet Sauvignon. Over 1,000 acres, all deeded to the Napa Valley Land Trust.

Nichelini Winery

2950 Sage Canyon Road
St. Helena
707.963.0717
www.nicheliniwinery.com

The Nichelini family has been growing grapes since the 1890's, and their winery in Sage Canyon is the oldest family-owned continuously operating winery in the county. They produce Zinfandel, Cabernet Sauvignon, Merlot, Sauvignon Vert and Petite Sirah. Open daily for sales and complimentary tasting. Picnic area and bocci ball court.

RustRidge Winery

2910 Lower Chiles Valley Road
St. Helena, CA 94574
707.965.9353
www.rustridge.com

Family-owned winery on 450 acres, also offering a bed and breakfast inn. By appointment. Chardonnay, Sauvignon Blanc, Zinfandel, Cabernet Sauvignon, Late Harvest Riesling, Late Harvest Zinfandel.

Volker Eisele Family Estate

3080 Lower Chiles Valley Road
St. Helena CA 94574
707.965.2260
www.volkereiselevineyard.com

Family-owned winery producing organically grown and highly-acclaimed Cabernet Sauvignon and Merlot. By appointment.

Lake Berryessa

Bureau of Reclamation Lake Berryessa Field Office

5520 Knoxville Road
Napa, CA 94558
707.966.2111
www.recreation.gov then search for "Lake Berryessa"

Lake Berryessa is less than 45 minutes from the Napa Valley in the eastern part of Napa County.

Prior to 1957, the lake was Monticello Valley and the town of Monticello. When Monticello Dam was completed, the lake started filling. Today it is one of the largest man-made lakes in California, 25 miles long, 3 miles wide and 275 feet deep at its deepest point, with 168 miles of shoreline.

A wide variety of fish can be found in the lake, including bass, rainbow trout, brown trout, bluegill, crappie and catfish. Campgrounds and picnic areas are abundant.

Cucina Italiana

4310 Knoxville Rd
Lake Berryessa, CA 94558
707.966.2433
www.lakeberryessanews.com/cucina italiana.html

Italian comfort food. Very popular with locals and others lucky enough to discover it.

Lake Berryessa Marina Resort

5800 Knoxville Road
Napa CA 94558
707.966.2161 Fax: 707.966.0761
www.lakeberryessa.com
15 cabins $75 - $150

All lake-view cabins (non-housekeeping), 45 RV sites, 70 primitive tent camping sites. Convenience store with food, clothing and camping supplies.

A variety of facilities and services including four-lane launch ramp, tackle shop, volleyball, restaurant, picnic areas with BBQ and tables, convenience store, fuel dock and courtesy dock. Houseboat rentals, along with other watercraft including jetskis, ski boats, runabouts, pontoon boats and fishing boats.

Lake Berryessa News

www.lakeberryessanews.com

Local newspaper published twice a month.

Markley Cove Boat Rentals

PO Box 987
Winters CA 95694
707.966.2134 800.242.6287

Houseboat and fishing boat rentals. Annual berth rental. Rental houseboats include dinette, gas oven and range, bathroom with tub/shower, bunks, refrigerator, gas BBQ, air conditioner, 110-volt generator, microwave, and 140 hp I/O engine. More deluxe models include such things as wet bars, second full bath, second refrigerator and/or trash compactor.

Oak Shores Park

Knoxville Road
707.966.2111

A recreation development operated by the U.S. Bureau of Reclamation. Eight different areas with a total of 100 picnic sites with tables and barbecue grills, swimming beaches, cartop boat facility for non-powered boats, and shore fishing. $4.00 per car fee for day use.

Putah Creek Resort

7600 Knoxville Road
Napa CA 94558
707.966.2116

Full marina, tackle shop, 200 campsites, 55 RV sites, 26 air-conditioned motel kitchenettes, grocery, delicatessen, snack bar, restaurant with cocktail lounge and dancing to live music.

Quail Ridge Reserve

530.758.1387
www.quailridge.org

Overlooks Lake Berryessa. Operated by the non-profit Quail Ridge Conservancy, it is 2000 acres of black oak, blue oak, interior live oak, oracle oak, scrub oak and valley oak —one of the new nearly untouched natural areas remaining in the California Coast Ranges. The reserve is home to a wide variety of native plants and animals including as many as 15 different native California grasses.

Quail Ridge is primarily a research site. However, with advance reservations the public can participate in monthly interpretive walks as well as four-hour and day-long boat ecotours. The boat tours offer bird watching and information on the history, plants and animals of the area.

Rancho Monticello Resort

6590 Knoxville Road
Napa CA 94558
707.966.2188
www.ranchomonticelloresort.com
Cabins - $75/night

Located on Lake Berryessa, the resort offers picnicking, boat launching, fishing from shore or boats, and fifty campsites for tents or RVs. All campsites have picnic tables and barbecues, with water faucet access, restrooms and showers nearby. Trailer sites have full hookup with electrical, water and sewer. Long-term sites based on annual leases are also available for mobile homes, travel trailers and RVs.

Spanish Flat Resort

4290 Knoxville Road
Napa CA 94558
707.966.7700 Fax: 707.966.7704
www.spanishflatresort.com
12 cabins $75 - $100

An RV/campground on Lake Berryessa. Camping is $22 per night and RV camping is $26. Or you can stay in a yurt for $60.
    Complete marina facilities. Power boats, boat ramp, jet ski rental, open and covered berths, secure boat garages, gas, fishing boats and supplies. Less than one mile from grocery store, deli, sporting goods, beautiful shops, post office, service station, restaurant and bar. A popular launching point for fishermen (fisherpersons?). Spanish Flat Resort also provides an online fishing report.

Steele Park Resort

1605 Steele Canyon Road
Napa CA 94558
707.966.2123 800.522.2123 Fax: 707.255.2727
www.steelepark.com

Motel rooms and cottages with swimming pool and championship tennis courts, restaurant, bar, store, full service marina, launch ramp, campsites and RV park.

Willi's Water Ski Center

1434 Grayson Avenue
St. Helena CA 94574
707.963.4409
www.williwaterski.com/

Willi Ellermeier operates a water ski school at Lake Berryessa with instruction for students ranging from beginner to tournament level.

Silverado Trail

The Silverado Trail runs along the east side of the valley from Calistoga at the northern end to Napa at the southern end. Even though these attractions do have town mailing addresses, we've listed them here for convenience because they're all located on the Trail. Keep in mind that there are more wineries along the trail than the ones we've listed here.

Auberge du Soleil
180 Rutherford Hill Rd.
Rutherford CA 94573
707.963.1211 800.348.5406 Fax:
707.963.8764
www.aubergedusoleil.com
50 rooms and suites - $525-$2250

Auberge du Soleil Restaurant
800.348.5406 Fax: 707.967.3818
www.aubergedusoleil.com
French Mediterranean - Entrees
$34-$37

A renowned Relais & Châteaux property that includes a restaurant and 50-room inn. Even if you don't stay here, you can enjoy a breakfast with a spectacular view as the morning fog gradually burns off revealing the vineyards on the valley below. Or order one of the excellent burgers and salads from their "deck menu" for lunch.

As close to heaven as you can get, with beautiful views of the Napa Valley, wonderful food and the largest restaurant/wine selection in the Napa Valley; 1,280 selections and 14,000 bottles. A truly romantic place on a moonlit evening.

Calistoga Ranch
580 Lommel Road
Calistoga CA 94515
707.254.2800 800.942.4220
www.calistogaranch.com
200 rooms - $400 - $650

Auberge Resorts, which also owns Auberge du Soleil in Rutherford, has built a new "private residential resort" 157 acres east of the Silverado Trail and south of Calistoga. It includes 27 "owner lodges" and 47 guest lodges, for a total of 200 rooms. It also offers spa services, and a restaurant and lounge.

Chappellet Vineyard
1581 Sage Canyon Road
St. Helena CA 94574
707.963.7136
www.chappellet.com

Tours and tastings by appointment. Chardonnay, Chenin Blanc, Cabernet Sauvignon, Merlot, Sangiovese, Zinfandel. Molly Chappellet's highly-regarded books on gardening and cooking are available at the winery.

Château Boswell
3468 Silverado Trail
St. Helena CA 94574
707.963.5472
www.chateauboswellwinery.com

Tours and tastings by appointment. Chardonnay,Cabernet Sauvignon, Syrah. A European-style chateau.

Chimney Rock Winery
5350 Silverado Trail
Napa CA 94558
800.257.2641
www.chimneyrock.com

Open daily for tasting, tours by appointment. A Cape-Dutch style winery whose vineyards include the site of a former 18-hole golf course, gone in a links-to-vines sacrifice. Cabernet Sauvignon, Cabernet Franc, Fumé Blanc, Rosé of Cabernet Franc.

Clos Du Val Wine Co., Ltd
5330 Silverado. Trail
Napa CA 94558
707.259.2220 800.993.9463
www.closduval.com

Open daily for tasting, tours by appointment. Co-founder Bernard Portet established the winery in the Stag's Leap area after a two-year worldwide search for the ideal château location. Pétanque (French bocce ball) courts and picnic tables available to winery visitors. Cabernet Sauvignon, Merlot, Chardonnay.

Conn Creek Winery
8711 Silverado Trail
St. Helena CA 94574
707.963.9100
www.conncreek.com

Open daily for tasting. Cabernet Sauvignon, Merlot, Cabernet Franc.

Cuvaison Winery
4550 Silverado Trail
Calistoga 94515
707.942.6266
www.cuvaison.com
Open daily. Tasting fee includes logo glass. Free tours of wine caves.
Picnic grove with 350-year-old oaks.

Outstanding wines with a focus on Carneros Chardonnay, since Cuvaison was farsighted enough to buy Carneros land back when few people realized what an excellent winegrowing region it was. Chardonnay, Pinot Noir, Cabernet Sauvignon, Merlot, Syrah, Zinfandel.

Darioush Winery
4240 Silverado Trail
Napa CA 94558
707.257.2345
www.darioush.com

Open daily for tasting. The winery's architectural style was inspired by the Persepolis, the ancient Persian city founded by Darius, the first king of Persia. Cabernet Sauvignon, Merlot, Shiraz, Chardonnay, Viognier. They also produce an olive oil.

Duckhorn Vineyards
1000 Lodi Lane
St. Helena CA 94574
888.354.8885
www.duckhornvineyards.com

At the corner of Lodi Lane and the Silverado Trail. Open daily for tasting; tours by appointment. Founded in 1978 by Dan and Margaret Duckhorn. Gardens, waterfowl art collection. Sauvignon Blanc, Merlot, Cabernet Sauvignon, and a dry Vermouth.

Dutch Henry Winery
4300 Silverado Trail
Calistoga CA 94515
707.942.5771 888.224.5879
www.dutchhenry.com

Tours and tastings by appointment only during spring and summer. Cabernet Sauvignon, Merlot, Meritage, Zinfandel, Chardonnay, Syrah.

Hagafen Cellars

4160 Silverado Trail
Napa CA 94558 USA
707.252.0781 Fax: 707.252.4562
www.hagafen.com

Tours are by appointment only. Established in 1979, Hagafen (meaning "the vine") Cellars is the only kosher winery in the Napa Valley. Winemaker/owner Ernie Weir turns out award-winning wines, which have frequently been served at state occasions at the White House. Chardonnay, Pinot Noir, Syrah, Sauvignon Blanc, Merlot, Cabernet Sauvignon Brut Cuvée, White Riesling.

Joseph Phelps Vineyards

200 Taplin Road
St. Helena CA 94574
707.963.2745
www.jpvwines.com

Tours and tastings by appointment only. Taplin Road runs east off the Silverado Trail, 1/4 mile north of Zinfandel Lane. Founded in 1972 by Joseph Phelps, who currently has160 acres of vines on a 600-acre ranch. Phelps donated some of his land on the valley floor to be used for farmworker housing. Cabernet Sauvignon, Sauvignon Blanc, Chardonnay, Merlot, and dessert wines.

Meadowood Resort

900 Meadowood Lane
St. Helena CA 94754
707.963.3646 800.458.8080
www.meadowood.com
85 cottages, suites and lodges - $375-$3585

A Relais & Châteaux property. Croquet anyone? Meadowood, one of Napa Valley's most exquisite resorts, has the only professional croquet court in the Napa Valley and is the site of many tournaments. You can take lessons from the croquet pro, or enjoy any of the other activities at this luxurious 250-acre resort in a wooded park-like setting. Choose from tennis, golf, biking, swimming, hiking, sleeping or reading in the sun, or revitalizing yourself in the health spa.

In the quiet of the early morning, you may see deer wandering across the nine-hole golf course. Sumptuous breakfasts await early risers seven days a week. Meadowood's superb restaurants attract both locals and visitors from afar.

The resort's wine school offers unique wine and food courses. Not surprising considering that Meadowood each June hosts the prestigious Napa Valley Wine Auction - one of the most famous events of its kind in the world.

Meadowood is elegant, luxurious, comfortable, and convenient to many of the Napa Valley's most renowned wineries. It's *the* place to stay upvalley.

Grill at Meadowood

900 Meadowood Lane
St. Helena CA 94754
707.963.3646 800.458.8080
www.meadowood.com

Restaurant at Meadowood

900 Meadowood Lane
St. Helena CA 94754
707.963.3646 800.458.8080
www.meadowood.com

Miner Family Vineyards
7850 Silverado Trail
Oakville CA 94562
800.366.9463
www.minerwines.com

Open daily for tasting and tours by appointment. Cabernet Sauvignon, Merlot, Chardonnay, Petite Sirah, Sauvignon Blanc, Zinfandel. A beautiful view of the valley from the winery

Mumm Napa Valley
8455 Silverado Trail
Rutherford CA 94573
707.942.3434 Fax: 707.942.3470
www.mummnapavalley.com

Open daily for tours and tasting.On the west side of Silverado Trail, approximately two miles north of Oakville Cross Road.
    The Wine Spectator has called Mumm Napa Valley "perhaps the best sparkling wine producer in California." Very friendly staff and a beautiful view of the valley, particularly at sunset.

Pine Ridge Winery
5901 Silverado Trail
Napa CA 94558
800.575.9777
www.pineridgewinery.com

Open daily for tasting; tours by appointment. Tours include wine caves. Cabernet Sauvignon, Merlot, Chardonnay, Chenin Blanc-Viognier.

Poetry Inn
6380 Silverado Trail
Napa CA 94558
707.944.0646
www.poetryinn.com
4 rooms - $575-$1250

A very high-end bed and breakfast inn above the Silverado Trail in the Stags Leap District overlooking the valley. Private balconies, indoor and outdoor showers, three-course breakfast. Highly-praised.

Quintessa
1601 Silverado Trail
St. Helena CA 94574
707.967.1601
www.quintessa.com

Tours and tastings by appointment only. Founded by Agustin and Valeria Huneeus. Agustin was formerly CEO of Chile's largest winery, and head of Franciscan Estates. Valeria is an advocate of *biodynamics* and uses those agricultural techniques on their vineyards. Cabernet Sauvignon, Merlot, Cabernet Franc.

Quixote Winery
6126 Silverado Trail
Napa CA 94558
707.944.2659
www.quixotewinery.com

Carl Doumani, former owner of Stags' Leap Winery, brought in Austrian artist Friedensreich Hundertwasser to design his new winery. This is the only Hundertwasser-designed building in the United States, and follows such principles as: no straight lines; roofs are planted with grass and trees; every building is capped with a golden turret to elevate man's sense of himself; and, color is king.
    Produces small quantities of Petite Syrah and Cabernet Sauvignon under the Quixote and Panza labels. All grapes are grown organically. Winery visits by appointment only.

Regusci Winery

5584 Silverado Trail
Napa CA 94558
707.254.0403
www.regusciwinery.com

The Regusci family has been farming in the Napa Valley since 1932. Their Stags Leap District winery is located in a "ghost winery," built in 1878, and crafted from lava stone with two-foot thick walls. Their focus is on reds—Cabernet Sauvignon, Merlot and Zinfandel. All are delicious.

Reynolds Family Winery

3266 Silverado Trail
Napa CA 94558
707.258.2558
www.reynoldsfamilywinery.com

Open daily for tasting. Small family winery. Cabernet Sauvignon, Pinot Noir.

Robert Sinskey Vineyards

6320 Silverado Trail
Yountville CA 94599
707.944.9090   800.869.2030
www.robertsinskey.com

Open daily for tastings; tours by appointment. Sinskey is farming its vineyards organically, and also using the even stricter methods of *biodynamics*. Pinot Noir, Chardonnay, Merlot, Cabernet Sauvignon, Cabernet Franc.

Rombauer Vineyards

3522 Silverado Trail
St. Helena CA 94574
707.967.5120   800.622.2206
www.rombauervineyards.com

Tours and tastings by appointment only. Founded in 1982. Over one mile of caves. Chardonnay, Zinfandel, Merlot, Cabernet Sauvignon.

Rutherford Hill Winery

200 Rutherford Hill Road
PO Box 427
Rutherford CA 94573
707.963.1871
www.rutherfordhill.com

Rutherford Hill opened in 1976 producing Merlot, and still focuses on that varietal, although it makes many others as well.

The winery makes picnic areas available to visitors, and its winery tour includes a walkthrough of its extensive system of wine caves, perhaps the largest in North America.

The winery also offers *Blending in the Caves*, which allows participants to create their own blend of Rutherford Hill Merlot. After a tour, your wine instructor will assist you by informing you about vineyard locations, varietal characteristics, flavor, taste and a few basic principle of blending. Then, sampling three varietal wines taken directly form the barrel, you'll create your own blend that you will bottle and take home to enjoy. For a special experience, your group can enter team blends into a "Merlot Blend-Off" competition. Reservations required. Merlot, Chardonnay, Cabernet Sauvignon, Malbec, Port, Gewürztraminer, Sangiovese and Sauvignon Blanc.

Rutherford Wine Company

1680 Silverado Trail
St. Helena, CA. 94574
800.778.0424
www.rutherfordwine.com

Located at the intersection of Silverado Trail and Rutherford Cross Road. Sales room open daily, tasting by appointment. Offers Rutherford Ranch, Round Hill, and Reindeer Ranch wines. Cabernet Sauvignon, Chardonnay. Merlot, White Zinfandel, Shiraz, Sauvignon Blanc, Zinfandel

Shafer Vineyards

6145 Silverado Trail. Napa
707.944.2877
www.shafervineyards.com

Tours and tasting by appointment only. Vineyards were originally planted in 1922. Fifty years later John Shafer founded this winery, one of the first in the Stag's Leap area. Cabernet Sauvignon, Chardonnay, Merlot.

Silverado Resort

1600 Atlas Peak Road
Napa CA 94558
707.257.0200 800.523.0500 Fax: 707.257.5400
www.silveradoresort.com
280 cottage suites - $280-$1415

1,200 acres whose cornerstone is a mansion built in the 1870s. Two hundred and eighty deluxe cottage suites complete with living room, wood burning fireplace, full kitchen, master bedroom and bath, and private patio or terrace. Health spa. Nine swimming pools. Two championship 18-hole golf courses designed by Robert Trent Jones, Jr. Twenty-three tennis courts. Three excellent restaurants. Live music in the bar. It's *the* place to stay in Napa.

Silverado Trail Wineries Association

www.silveradotrail.com

Nearly 40 wineries on, or near, the Silverado Trail are members of the association.

Silverado Vineyards

6121 Silverado Trail
Napa CA 94558
707.257.1770
www.silveradovineyards.com

Open daily for tasting; tours by appointment. Jack Stuart, acknowledged to be one of the finest winemakers in the Napa Valley, has been producing outstanding wines for years at this winery founded by the family of Walt Disney. Beautiful views from the tasting room area. Sauvignon Blanc, Chardonnay, Merlot, Cabernet Sauvignon, Sangiovese.

Soda Canyon Store

4006 Silverado Trail
Napa CA 94558
707.252.0285

Delicatessen, picnic lunches, espresso, groceries. Picnic tables. Wine tasting bar, where you can taste three local wines. The tasting bar focuses on vineyards in Soda Canyon (such as Atlas Peak Vineyards) as well as wineries along the Silverado Trail. It's the only store on the Trail between Napa and Calistoga.

Stag's Leap Wine Cellars

5766 Silverado Trail
Napa CA 94558
707.944.2020
www.stagsleapwinecellars.com
Open daily for tasting; tours by
appointment.

Stag's Leap staggered the international wine community—and particularly the French part of it—when its 1973 Cabernet Sauvignon took first place in a blind wine tasting in Paris in 1976. The renowned (and very French) wine tasters were horrified that an upstart California winery would best France's finest wines. Some even tried to get their tasting notes back.

Stag's Leap Wine Cellars' place in history was secure. Other Napa Valley wineries have since won many awards in France and other international competitions, but owners Warren and Barbara Winiarski have never rested on their laurels, and continue to produce superb wines, including their celebrated Cask 23. It well deserves your visit. White Riesling, Sauvignon Blanc, Chardonnay, Merlot, Cabernet Sauvignon.

ZD Wines

8383 Silverado Trail
Napa CA 94558
800.487.7757
www.zdwines.com

Open daily for tastings. Founded in 1969 in Sonoma County, and moved to the Napa Valley in 1979. Chardonnay, Pinot Noir, Merlot, Cabernet Sauvignon.

Scenic Drives

Highway 29

Every road in the Napa Valley is scenic. Some are just more scenic than others. Highway 29, the main road up the (westish) center of the valley, takes you through all the valley towns and right by some of the area's most famous wineries and restaurants. From Napa to St. Helena it parallels the route of the Napa Valley Wine Train. Wave at the engineer and passengers. That's half the fun for everybody.

Passing through St. Helena, Highway 29 is called Main Street. Along most other stretches it's referred to as the Saint Helena Highway. In reality, it's all Highway 29—a divided highway from Napa to Yountville, and a two-lane highway (with frequent left-turn lanes) all the way from Yountville to Calistoga. Caltrans, the State of California's transportation department, would love to make "29" a divided highway the whole length of the valley, but the natives have fought valiantly and successfully to prevent this from happening. Even most of those who commute up or down the valley are willing to put up with the inconvenience of a two-lane road in order to preserve the beauty of the drive.

To get a full appreciation of the Napa Valley, you should definitely drive Highway 29, in one direction or the other.

Silverado Trail

The Silverado Trail runs along the east side of the valley. It goes outside most of the towns, and there are fewer wineries and much less traffic. Yet it still offers beautiful views, many wineries and quicker driving if you're in a hurry. Don't be in too much of a hurry, however. The view is too lovely and this road can be dangerous, because people drive much faster than on Highway 29 and seem to get more impatient, passing on stretches where it is unsafe to pass. Use caution and you'll enjoy "the Trail" immensely. We do.

The name "Silverado" comes from the road's history carrying quicksilver (mercury) wagons from the mines in northern Napa County. The quicksilver was eventually transported to the gold fields of California where it was used to separate gold from the ore or sand in which it was found. The Trail also led to the Silverado Silver Mine on Mt. St. Helena, where years later Robert Louis Stevenson gathered the notes for his story The Silverado Squatters.

Cross Roads

Crossing the valley from west to east, connecting Highway 29 with the Silverado Trail, are three major crossroads. Each road crosses the valley at the town that it's named after. They are: Yountville Cross Road, Oakville Cross Road, and Rutherford Cross Road. (Several other roads make this connection, too, but they don't quite have the flair that the crossroads do.) Each road passes wineries and beautiful homes, and all offer gorgeous views. Try any one of these to get off the beaten path.

Cuttings Wharf Road

Don't be too disappointed if after turning off Highway 121/12 south of Napa, you follow the "Napa River Resorts" signs to Cuttings Wharf and have trouble finding the "resorts." Perhaps once there were resorts in this area, although there appears to be no historical record that this was ever the case. Even California's Department of Transportation has no idea why the sign is there. Still, it's a pleasant drive, taking you through some of Napa County's section of the Carneros wine district, famous for its Chardonnays and Pinot Noirs.

Solano Avenue and Washington Street

Between Yountville and Napa is an 8-mile stretch of divided highway. The highway provides beautiful views, but for more leisurely sightseeing we offer two tips. Northbound from Napa, turn right (east) at the Washington Street turnoff, then turn immediately left to go north again. Follow the frontage road to Yountville, enjoy the view of the vineyards by the side of the road, and take pictures of the beautiful views toward the mountains to the east.

Coming back at the end of the day, skip the divided highway again. Instead go west off Highway 29 at the Veterans Home turnoff, cross the tracks and turn left on the frontage road (Solano Avenue) to go south toward Napa. This will give you beautiful views of homes, vineyards and wineries to the west toward the Mayacmas Mountains. If this is at sunset, it's even more beautiful. Follow Solano into Napa and then, when you reach the business and residential areas, turn back onto the highway again and continue your journey south on the main highway.

Yount Mill Road

A beautiful drive that will take you from Yount Street in Yountville to Highway 29 north of town. You'll pass the site of the original mill built by town founder George Yount in 1836.

Other Scenic Drives

There are many other drives, particularly in the eastern part of Napa County, that offer beautiful scenery and relatively uncrowded roads. The best online source we've found is California Motorcycle Roads (www.pashnit.com/motoroads.htm). It includes lengthy write-ups and extensive photographs. While the writer is speaking to motorcycle riders, the routes he describes can all be driven by car. Look at the listings under the Napa—Sonoma—Solano section. They include Berryessa—Knoxville Road, Highway 128, Highway 121, Chiles—Pope Valley Road, Howell Mountain Road, and Spring Mountain—St. Helena Road.

Just Outside the Valley

They're not in the Napa Valley but they're close by and might interest you. Most of these destinations are a 20-30 minute drive from the valley.

Anheuser-Busch Brewery

3101 Busch Drive
Fairfield CA 94533
707.429.7595
www.budweisertours.com
Open September-May Tuesday through Saturday from 9 a.m. to 4 p,m. June-August open Monday through Saturday. Free 45-minute tours depart on the hour.

The world's largest brewer. Enjoy samples of fine beers and snacks. Visit the production floor to see packaging lines that fill thousands of cans and bottles every minute.

Calpine Geothermal Visitor Center

15500 Central Park Road
Middletown CA 95461
866-GEYSERS
www.geysers.com

The Geysers is the world's largest geothermal energy source, and is operated by Calpine. Wells drill deep into the earth to tap the natural steam, which is used to power turbines, generating energy for customers in Northern California. The energy efficient visitor center is heated and cooled by geothermal energy, and features interactive exhibits, a gift shop and picnic area, and free bus tours to an operating geothermal power plant. Advance registration is required for the bus tours. Free. Open Thursday through Monday.

Jelly Belly

Herman Goelitz Candy Company
2400 North Watney Way
Fairfield CA
800.9JELLYB
www.jellybelly.com

Take Interstate 80 north toward Sacramento. At Fairfield, exit freeway at Highway 12/Chadbourne Road, and exit at Chadbourne. Turn right at stop sign onto Chadbourne, then left onto Courage Drive. Turn left onto North Watney Way. Tours Monday through Friday from 9 a.m. to 2 p.m. Closed holidays, April 1, and the last week of June through the first week of July.

The makers of Ronald Reagan's favorite snack—the first jelly beans in outer space—and another long-time favorite, *Candy Corn*. The factory makes up to 40,000,000 jelly beans a day and sells enough each year to circle the earth's equator 2.5 times. It's the only place in the world where you can buy *Belly Flops*, beans that don't meet Goelitz's high standards for size or color, but they're still delicious. A fun tour and great for kids.

Safari West

3115 Porter Creek Road
Santa Rosa CA
707.579.2551 800.616.2695
www.safariwest.com

From the Napa Valley, go north on Highway 128/29. Do not turn right into Calistoga. Continue to Petrified Forest Road. Turn left, pass the Petrified Forest and turn right on Porter Creek Road. Go 2.5 miles, cross the bridge, and immediately turn right onto Franz Valley Road. Turn into the very first driveway.

Daily tours by appointment. Tours last 2 1/2 hours and cost $58 for adults, $28 for children 12 and under.

A private wildlife preserve of 400 acres that is home to 350 exotic mammals and birds. Includes antelope, cheetah, eland, gazelle, zebra, giraffe and many more. Bring your cameras.

Discovery Kingdom

Marine World Parkway
Vallejo CA 94589
707.643.6722
www.sixflags.com/discoveryKingdom/

Formerly Marine World. Open all year, Wednesday through Sunday from 9:30 a.m. to 5 p.m., and every day during the summer from 9:30 a.m. to 6:30 p.m. (Memorial day to Labor Day). Kids under 48 inches $27, general admission $43.

Whales, tigers, elephants, sharks, kangaroos, water-skiing shows, trained seals, giraffes, butterflies and scads of other animals and performances. Plus lots of thrill rides, including five roller coasters. It's probably the premier place in the entire San Francisco Bay Area for a family outing.

Smith's Mount St. Helena Trout Farm

Ida Clayton Road
Calistoga CA 94515
707.987.3651

Take Highway 128 from Calistoga toward Healdsburg/Geyserville, turn right on Ida Clayton Road. Also accessible from Middletown in Lake County, and from Santa Rosa via Mark West Springs Road and Franz Valley Road.

Fishing for the entire family for rainbow trout raised in cold mountain water. No license. No limit. Bait and poles available. Open Saturday, Sunday and observed holidays, February through October. Hours 10 a.m.-6 p.m.

Traintown

20264 Broadway - Highway 12
Sonoma, CA 95476
707.938.3912
www.traintown.com
Open daily 10 a.m. to 5 p.m .June 1-
Labor Day. Friday, Saturday and
Sunday September 1-May. $3.75
adults, $3.25 children.

There's not much for young kids to do in the Napa Valley. Fortunately Traintown is only twenty minutes away from Napa. It's located in the town of Sonoma on 10 acres, with one and a quarter miles of railroad track.
   During the twenty-minute trip on the small-scale train, you'll travel over five bridges and trestles and through two tunnels, one of them 140 feet long. Admission includes a petting zoo and three full-size cabooses to explore. Extra charge for ferris wheel and carousel.

Twin Pine Casino

Highway 29 at Rancheria Road
Middletown, CA 95461
707.987.0197 Fax 707.987.9786
www.twinpine.com

A casino owned by the Middletown Rancheria band of Pomo Indians. Open 24 hours a day, seven days a week. Nearly 500 slot machines, blackjack, pai-gow poker, keno, electronic bingo, video poker and Digital 21 games.

Foods of the Napa Valley

For information on specific Napa Valley restaurants, see the Town sections earlier in this book.

What Is Napa Valley Cuisine?

It's fresh, it's artistic, and it's often a blend of cultures.

Most produce is locally grown, if not in the Napa Valley, then in Northern California. It's also frequently organic and often grown right at the restaurant.

Entrees can include anything from beef to fish to vegetarian. Most chefs tend toward the light side, without heavy sauces and large amounts of meat. However, there is currently a noticeable trend in many restaurants toward the heavier "comfort food."

Meals are customarily prepared to complement local wines, although with the variety of wines offered in the Napa Valley, it's likely you can find a bottle to go with any kind of food.

California cuisine is generally regarded to have started with Chez Panisse in Berkeley, although the Napa Valley was quick to join in. The legendary, and now departed, Diner in Yountville was the first in the valley to serve the lighter and fresher food now known as "California cuisine" or, more recently, "wine country cuisine." The still-famous *Mustard's Grill* was another early pioneer.

"Fusion" is a popular style where ingredients and seasonings from two or more countries are blended into a unique dish. "Pan-Pacific" is a popular subset of fusion in which chefs blend dishes and ingredients from various locations around the Pacific Rim, including Japan, China, the Philippines, Hawaii, Australia and South America.

Despite its strong ties with Spain and Mexico, the Napa Valley seems to have turned into "Tuscany West", although to be fair it *was* largely the Italians that established the modern wine industry in the valley. Tuscan-style wineries, homes and restaurants abound, and you'll have no problem finding Italian and Cal-Italia cooking in the style you like.

Prices are not cheap. While you can find "fair" prices, you'll have a hard time find inexpensive ones. IIn the majority of upscale valley restaurants, you'll be lucky if two of you can leave a restaurant—after having had an entrée, an appetizer or a dessert, and a glass of wine—for less than eighty dollars, although it's possible if you stick to the low end of the menu selections. One hundred dollars and up is more common. But you'll more than likely have enjoyed an excellent meal with fine service and attractive surroundings.

We discuss restaurants in the various town sections of this book. We don't list them all, but we have tried to present the best known, most typical or unique. Not all aspire to be Yountville's *French Laundry*—considered by many to be the top restaurant in the United States—but almost all have highly trained chefs deeply committed to their art.

Don't hesitate to ask the locals for their restaurant recommendations. You'll find the staff of winery tasting rooms particularly helpful. They like to eat as much as they like to drink.

Cooking Classes

Camp Napa Culinary
PO Box 114
Oakville CA 94562
707.944.9112 888.999.4844
www.hughcarpenter.com

Chef/cooking teacher Hugh Carpenter has written over a dozen popular cookbooks. His articles have appeared in numerous newspapers and magazines, including Cook's Illustrated and Bon Appetit. Carpenter and his photographer wife Teri Sandison conduct 6-day tours that include cooking classes and visits to wineries and private estates throughout the valley.

CasaLana
1316 South Oak Street
Calistoga 94515
707.942.0615 877.968.2665
www.casalana.com

A bed and breakfast inn that also offers hands-on cooking classes in a professionally equipped kitchen. Classes range from essential skills to advanced techniques. Personalized courses for groups are also available.

Cooking with Julie
P.O. Box 5412
Napa CA 94581
707.227.5036
www.cookingwithjulie.com

Wine country cooking classes given at Churchill Manor in Napa

Copia - American Center for Wine, Food and the Arts (Napa)
www.copia.org

Culinary Institute of America at Greystone (St. Helena)
www.ciachef.edu/greystone

Napa Valley Cooking School (St. Helena)
www.napavalley.edu/apps/comm.asp?Q=29
707.967.2930

Located at the upvalley branch of Napa Valley College. Excellent school offering a two-semester course. Graduates currently have 100% full employment rate.

Beer

People don't drink just wine here, particularly in the summer. In fact, everyone will admit that the beverage of choice for people working during the harvest is beer.

The Napa Valley currently has three microbreweries. You'll find more information in their entries in their respective town sections.

Microbreweries

Downtown Joe's (Napa)

Napa Valley Brewing Company at the Calistoga Inn (Calistoga)

Silverado Brewing Company (St. Helena)

Cheese

Goat's Leap Cheese

3321 St. Helena Highway
St. Helena CA 94574
707.963.2337
www.goatsleap.com

Currently produces four varieties of goat cheese, available at fine cheese shops throughout the Napa Valley and the San Francisco Bay Area. Not open to the public.

Skyhill Napa Valley Farms

2431 Partrick Road
Napa CA 94558
707.255.4800

Produces goat cheese and yogurt at its farm in the Carneros hills. Retail outlets include Trader Joe's and Costco. Not open to the public.

Family Farms

Some of this information is courtesy of the University of California, Small Farm Center. The center publishes *Napa Yolano Harvest Trails*—a map and directory of farms, wineries, trails, bed-and-breakfast inns, and parks in Napa, Yolo and Solano counties.

University of California, Small Farm Center
530.752.8136
www.sfc.ucdavis.edu

Forni Brown Gardens

900 Foothill Boulevard
Calistoga CA 94515
707.942.6123

Forni Brown provides vegetables to some of the country's finest restaurants. Not open to the public, except for their annual Spring Garden Sale every April, but you can phone in advance for special orders throughout the year.

Grandpa Jack's Farm

707.226.9291
www.grandpajacksfarm.com

Seven-acre farm in Napa producing heirloom and unusual vegetable varities, free range eggs, and occasional surprises like homemade pies and Thanksgiving turkey. Weekly box provides average family of four with all the fresh vegetables and eggs it can handle. Home delivery.

Hoffman Farm

2125 Silverado Trail
Napa CA 94558
707.226.8938
Open daily August-November.

On the west side of the Silverado Trail, 1/4 mile north of Trancas Street.

Twenty-three acres of prunes, pears, persimmons and walnuts. You can pick yourself if you wish.

Omi's Farm

4185 Silverado Trail
Napa CA 94558
707.224.0954
kniesar@napanet.net

Located on the Silverado Trail 3.5 miles north of Trancas Street. Open year-round, by appointment only. Sustainable family farm offering seasonal produce, eggs, walnuts and berries. Also sells sheep and Australian cattle dogs.

Rancho Gordo
1755 Industrial Way #26
Napa CA 94558
707.259.1935
www.ranchogordo.com

Specialty produce organically grown (but not yet organically licensed) to support "rancho" cooking, a blend of Mexican, Native American and California cooking. Tomatoes, chile peppers, beans and corn, tomatillos, squash and cucumbers, amaranth, Persian cress, culantro, quelite, cilantro, chard and other Mexican herbs, greens and grains. Available at farmers markets in the area.

Rutherford Gardens (St. Helena)
See page 93.

Stewart's Farm
Silverado Trail at Deer Park Road
St. Helena CA 94574
707.967.8360
Open daily May-November.

A roadside stand that sells produce grown on the site and at nearby farms. Depending on the season, you'll find zucchini, squash, cherries, apricots, green beans, pumpkins, tomatoes and corn.

Slow Food

Napa Valley Convivium
www.napavalleyslowfood.com

Slow Food began in Italy in 1986 as a reaction to (and protest against) the primarily American fast food industry, which has contributed not only to fast, mass-produced meals but a fast, mass-produced society in most developed countries. Slow Food's manifesto states that it is a "movement for the protection of the right to taste."

Slow Food supports and encourages quality foods and beverages, and supports local growers, chefs, winemakers and others who share their goals. Slow Food USA's mission is to "rediscover pleasure and quality in everyday life precisely by slowing down and learning to appreciate the convivial traditions of the table." It does this through local chapters called "convivia" that organize educational, cultural and, most important, gastronomic events.

There is an active Slow Food group in the Napa Valley. It has monthly events focusing on small food producers and the chefs who use their products.

Tea

Drink the Leaf
Napa
707.255.1057
www.drinktheleaf.com

Loose leaf teas from around the world.

Vegetarian Restaurants

Currently there is only one vegetarian restaurant (Ubuntu Restaurant in Napa – see page 73) in the Napa Valley.

However, there is such a focus on fresh fruit and vegetables at most valley restaurants, that it really doesn't matter. You should have no trouble ordering vegetarian dishes from the menu at almost any restaurant you visit. If you have any doubts, just ask your waiter.

Events

April in Carneros

800.825.9457
www.carneroswineries.org

Annual open house and festival sponsored by wineries in the Carneros District.

Auction Napa Valley

PO Box 141
St. Helena CA 94574
707.963.3388
www.napavinters.com

Auction Napa Valley (formerly known as Napa Valley Wine Auction) has been held every year since 1981. It is the world's largest wine charity event, with all of the auction's proceeds staying within Napa County.

During that time, the auction's sponsor, the Napa Valley Vintners Association, has donated more than $65 million to Napa County hospitals, clinics, youth and housing organizations. The association is the primary donor to the Napa Valley Vintners Community Health Center in Napa. The center offers a variety of medical, dental and counseling services for low income, medically uninsured or underinsured county residents.

Auction goers are well-primed with Napa Valley wines as they vie to outbid each other for some of the finest wines in the world—and some of the most unusual auction packages. The auction is very elegant and very expensive, and admission is by prior registration only.

Carols in the Caves
707.224.4222
www.carolsinthecaves.com

Weekends during November and December in the wine caves of various wineries.

David Auerbach, who should be declared a Napa Valley treasure, plays sacred music on rare and unusual instruments. As David says, "If you've heard of it, I probably don't play it." A rare treat.

Chamber Music in the Napa Valley
707.252.7122
www.chambermusicnapa.org

Outstanding performances usually held in the beautiful and acoustically excellent First Methodist Church in Napa. Call for schedule.

Domaine Chandon Bastille Day Celebration
Domaine Chandon
Yountville
707.944.2280
Held every July 14.

Festival Of Lights
Town of Yountville
707.944.0904
December

Beautiful Christmas display, music, entertainment.

Harvest (Crush)

The grape harvest takes place every year in the fall. Depending on the weather, it can start in early August for sparkling wine grapes, which are picked at lower sugar levels. It picks up steam in late August and is in full swing during most of September and

October. This is the time to actually see how wine is made. The stemmer-crushers are operating throughout the day, the fermentation tanks are full and bubbling with carbon dioxide, and gondolas overflowing with grapes are travelling along every countryside road in the valley.

Home Winemakers Classic
Held at St. Supéry Winery
www.homewine.com

The Home Winemakers Classic is an annual tasting and judging of award-winning home wines by Napa Valley enologists and viticulturists, with music, silent auction of vintage wines, raffle and food. Held every July, it is an extremely popular event for residents and the local wine community.

Land Trust Hikes
Napa County Land Trust
1040 Main Street
Napa CA 94559
707.252.3270
www.napalandtrust.org

Hikes held throughout the year, usually at locations that are normally closed to the public.

Magical Moonshine Puppet Theater
PO Box 2296
Yountville CA 94599
707.257.8007
www.magicalmoonshine.org

This is a Napa Valley treasure. Unfortunately, performances are only held sporadically. Fortunately for locals, they're frequent enough to be a favorite, and held at locations throughout the valley. A wonderful experience for kids, no matter what their age.

Mountain Men
Skyline Park
Napa
707.252.0481

Mountain men in furs and deerskin with muzzle-loading rifles. An annual event, open to the public. Call the park to find out when this takes place.

Music in the Vineyards
PO Box 432
St. Helena CA 94574
707.258.5559
www.napavalleymusic.org

Napa Valley Chamber Music Festival held every August at locations, primarily wineries, throughout the valley.

Napa Country Iris Gardens
9087 Steele Canyon Road
Napa CA 94558
707.255.7880
www.napairis.com

Near Lake Berryessa. From Highway 29 in north Napa take Trancas Street east. Past the Silverado Trail Trancas becomes Monticello Road and Highway 121. Continue on 121 to Highway 128. Turn left on Highway 128 and then right on Steele Canyon. The gardens are 1.5 miles on the right.

A commercial one-acre garden of tall bearded irises. Mail order for bare-root iris. The garden is open to the public for five weeks every spring in April and May. No charge. Picnic tables available.

Napa County Fair
Napa County Fairgrounds
1435 Oak Street
Calistoga CA 94515
707.942.5111
www.napacountyfairgrounds.com

The annual county fair with a parade, exhibits, carnival rides, food, music and lots of other events, always held over the 4th of July holiday.

Napa Town & Country Fair
Napa Valley Exposition
Napa
707.253.4900
www.napavalleyexpo.com

The really big fair in Napa County. Held in early August.

Napa Valley Cinco de Mayo
www.napavalleycincodemayo.com

Held every year on, or near, May 5th. The parade and festival is the largest event of its kind in the Napa Valley. It celebrates the Mexican victory over superior French forces by 5,000 untrained and outnumbered Mestizo and Zapotec Indian guerilla troops under General Zargosa at the Battle of Puebla on May 5, 1862.

Napa Valley College Theatre
2277 Napa-Vallejo Highway
Napa CA 94558
707.253.3200
www.napavalley.edu

South of Napa on Soscol Avenue just south of Imola.

The *Napa Valley College Division of Fine and Performing Arts* sponsors approximately 100 events each year: plays, musicals and concerts (choral, jazz, and instrumental), including events for young audiences.

Tickets at the NVC Cashier, Blumer's Music Center in Napa and Main Street Books in St. Helena. Or use Visa/MasterCard and phone the college for tickets. Free parking; wheelchair access.

Napa Valley Marathon
PO Box 4307
Napa CA 94558
www.napavalleymarathon.org

Held every spring. One of the top marathons in the United States. Route goes from Calistoga south on Silverado Trail to Napa.

Napa Valley Model Railroad Club
Napa Valley Exposition
Third Street Gate
Napa CA 94559
707.253.8428
www.nvmrc.org
Open Friday evenings from 7:30 p.m. on and during major fairground events.

This elaborate model railroad occupies a 3,600 square foot room at the Napa Valley Exposition.

The "Napa Valley Northern" runs from Napa north through Lake County with northbound connections to Portland, and southbound connections to Stockton. The layout has more than 1,500 feet of track and the time period is from 1940 to present. Great for kids and railroad fans of any age.

Napa Valley Mustard Festival
707.942.9762
www.mustardfestival.org

Held in February and March at locations throughout the valley.

Napa Valley Symphony
2407 California Boulevard
Napa CA 94558
707.226.6872
www.napavalleysymphony.org

The Napa Valley has developed an outstanding group of musicians. Most concerts are held in the Lincoln Theater at the Veterans Home in Yountville. There's also an annual free concert by the river at Veterans Park in downtown Napa. Call the Symphony for a schedule of all performances.

Napa Valley Wine Festival
Napa Valley Exposition, Napa

This is a major annual event, held every November and sponsored by the Napa Valley Unified Education Foundation as a benefit for Napa public schools. Over 50 wineries participate, so it's a unique opportunity to try a wide variety of Napa Valley wines.

Napa Valley Wine Library Tasting
PO Box 328,
St. Helena CA 94574
707.963.5145
www.napawinelibrary.org

Every August more than 100 Napa Valley wineries pour a particular wine at this special wine tasting benefitting the wine library. Held each year at Silverado Resort in Napa. Open to members only, but membership is available at the door for $40.

Open Studios

Arts Council of Napa Valley
1041 Jefferson Street, Suite 4
Napa CA 94559
707.257.2117
www.artscouncilnapavalley.org

Open house at several hundred artists' studios, held every September and October on two weekends. The first weekend is upvalley, the second in Napa.

Robert Mondavi Summer Festival

Robert Mondavi Winery
Oakville CA
707.226.1395
www.robertmondaviwinery.com

Margrit Biever Mondavi, vice president of cultural affairs at the Robert Mondavi Winery and wife of the founder, has made this her pet project since 1969. Concerts are open-air, held on the winery's main lawn, and take place in June, July and August. Most concerts begin at 7 p.m., with gates open for picnicking.

A past entertainment lineup gives an idea of the outstanding quality of the performers: New Orleans' Preservation Hall Jazz Band, Cesaria Evora, Buena Vista Social Club, Dan Fogelberg, and Dave Koz.

Wine and cheese tasting are offered at intermission. 2001 tickets ranged from $42-$75, depending on the performer. While children are allowed, we've seldom seen any there.

It's an elegantly casual affair, with most attending in jeans and shorts but some finely dressed. Picnic baskets brought by guests range from French bread and cheese to elegantly prepared meals served with fine china and crystal. It's great fun and outstanding entertainment. Tickets, which go on sale the end of April, go fast. They're available at the winery and all BASS outlets. A sign at the front of the winery, easily visible from Highway 29, shows the season's schedule and ticket availability.

Society for Creative Anachronism

Skyline Wilderness Park
Napa
707.252.0481
www.vinhold.org

The Society for Creative Anachronism (SCA) meets annually at Skyline Park in Napa for a day of jousting, swordsmanship, wenching, dining, and general rollicking fun, all sponsored by the local Barony of Vinhold. Open to the public for a small donation. Call Skyline Park to find the date of the SCA's next visit.

Symphony on the River Festival

Downtown Napa at the Third Street Bridge.
Sponsored by Friends of the Napa River
707.254.8520
www.friendsofthenapariver.org

A free event held every September. The Napa Valley Symphony performs early in the evening and is followed by fireworks at dark. Activities include local entertainment, food and drink, and a boat parade on the river.

Valley Men Who Cook
Upvalley location
707.255.5911

Held on Father's Day each year. Amateur but well-known chefs from around the valley compete in a wide variety of food categories. A very popular and fun event.

Veterans Home Fourth of July Fireworks
Veterans Home
Yountville
707.944.4600

The biggest fireworks display in the valley.

Victorian Holiday Candlelight Tour
707.255.1836

Annual tour in December of some of Napa's most beautifully restored Victorian homes by Napa County Landmarks.

White Barn
2727 Sulphur Springs Avenue
St. Helena CA 94574
707.251.8715

A favorite for locals who attend theatrical and musical performances held throughout the year in an 85-seat theater that was originally a carriage house. All proceeds go to charity. A labor of love for founder Nancy Garden and her family.

Wine and Crafts Faire
Downtown Napa
707.257.0322

Wine tasting, crafts, food, entertaining. Held in September, it's the big street fair of the year.

Wine Country Film Festival
www.winecountryfilmfest.com
707.935.3456 for program information, advance tickets to al fresco screening, and passes. Tickets are available at BASS outlets.

Founded in 1986, the Wine Country Film Festival stretches over four weekends in July and August. It has a true, casual, wine country feeling. Many of the films are screened outdoors, at wineries in the Napa and Sonoma Valleys.

The program always includes new features from major studios and the latest in independently produced features, documentaries and shorts from around the world. It has premiered such films as *A Fish Called Wanda*; *Honeymoon in Vegas*; *sex, lies and videotape*; and *Married to the Mob*, and held tributes to such stars as Anthony Quinn and Gregory Peck.

Lodging Reservations

Bed and breakfast inns are listed here. We list major hotels, inns and resorts in our Town sections. For an online listing, we suggest you go to www.napanow.com/lodging.html.

Lodging Reservations

The Napa Valley is filled with bed and breakfast inns, hotels, resorts, and spas. The easiest way for you to find a place to spend the night is through one of the reservation services. They'll know which places have rooms available, and can recommend accommodations suitable for your needs. Plus there's no extra charge for their services.

Wine Country Reservations
PO.Box 5059
Napa CA 94581
707.257.7757
www.winecountryreservations.com

Napa Valley Reservations Unlimited
1819 Tanen Street
Napa CA 94559
707.252.1985 800.251.6272
www.napavalleyreservations.com

Bed & Breakfast Inns of the Napa Valley
PO Box 2937
Yountville CA 94599
707.944.4444

Hotel Hotline
707.963.8466 • 800.499.8466
(California)

B&B Style
707.942.2888 • 800.995.8884

Bed and Breakfast Inns

Note: Rates have likely increased since publication of this book. Most rates given do not include tax. Rates represent the range of prices, from the lowest during off-season to the highest during the high season.

Angwin

Forest Manor
415 Cold Springs Road
Angwin, CA 94508
800.788.0364 Fax 707.965.1962
www.forestmanor.com
6 suites - $210-$395

Located in the hills above St. Helena on 20 acres, just minutes from wineries, shops, restaurants and attractions. Six spacious suites, a gourmet breakfast each morning, an outdoor pool and jacuzzi.

Calistoga

Bear Flag Inn
2653 Foothill Boulevard
Calistoga 94515
800.670.2860
www.bearflaginn.com

Brambles, The
1322 Berry St.
Calistoga 94515
707.942.4781 707.942.5919

Brannan Cottage Inn
109 Wappo Avenue, PO Box 81
Calistoga 94515
707.942.4200
www.brannancottageinn.com
6 rooms - $125-$160

A Victorian country cottage built in the 1860s and listed on the National Register of Historic Places. All rooms have private entrances and garden views.

Calistoga Country Lodge
2883 Foothill Blvd.
Calistoga, CA 94515
707.942.5555 707.942.5864 fax
www.countrylodge.com
6 rooms - $120-$195

Secluded inn nestled in the western foothills of Calistoga. Beautifully decorated with American antiques, bleached pine and contemporary art. Outside is a heated pool and spa, inside is a large living room with a fieldstone fireplace. Prices include a glass of local wine with cheese in the evening and a buffet breakfast for two in the morning. Located five minutes from the spas, restaurants and shops of downtown Calisotoga.

Calistoga Wayside Inn
1523 Foothill Boulevard
Calistoga 94515
707.942.0645 707.942.4169
www.calistogawaysideinn.com
3 rooms

Carlin Cottages
1623 Lake Street
Calistoga 94515
800.734.4624 707.942.9102
www.carlincottages.com
15 cottages - $110-$205

Spring-fed mineral baths and pool. Shaker-style furniture, Irish country motif.

CasaLana

1316 South Oak Street
Calistoga 94515
707.942.0615 707.942.0204
www.casalana.com
2 rooms - $175-$225

A river setting just a short walk from downtown Calistoga. Also offers culinary tours, and gourmet weekends and cooking classes in the B&B's professional kitchen.

Chateau de Vie

3250 Highway 128
Calistoga 94515
707.942.6446 877.558.2513
www.chtaeaudv.com
3 units - $189-$279

Right in the vineyards with a spectacular view of Mount St. Helena.

Chien Blanc Lodging, a Vacation Rental

1441 Second Street
Calistoga, CA 94515
800.676.4205 Fax 707.942.8682
www.chienblanc.com
3 suites with private gardens - $125-$175

Three bungalows with private entrance, living room, bedroom (queen), bath with standard tub-shower arrangement and very functional kitchen. Each unit has a small garden. TV, telephones, and all the comforts of home, including washer and dryer. An easy walk to the spas, restaurants and shops. Wineries are located throughout the area.

Christopher's Inn

1010 Foothill Boulevard
Calistoga 94515
707.942.5755

www.christophersinn.com
22 units - $175-$425

All rooms with private baths, most with fireplaces, many with patio gardens, several with whirlpool tubs.

Cottage Grove Inn

1711 Lincoln Avenue
Calistoga 94515
800.799.2284 707.942.8400
www.cottagegrove.com
16 cottages $235 - $295

Private cottages with king-size beds, 2-person deep whirlpool tubs and wood burning fireplaces. Listen to a favorite CD or watch your favorite movie as you relax. Located within walking distance to town, on a beautifully landscaped property.

Culver Mansion

1805 Foothill Boulevard
Calistoga 94515
877.281.3671 707.942.4535
707.942.4557
www.culvermansion.com
6 rooms - $170-$190

A three-level Victorian built in 1867. The bedrooms are decorated in period styles such as Victorian, Edwardian, Art Deco, Art Nouveau and Early Twentieth Century. Great view of Mount St. Helena, the Palisades and the valley. A short walk from downtown.

Czech Inn

1102 Pine St.
Calistoga 94515
707.942.9341

Fanny's

1206 Spring Street
Calistoga 94515
707.942.9491

Foothill House
3037 Foothill Boulevard
Calistoga 94515
800.942.6933 707.942.6933
www.foothillhouse.com
1 room, 2 cottages, 2 suites - $175-
$325

In the foothills just north of
Calistoga.

Garnett Creek Inn
1139 Lincoln Avenue
Calistoga 94515
707.942.9797 707.942.5288
www.garnettcreekinn.com
5 rooms $155 - $295

On Calistoga's main street.

Hacienda Guest House
707.942.5259
www.napavalleybnb.com
1 house - $350-$425

A Mexican-style hacienda vacation
rental just minutes from Calistoga.

Hillcrest Country Inn
3225 Lake County Hwy. (Highway
29)
Calistoga CA 94515
707.942.6334
www.bnbweb.com/hillcrest
6 rooms $69 - $193

Small lake for fishing. Hiking,
barbeque area

Holiday House
3514 Highway 128
Calistoga 94515
707.942.6174

Hotel d'Amici
1436 Lincoln Avenue
Calistoga 94515
707.942.1007 707.963.3150

www.rutherfordgrove.com/hotel.ht
ml
4 suites - $150-$225

La Chaumiere
1301 Cedar Street
Calistoga 94515
800.474.6800 707.942.5139
www.lachaumiere.com
2 rooms, 1 cottage - $165-$250

One half-block from downtown.
Patio gardens.

Larkmead Country Inn
1103 Larkmead Lane
Calistoga 94515
707.942.5360
www.larkmeadinn.com
3 rooms - $150

Built in the early 1900s. Vineyard
setting.

Meadowlark Country House
601 Petrified Road
Calistoga 94515
800.942.5651 707.942.5651
www.meadowlarkinn.com
7 rooms - $165-$265

Secluded 20-acre estate, magnificent
views, privacy, naturist pool, deck,
sauna and hot tub, massage,
fireplace, AC, gourmet breakfast, gay
friendly, dogs welcome, one mile to
shops and dining.

Mora Lane
2087 Mora Avenue
Calistoga 94515
707.942.1395

Oakwood
1503 Lake Street
Calistoga 94515
707.942.5381

Pink Mansion, The
1415 Foothill Boulevard
Calistoga 94515
800.238.7465 707.942.0558
www.pinkmansion.com
6 rooms - $155-$295

Built in 1875 by William Fisher, who founded Calistoga Water. It was purchased by the Semic family in the 1930s, who painted it pink and added the indoor heated pool. Most suites have fireplaces, king beds and whirlpool tubs. The Pink Mansion is two blocks north of Lincoln Avenue and within walking distance to most of the spas and restaurants.

Quail Mountain
4455 North St. Helena Highway
Calistoga 94515
707.942.0316 707.942.0315

Scarlett's Country Inn
2918 Silverado Trail, N.
Calistoga 94515
707.942.6669
members.aol.com/scarletts
1 room, 2 suites

1890 country house in a private canyon.

Stevenson Manor Inn
1830 Lincoln Avenue
Calistoga 94515
707.942.1112 707.942.0381
34 rooms - $134-$234

Trailside Inn
4201 Silverado Trail
Calistoga 94515
707.942.4106 707.942.4702
www.trailsideinn.com
3 suites - $165-$185

A 1930s farmhouse. Pool, hot tub, neighboring vineyards and two acres of flower-filled lawns.

Washington Street Lodging
1605 Washington Street
Calistoga 94515
707.942.6968
www.napalinks.com/wsl/
5 cottages - $90-$135

Large oaks, lovely garden, close to downtown and overlooking the Napa River.

Wine Way Inn
1019 Foothill Boulevard
Calistoga 94515
800.572.0679 707.942.0680
707.942.4656
www.napavalley.com/wineway
6 rooms - $115-$175

Napa

1801 Inn, The
1801 First Street
Napa, CA 94559
707.224.3739
www.the1801inn.com
8 cottages and suites - $165-$325

An intimate urban retreat located in the heart of downtown Napa, strolling distance to fine restaurants, quaint shops and historic sites. The beautifully restored Queen Anne Victorian now offers resort style accommodations and contemporary amenities, catering to savvy travelers who demand excellence.

Features include romantic fireplaces and gracious sitting areas; large, private baths with two-person tubs or whirlpool tubs; gourmet breakfast; evening wine and hors d' oeuvres; and a 24-hour complimentary minibar. Guests can linger on the sun porch with a cup of custom-blend 1801 Inn coffee, or enjoy the evening breeze and a glass of wine on the delightful patio and shade garden.

Arbor Guest House

1436 G St.
Napa, CA. 94559
707.252.8144 866.627.2262 (Toll free)
www.arborguesthouse.com
5 rooms - $175-$250

Located on a quiet residential street just 10 minutes walking distance from downtown Napa and a short four blocks from Highway 29. The beautiful gardens, where three- to four-course gourmet breakfasts are usually served, have many areas where you can relax and listen to the birds, read or enjoy a bottle of wine.

Beazley House

1910 First Street
Napa CA 94559
800.559.1649
www.beazleyhouse.com
11 rooms - $125-$295

Napa's oldest B&B. A 1902 mansion. Gardens and private whirlpool tubs.

Blackbird Inn

1755 First Street
Napa CA 94559
707.226.2450 888.567.9811
www.foursisters.com/inns/blackbird inn.html
8 rooms - $135-$275

Beautifully handcrafted restoration in the early 20th Century Craftsman style. A short drive to downtown Napa.

Blue Violet Mansion

443 Brown Street
Napa CA 94559
707.253.2583 800.959.2583

www.bluevioletmansion.com
17 rooms - $199-$359

An 1886 Queen Anne Victorian mansion in Old Town Napa. Each room is painted in *trompe l'oeil* fashion. Surrounded by an acre of manicured gardens, including a rose garden centered by a period gezebo with swing, expansive porches and swimming pool. A short walk to downtown Napa.

Candlelight Inn

1045 Easum Drive
Napa CA 94558
707.257.3717 800.624.0395
www.candlelightinn.com
10 rooms - $135-$295

A lovely English Tudor built in 1929 on a quiet park-like one-acre garden setting. Nestled among redwood groves and trees along Napa Creek. Beautiful landscaping and large swimming pool.

Cedar Gables Inn

486 Coombs Street
Napa CA 94559
707.224.7969 Fax 707.224.4838
www.cedargablesinn.com
9 rooms - $189-$ 329

Styled after a 16th century English country manor, this dark brown shingled mansion is located just four blocks from downtown Napa. Winding staircases lead to antique appointed rooms. Full breakfast, wine and cheese hour, whirlpool tubs, fireplaces, queen size beds, comfy robes. Luxurious surroundings and warm hospitality.

Churchill Manor

485 Brown Street
Napa CA 94559
707.253.7733

www.churchillmanor.com
10 rooms - $155-$255

A three-story, 10,000-square foot mansion built in 1889 by one of Napa's founders and listed on the National Register of Historic Places.

Daughters Inn
1938 First Street
Napa CA 94559
866.253.1331
www.thedaughtersinn.com
10 rooms - $235 - $325

All rooms have fireplaces and whirlpool tubs. English country garden setting.

Frog Hollow House
472 Seminary St
Napa, CA 94559
925.831.4989
www.froghollowhouse.com
2 bdrm 1 bath home - $225-$275

Vacation rental. A charming and beautifully decorated 18th-century Victorian home located in historic downtown Napa. The bedrooms are decorated with antique iron beds, down comforters and pillows and lovely furniture. A lovely backyard and front yard for sipping wine and outdoor cooking. Full kitchen and all the amenities of home. Shops, restaurants, antiques and Copia are all within walking distance.

Hennessey House
1727 Main Street
Napa CA 94559
707.226.3774
www.hennesseyhouse.com
10 rooms - $145-$295

A Queen Anne Victorian built in 1889. Just minutes from the downtown Napa's restaurants, shops and Copia.

Hillview Country Inn
1205 Hillview Lane
Napa CA 94558
707.224.5004 707.224.6422
www.hillviewinnnapa.com

Inn of Imagination
470 Randolph Street
Napa, CA 94559
707.224.7772 Fax 707.257.9827
www.innofimagination.com
3 rooms - $240.00-$280.00

Rooms capturing the lives and works of Lewis Carroll, Dr. Seuss and Jimmy Buffett. Features many murals, period furniture, expansive grounds, sculpture gardens, rain forest library, private baths and a whimsical feel. A classic example of Spanish Revival architecture, the inn is on the National Registry of Historic Places, and is located in the historic Arroyo Grande section of Old Town Napa.

Inn on Randolph
411 Randolph Street
Napa, CA 94559
707.257.2886 800.670.6886
www.visitsoon.com
5 rooms - $119-$229

A Gothic Revival Victorian built in 1860.

La Belle Epoque
1386 Calistoga Avenue
Napa CA 94559
707.257.2161 800.283.8070
www.labelleepoque.com
7 rooms, 2 suites - $160-$325

Built in 1893. In the center of Old Town Napa.

McClelland - Priest B&B Inn, The

569 Randolph Street
Napa CA 94559
707.224.6875 800.290.6881
www.historicinnstravel.com
5 suites

In Old Town Napa. Built in 1879.

Milliken Creek Inn

1815 Silverado Trail
Napa CA 94558
888.622.5775
www.millikencreekinn.com
10 rooms - $295-$525

A luxury inn on the Napa River. Three acres of gardens, fountains and trails. River and garden views. Concierge services, massage and spa treatments, live jazz piano, breakfast in bed, even private yoga classes. *Travel & Leisure Magazine* said it's one of the top 30 inns in the country, and *Travel Holiday* called it Napa Valley's finest inn.

Napa Inn, The

1137 TheWarren
St. Napa CA 94559
707.257.1444 800.435.1144
www.napainn.com
14 rooms/suites - $120-$300

Oak Knoll Inn

2200 E. Oak Knoll Avenue
Napa CA 94558
707.255.2200
www.oakknollinn.com
4 rooms - $250-$450

Surrounded by 600 acres of vineyards just minutes north of Napa. Swimming pool and whirlpool tubs.

Old World Inn

1301 Jefferson St.
Napa CA 94559
707.257.0112 800.966.6624
www.oldworldinn.com
10 rooms - $150-$265

All room rates include a full gourmet breakfast, afternoon tea, a wine and cheese social hour, and their evening chocolate lover's desserts.

Stahlecker House

1042 Eastum Drive
Napa CA 94558
707.257.1588 800.799.1588
www.stahleckerhouse.com
3 rooms, 1 suite - $160-$268

Located on one and a half acres of manicured lawns and flowering gardens.

Tall Timbers Chalet

1012 Darms Lane
Napa 94558
707.252.7810 707.252.1055
www.talltimberscottages.com

Pope Valley / Chiles Valley

Rustridge Bed & Breakfast Inn

2910 Lower Chiles Valley Road
St. Helena 94574
800.788.0263 707.965.9353
707.965.9263
www.rustridge.com
3 rooms - $165-$225

Tennis, hiking. On the grounds of RustRidge Ranch & Winery

St. Helena

Adagio Inn

1417 Kearney Street
St. Helena, CA 94574
707.963.2238 888-8ADAGIO Fax
707.963.5598
www.adagioinn.com
3 rooms - $220-$315

Located in a quiet area, this luxuriously decorated Edwardian residence is two blocks from world-class restaurants and unique shops. A lavish breakfast is served in the sunroom or on the veranda. Afternoon refreshments are served in the parlor with its baby grand piano. Extra large rooms/suites all have a European elegance along with king-sized beds, air conditioning and cable TV.

Ambrose Bierce B&B

1515 Main St.
St. Helena CA 94574
707.963.3003
www.ambrosebiercehouse.com
3 rooms - $199-$269

Former residence of the 19th century author of short stories and "The Devil's Dictionary"

Bartels Ranch & Country Inn

1200 Conn Valley Road
St. Helena CA 94574
707.963.4001
www.bartelsranch.com
4 rooms - $235-$455

60 acres, hiking/biking trails, lake, pool, whirlpool tub.

Bylund House

2000 Howell Mountain Road
St. Helena CA 94574
707.963.9073
www.bylundhouse.com
2 rooms $95 - $200

A northern Italian Villa tucked into a "Tuscan" valley just two miles outside of downtown St. Helena in the heart of the wine country. A separate tower, with a private entrance into a parlor with a fireplace, houses two rooms with private baths, balconies and sweeping views. Complimentary wine and hors d'oeuvres at poolside or starlight in the spa. Gourmet continental breakfast.

Cinnamon Bear

1407 Kearney St.
St. Helena CA 94574
707.963.4653
$115-$185

Historic home. Walk to town.

Eagle & Rose Inn

1189 Lodi Lane
St. Helena CA 94574
707.967.0466
www.eagleandroseinn.com
5 rooms - $99-$169

Erika's Hillside B&B

285 Fawn Park Drive
St. Helena CA 94574
707.963.2887

Vineyard views, hillside retreat, whirlpool tub.

Glass Mountain Inn

3100 Silverado Trail
St. Helena CA 94574
707.968.9400 877.968.9400 (toll free)
www.glassmountaininn.com
3 suites, 1 cottage

Victorian home, century-old wine cave, gazebo, private decks. On the mountainside east of St. Helena.

Hilltop House B&B
9550 St. Helena Road
St. Helena CA 94574
707.944.0880
4 rooms - $135-$195

On the mountain. Hiking, spa.

Ink House, The
1575 St. Helena Highway
St. Helena CA 94574
707.963.3890
www.inkhouse.com
7 rooms - $110-$215

Historic home with observatory with 360-degree view. Built in 1884, and listed on the National Registry of Historic Places.

La Fleur
1475 Inglewood Avenue
St. Helena 94574
707.963.0233
www.lafleurinn.com
$150-$195

Napa Valley Spanish Villa Inn
474 Glass Mountain Road
St. Helena CA 94574
707.963.7483
www.napavalleyspanishvilla.com
3 rooms - $155-$275. Entire home available at reduced rate.

Country villa, two-mile drive from town.

Oliver House
2970 Silverado Trail
St. Helena CA 94574
800.682.7888 707.963.4089
www.oliverhouse.com

4 rooms, 1 cottage - $165-$295

European-style chalet located on the historic Silverado Trail. Nestled on a hillside above St. Helena and within walking distance of five major wineries. Relax on private balconies or in beautiful common areas, or enjoy the views of the valley from the extensive grounds. Vibrant colors, unique custom painting and beautiful antiques throughout the guestrooms and living areas. All rooms and suites include private baths, down comforters, luxurious 100% cotton linens, and individual heat and air conditioning controls. A full gourmet breakfast is served every morning.

Prager Winery B & B
1281 Lewelling Lane
St. Helena CA 94574
707.963.3720
www.pragerport.com
Two 3-room suites - $225

Next to Prager Winery and Port Works.

Shady Oaks Country Inn
399 Zinfandel Lane
St. Helena CA 94574
707.963.1190
www.shadyoaksinn.com
4 rooms - $189-$239

Sunny Acres
397 Main Street
St. Helena CA 94574
707.963.2826
www.sunnyacresbandb.com
2 rooms - $195

Restored building originally constructed in 1879. In the middle of a 20-acre vineyard. All rooms have private bath.

Vineyard Country Inn

201 Main St.
St. Helena CA 94574
707.963.1000
www.vineyardcountryinn.com
21 suites - $160-$240

Vineyard setting, woodburning fireplaces, wet bars. Pool, whirlpool tub. Close to wineries and restaurants.

Wine Country Inn

1152 Lodi Lane
St. Helena CA 94574
707.963.7077
www.winecountryinn.com
24 rooms, 5 cottages - $185-$430

Wine Country Victorian & Cottages

400 Meadowood Lane
St. Helena CA 94574
707.963.0852
1 suite, 2 cottages - $205-$255

Turn-of-the-century Victorian and cottage, vineyard and woodland setting.

Zinfandel Inn

800 Zinfandel Lane
St. Helena CA 94574
707.963.3512
www.zinfandelinn.com
3 rooms - $175-$330

English Tudor on two beautifully landscaped acres. Fireplaces, whirlpool tub, gazebo and aviary.

Yountville

Bordeaux House

6600 Washington Street
Yountville 94599
707.944.2855
www.bordeauxhouse.com
5 rooms - $135-$165

A very short walk to all Yountville shops and restaurants.

Burgundy House

6711 Washington Street
Yountville 94599
707.944.0889
www.burgundyhouse.com
6 rooms - $125-$175

A French country stone building from the early 1890s. Just a short walk to Yountville shops and restaurants.

Castle in the Clouds

7400 St. Helena Highway
Yountville CA 94599
707. 944.2785
www.castleintheclouds.com
4 rooms - $235-$325

Perched high atop a hill on eight acres in the heart of Napa Valley. Looks down upon world famous wineries and vineyards, and provides easy access to fine dining and wine tasting. Decorated with museum quality antiques, the B&B offers luxurious comforts including king or queen beds with down comforters, plush robes, private baths and air conditioning.

The large parlor has a 52-inch digital satellite TV, fireplace, guest refrigerator with complimentary beverages and snacks, coffee/tea bar and a variety of board games. A hot tub carved into the side of the mountain, patio with gardens and fountains, a picnic area, a balcony and rooftop sitting area offer many ways to enjoy the best views in Napa Valley.

Oleander House

7433 St. Helena Highway
Yountville, CA 94599
707 944-8315 / 800 788-0357
www.oleander.com
5 rooms - $145-$195

Oleander House is just north of
Yountville, set amongst the
vineyards and countryside. Guest
rooms are spacious and antique
filled, with Laura Ashley
wallcoverings. Within five minutes
of world-class restaurants, wineries
and shopping.

Petit Logis

6527 Yount Street
Yountville 94599
707.944.2332
www.petitlogis.com
5 rooms - $105-$200

In the very heart of Yountville. Each
room has a fireplace and large
bathroom with double whirlpool tub.

Other Lodging

Horse Camping

Skyline Wilderness Park

2201 Imola Avenue
Napa CA 94559
707.252.0481
www.ncfaa.com/skyline/horse_cam
ping.htm

10 spacious horse camping sites,
each accommodating two horse and
two rigs, with water and picnic table.
Bathrooms with showers within a
short walking distance. Fifteen miles
of trails through wooded forest,
valleys and hilltops.

RV Camping

Napa Valley Exposition

575 Third Street
Napa CA 94559
707.253.4900
www.napavalleyexpo.com/f-rvs.html

RV parking is $20 per night, and
includes water and electrical hook
ups, and the use of the dump station.
Spaces are available on a first
arrived, first filled basis

Rancho Monticello Resort

6590 Knoxville Road
Napa CA 94558
707.966.2188
www.ranchomonticelloresort.com

Located on Lake Berryessa, the
resort offers picnicking, boat
launching, fishing from shore or
boats, and fifty campsites for tents or

RVs. All campsites have picnic tables and barbecues, with water faucet access, restrooms and showers nearby. Trailer sites have full hookup with electrical, water and sewer. Long-term sites based on annual leases are also available for mobile homes, travel trailers and RVs.

Skyline Wilderness Park
2201 Imola Avenue,
Napa CA 94559
707.252.0481
www.ncfaa.com/skyline/rvcamp.htm

Thirty-nine spaces available in the park, 19 with full hookups at $27 per night, and 20 with water and electricity only at $25 per night.

RV camping is also available at the following locations.

Calistoga – Napa County Fairgrounds (see page 118)

Lake Berryessa - Lake Berryessa resorts (see page 129)

Napa - Napa Valley Exposition (see page 62)

Time Share

River Pointe
500 Lincoln Avenue
Napa CA 94558
888.430.9988
www.riverpointenapa.com
180 rooms - $85-$350

Cottage resort next to the Napa River in the heart of the city of Napa. Swimming pool, hot tub, sauna, workout facility.

Vino Bello Resort
865 Bordeaux Way
Napa CA 94558
www.vinobelloresort.com
180 rooms

Shares property with The Meritage Resort at Napa. Swimming pool, jacuzzi, children's pool, one- and two-bedroom units, exercise facility.

Tours

Tour Planning Agencies

If you're bringing a corporate group to the valley, or just want to organize things before you arrive, here are some companies that will assist you in making your visit both productive and enjoyable.

Destination: Napa Valley Tours
295 West Lane
Angwin CA 94508
707.965.1808
www.tournapavalley.com

Personalized tours for individuals, couples, groups and business events.

Wine Country Concierge
PO Box 789
Napa CA 94559
707.252.4472
www.winecountryconcierge.com

Wine Country Concierge can arrange lodging, restaurants, spas, tours, and small events, including getting you in to visit wineries not normally open to the public.

Wine & Dine Tours
P.O. Box 513
345 La Fata Suite E
St. Helena CA 94574
707.963.8930 •
800.WINETOUR
www.wineanddinetour.com

Designs, organizes, and conducts winery tours and events for groups as small as two and as large as 25,000. Focuses on such things as wine and food pairing meals, off-the-beaten-path wineries, educational seminars, enology lectures, meet the winemaker special events, and cooking demonstrations.

Meeting Facilities

Calistoga

Calistoga Village Inn & Spa - Conference space for 70

Napa County Fairgrounds – Three meeting halls for total of 1,060 people and 15,300 square feet

Silver Rose Inn - Conference space for 50

Napa

Chateau Hotel - 10,000 square feet of meeting space

Christian Brothers Retreat & Conference Center - Meeting space for up to 150

Embassy Suites - Up to 8 meeting rooms and more than 6,900 square feet of meeting space

Marriott Napa Valley - 11 meeting rooms, 11,000 square feet

Meritage Resort at Napa – 10 meeting rooms with 13,500 square feet

Napa River Inn - 2 meeting rooms for a total of 124 people and 2,200 square feet

Napa Valley Exposition - 4 meeting halls, each holding from 250 - 350 people with tables and chairs

River Terrace Inn – 2,500 sq. ft. of meeting space, including one board room, one breakout room, and one 900 square foot conference room.

Rutherford

Rancho Caymus Inn - Meeting space for up to 75

Silverado Trail

Auberge du Soleil - Meeting space for up to 150 (Rutherford)

Meadowood - Over 3,300 square feet of meeting space in four buildings (St. Helena)

Silverado Resort - 25,000 square foot executive conference center (Napa)

St. Helena

Harvest Inn - 8 meeting and special event spaces (over 3,000 square feet)

Yountville

Napa Valley Lodge - Meeting space for up to 60

Villagio Inn - Up to 7 meeting rooms with more than 3,700 square feet

Vintage Inn - Meeting space for up to 150

Yountville Inn - Meeting space for up to 60

Recreation and Outdoors

Archery

Silverado Archery Club
www.ncfaa.com/skyline/archery.htm
Silverado Archers
www.ncfaa.com/silverado.html

Silverado Archery Club is located on 25 acres within the boundary of Skyline Wilderness Park (see page 70) in Napa. The club is NFAA charted with three separate NFAA marked yardage ranges, each range having 14 permanent targets as well as an area for 14 unmarked distance targets utilizing McKenzie 3-D's.

The club hosts a number of tournaments each year for target archers and hunters, including a 16 week un-marked distance series (open to the public) on Thursday evenings from April through July for hunters in preparation for the hunting season. Their facilities are open to the public on the second Sunday of each month.

Bicycling

Bicyclists can be found throughout the Napa Valley. Highway 29 is a popular stretch. There is a bike lane on the frontage road (Solano Avenue) that runs along the west side of Highway 29 from Napa to Yountville. North of Yountville you're on your own. If you're going to continue north, watch out for the railroad tracks crossing Highway 29 at Whitehall Lane south of St. Helena. Many inattentive cyclists have hit the asphalt here.

Silverado Trail has bike lanes all the way from Napa to Calistoga. The main caution here is the drivers, who travel much faster on this road than on Highway 29.

South of Napa, in the Carneros District that overlaps both Napa and Sonoma counties, you'll find the least traffic—and cooler temperatures. There are low, rolling hills covered with vineyards, lots of wineries and far fewer tourists.

To give you an idea how bicyclists feel about the Napa Valley, it was proposed that the Napa Valley host the bicycling events if San Francisco was awarded the 2012 Summer Olympics. (It wasn't.) It's not known if San Francisco Olympic organizers were aware that the Olympics occur at the same time as Crush, and what effect tens of thousands of visitors would have on a successful harvest.

Bicycle Shops

Bicycle Madness (Napa)
707.253.2453

Bicycle Works (Napa)
707.253.7000

Bike Tours of Napa Valley (Napa)
707.255.3380

Napa River Velo (Napa)
707.258.8729
www.naparivervelo.com

Palisades Mountain Sport
(Calistoga) 707.942.9687
www.bikeroute.com/Palisades/

Pedals Past (Calistoga)
707.942.9469

St. Helena Cyclery (St. Helena)
707.963.7736
www.sthelenacyclery.com

Bicycle Rentals

Getaway Wine Country Bicycle Tours and Rentals
707.942.0332 800.499.2453

Napa Valley Bike Tours and Rentals (Napa) 707.255.3377
www.napavalleybiketours.com

Napa River Velo (Napa)
707.258.8729
www.naparivervelo.com

Palisades Mountain Sport
(Calistoga)
707.942.9687

Pedals Past (Calistoga)
707.942.9469

St. Helena Cyclery (St. Helena)
707.963.7736
www.sthelenacyclery.com

Other Bicycle Contacts

Napa Valley BMX 707.224.8269

Bicycle Events Information
707.226.7066

CalTrans Highway Information
800.427.7623

California Highway Patrol
707.253.4906

Napa Police Department
707.257.9550

Napa Valley Transit 707.255.7631

Napa Valley Transit buses are equipped with front-mounted bike racks that can accommodate up to two bikes very quickly and easily.

Boating

Boating is available at Lake Berryessa and on the Napa River.

Lake Berryessa Resorts (see page 129) offer rentals of fishing boats, ski boats, patio boats, houseboats, and jet skis.

Napa River Adventures (see page 58) offers cruises on a slow-paced electric-powered boat.

Disc Golf

Disc Golf Course
Skyline Wilderness Park
707.252.0481
www.ncfaa.com/skyline/disc_golf.htm

A short but technical course. 18 holes with dirt tees and disc-catcher baskets. Framed signs at the tee show alternate pin placements. Can be easily played in two hours. Discs (like Frisbees) are available at the kiosk as you enter Skyline Park. Entrance to the park is $4 per vehicle.

Fishing

Napa County offers fishing at Lake Berryessa and its surrounding streams, and on the Napa River. Here's the place to find all the information you need, including what's biting, where, and what on.

Sweeney's Sport Store
River Park Shopping Center
1537 Imola Avenue West
Napa CA 94559
707.255.5544

www.sweeneyssports.com

Open 7 days a week. Sweeney's is *the* place for fishing tackle and information. Free flycasting classes every Saturday morning at 9 a.m.

Lake Berryessa Resorts

The resorts at Lake Berryessa (see page 129) offer everything you need from lodging to boats to tackle, and the very latest information on fishing the lake.

Spanish Flat Resort provides a current Berryessa fishing report at: www.spanishflatresort.com/fishing.php

State of California Department of Fish and Game
7329 Silverado Trail
Yountville CA 94599
707.944.5500

Napa Valley Fly Fishermen
PO Box 2373
Napa CA 94558

Geocaching

Geocaching (pronounced "GEO-cashing") combines the high-technology of Global Positioning System (GPS) satellites and the low-technology of walking around on the ground. Geocachers hide a "cache" somewhere in a publicly-accessible area (perhaps a park, forest, beach area) and then use an electronic GPS unit to determine the precise location of the cache in latitude and longitude. That location is posted on the Web, and others can then hunt for the cache, using the provided coordinates. The cache may contain some sort of object, but will always contain a logbook, in which the finder will note his or her discovery of the cache.

Geocachers have naturally discovered the Napa Valley and there are caches hidden throughout the area. Use the following web site to get their coordinates.

Geocaching
www.geocaching.com

The primary web site for geocachers. It gives information about the hobby of geocaching, provides discussion forums, and lists cache locations all over (currently more than 180 countries) the world.

Golf

Aetna Springs Golf Course
9 holes (Pope Valley)
1600 Aetna Springs Road
Pope Valley, CA 94567
707.965.2115
www.aetnasprings.com

9-hole, par 70. Beautiful setting. Reputedly the oldest golf course west of the Mississippi.

Chardonnay Golf Club
27 holes (Napa)
2555 Jamieson Canyon Road
(Highway 12 between Highway 29 and Highway I-80)
PO Box 3779
Napa CA 94558
707.257.1900
www.chardonnaygolfclub.com

27 holes through 130 acres of Chardonnay and Merlot vineyards, lakes and creeks.

Eagle Vines Golf Club
18 holes (Napa)
580 South Kelly Road
PO Box 2398
Napa CA 94558
707.257.4470
www.eaglevinesgolfclub.com

18-hole, par 72. Open to the public. 7,283 yards - six sets of tees including two ladies'.

Meadowood Resort
9 holes (St. Helena)
900 Meadowood Lane
St. Helena CA 94574
707.963.3646 800.458.8080
www.meadowood.com

9-hole, par 31. 2,014 yards. A walking course.

Mt. St. Helena Golf Course
9 holes (Calistoga)
P.O. Box 344
Calistoga CA 94515
707.942.9966
www.napacountyfairgrounds.com

9-holes, par 34. Men - 2,759 yards. Women - par 35 - 2,650 yards. Public course located at Napa County Fairgrounds.

Napa Golf Course
18 holes (Napa)
2295 Streblow Drive
Napa CA 94558
707.255.4333
www.playnapa.com

18-hole, par 72. 6,730 yards Public golf course located in Kennedy Park off Highway 221 at the south end of Napa. Reasonable fees, uncrowded.

Discounts for residents of Napa city and county.

Napa Valley Country Club
18 holes (Napa)
3385 Hagen Road
Napa, 94558
Golf Shop 707.252.1114. Business Office 707.252.1111.
www.napavalleycc.com

Private course. Members and guests only. Reciprocal with other private clubs. Guest Fees - $90, includes cart. 18-holes. 5,285/6,148 yards - par 72. Three tees.

Silverado Country Club
36 holes (Napa)
1600 Atlas Peak Road
Napa CA 94558
707.257.5460
www.silveradoresort.com

South Course - 6,500 yards par 72. North Course - 6,700 yards par 72. Designed by Robert Trent Jones, Jr. Home of the Senior PGA "Transamerica" tournament.

Vintner's Golf Club
9 holes (Yountville)
7901 Solano Avenue
Yountville, CA 94599
707.944.1992
www.vintnersgolfclub.com

9-hole, par 34. 4,258/5,573 yards. Three sets of tees. Located just off Highway 29 at the Veterans Home.

Hiking

There is some beautiful country in the Napa Valley, but most of it is privately owned. There are only a few places where members of the public can hike whenever they wish.

However, there are several organizations that schedule hikes throughout the year on private lands. Anyone can go on these hikes, as long as they reserve a space.

Because Napa is one of the nine San Francisco Bay Area counties, it is also part of two Bay Area-wide hiking projects: the Ridge Trail and the San Francisco Bay Trail, also called the "Wetlands Trail".

Bay Area Ridge Trail
415.561.2595
www.ridgetrail.org

The Ridge Trail is a 400-mile multiple-use trail connecting parks and preserved open spaces along the ridgelines surrounding California's San Francisco Bay.

In Napa County it currently passes through Skyline Wilderness Park heading east to Solano County. The trail segment west to Sonoma County is not yet in place.

Ridge Trail—Napa County Segment

Length is about 4.4 miles with an elevation change of about +900 feet.

Leave the picnic area near the Skyline Wilderness Park entrance and take gravelled Lake Marie Road, which crosses a causeway between two ponds, Lake Louise and Lake Camille. Lake Marie Road bends left (east), and in about 600 feet you turn right (southeast) off it onto Skyline Trail. In a few yards you pass the junction with Buckeye Trail.

Skyline Trail zigzags up a steep hill and soon enters oak and buckeye woods where the trail straightens, levels off a bit, and heads south. Pass the junction with Bayleaf Trail by staying right on Skyline Trail. Soon, pass the spur road which goes to the right through Passini Gate. Just beyond, you begin climbing to high grasslands. Traverse a steep hillside, pass the skeleton of a house in a small clearing, and continue to follow Skyline Trail on an old, rocky roadbed through oaks and firs. Pass the junction with Chaparral Trail on the left, following a creek on Skyline Trail. Cross to the south side of Marie Creek, draining into Lake Marie below. Soon you reach the locked boundary gate near the southeast corner of the park.

San Francisco Bay Trail
baytrail.abag.ca.gov/

The Bay Trail is a planned recreational corridor that, when complete, will encircle San Francisco and San Pablo Bays with a continuous 400-mile network of bicycling and hiking trails. It will connect the shoreline of all nine Bay Area counties, link 47 cities, and cross the major toll bridges in the region.

To date, approximately 210 miles of the alignment—or slightly more than half the Bay Trail's ultimate length—has been completed. The Trail is frequently referred to as the "Wetlands Trail" since, unlike the Ridge Trail which travels along the mountain ridges encircling the bay, this trail passes through the shoreline/wetland areas.

When completed, the trail will enter Napa County from the west through the Carneros Region, go to the southern edge of the city of Napa at John F. Kennedy Park, and then proceed south to American Canyon and onto Vallejo.

Napa River Trail
www.cityofnapa.org/commres/river/river.htm

The City of Napa is also creating its own trail, running along the banks of the Napa River from Trancas Street at the northern end of town to John F. Kennedy Park at the southern end.

Currently, the segment from Trancas Street to Lincoln Avenue is in place, as is the area at Kennedy Park. The downtown restoration and flood control project will result in the completion of the other segments.

The Napa County Land Trust and the Sierra Club offer scheduled hikes.

Land Trust of Napa County
707.252.3270
www.napalandtrust.org

Offers scheduled hikes during the year throughout the valley. An opportunity to see creeks, waterfalls and views on private property.

Napa Sierra Club
www.redwood.sierraclub.org/napa

Offers scheduled hikes during the year throughout the valley.

Napa County Hiking Trails

For detailed information on trails, see our parks section (page 174).

Bale Grist Mill State Historic Park (St. Helena)

Bothé-Napa Valley State Park (Calistoga)

Robert Louis Stevenson State Park (Calistoga)

Skyline Wilderness Park (Napa)

Horseback Riding

Napa Valley Equestrian Center
1132 El Centro
Napa CA 94558
707.255.0302
www.napahorses.com

Ten-acre English hunt seat riding facility. Lessons, dressage, boarding, tack shop

North Bay Natural Horsemanship
707.479.8031
Napa
www.northbaynaturalhorsemanship.com

Training, lessons, camps.

Sunrise Stables
1098 Lodi Lane
St. Helena CA 94574
707.963.7783
www.srshorsesnapavalley.com

A family-centered facility for horse lovers of all ages. Lessons, day camps, boarding.

Triple Creek Horse Outfit
707.887.8700
www.triplecreekhorseoutfit.com

Guided horseback rides in Bothé-Napa State Park. Minimum age 8 years old. Seven days a week, April through October. Reservations required.

Horse Camping

Skyline Wilderness Park
707.252.0481
www.ncfaa.com/skyline/horse_camping.htm

10 spacious horse camping sites, each accommodating two horse and two rigs, with water and picnic table. Bathrooms with showers within a short walking distance. Fifteen miles of trails through wooded forest, valleys and hilltops.

Hot Air Balloons

A balloon glides silently on a morning in the vineyards.

Hot air ballooning is something you have to experience to truly appreciate. Drifting almost soundlessly over the hills and vineyards of the valley, you'll come to experience the breathtaking beauty of this famous part of the world.

Most balloons launch from the Yountville area early in the morning. The first "shift" rides in the balloon gondola while the second shift pursues the balloon in the "chase" vehicle. Then, after the balloon sets down at the end of its voyage, the two crews switch for the second flight. Almost every morning's flight ends in a champagne brunch. You can even get married in a balloon. Cost, including brunch, ranges from $150-$175 per person for a one-hour flight.

Above the West Ballooning
707.944.8638
www.nvaloft.com

Adventures Aloft
800.944.4408 707.944.4409
www.nvaloft.com

Balloons Above the Valley
800.464.6824
www.balloonrides.com

Balloon Aviation of Napa Valley
707.944.4400 800.367.6272
www.nvaloft.com

Bonaventura Balloon Company
800.359.6272
www.bonaventuraballoons.com

Napa Valley Balloons Inc.
707.944.0228 800.253.2224
www.napavalleyballoons.com

Napa Valley Drifters
707.252.7210 877.463.7438
www.napavalleydrifters.com

Paintball

American Canyon Paintball Jungle
See page 30.

Water Skiing

Lake Berryessa Resorts
See page 129.

Lake Berryessa is one of the most popular places in Northern California for water skiing. All resorts provide boats and other equipment.

Willi's Water Ski Center
1434 Grayson Avenue
St. Helena CA 94574
707.963.4409
www.williwaterski.com/

Willi Ellermeier operates a water ski school at Lake Berryessa with instruction for students ranging from beginner to tournament level.

Parks and Camping

Most of the land in the Napa Valley is privately owned, so parks, hiking and camping are limited. Although there is no county park system, cities have a variety of neighborhood and community parks.

The State of California operates two state parks, Bothé-Napa Valley and Robert Louis Stevenson, and one state historical park, Bale Grist Mill. There is also a large equestrian, hiking and limited camping park run by a private, non-profit organization, Skyline Wilderness Park. In the northeastern part of the county, the

U.S. Bureau of Reclamation oversees Lake Berryessa.

State Parks

Bale Grist Mill State Historic Park

3369 North Saint Helena Highway (Highway 29)
St. Helena CA 94574
707.942.4575
www.parks.ca.gov/default.asp?page_id=482
Three miles north of St. Helena
Hours 10 a.m. to 5 p.m.

Open daily throughout the year except New Year's Day, Thanksgiving and Christmas. Built in 1846 by Edward Bale, the mill has been restored to operating condition complete with its 36-foot wooden waterwheel and big millstones. On weekends, you can watch the mill in action, grinding grain to produce stone ground flour. Schedule your visit in October for *Old Mill Days* or December for *Pioneer Christmas*.

The "Bears" who were involved in the Bear Flag Revolt at Sonoma (when Yankees living in California caused it to split off from Mexico and join the United States) gathered here beforehand. A fun and educational experience for the kids and parents, too. Limited picnic facilities.

In addition to scheduled tours and demonstrations at the mill on weekends at 11:30 a.m., 1:00 and 2:30 p.m., groups may schedule visits for Tuesdays or Wednesdays by calling the park at least 30 days in advance.

Bothé-Napa Valley State Park

3801 North Saint Helena Highway (Highway 29)
Calistoga CA 94515
707.942.4575
www.napanet.net/~bothe/

Bothé is just north of Bale Grist Mill, and the two parks are connected by a one-mile trail.

The nearly 2,000-acre park has excellent trails along Ritchey Creek and through beautiful redwood groves. It offers 50 camping areas either near redwoods along the creekside, or among the oaks and manzanita on sunny slopes above the creek. Campsites are also available for groups, hikers and bicyclists, and one site is fully wheelchair accessible. Picnic areas and an outdoor swimming pool are available.

The Native American Garden, is located next to the Visitor Center. Many of these plants are still used today by the Wappo People.

Day use fees are $5.00 per car. Camping is $16 on the weekends, $15 during the week. It's a wonderful place for all ages and the loveliest public place to hike in the entire valley.

Hiking at Bothé-Napa Valley State Park

1. **Ritchey Canyon Trail** takes you through the heart of the park on historic routes and paths that parallel a year-round stream shaded by redwoods, firs and other plants that prefer cool, moist environments. The trail becomes steeper after a half mile, but offers solitude and a pleasant picnic spot at the homestead site.

2. **Redwood Trail** skirts the south side of Ritchey Creek. Along its upper section, the path is heavily shaded by redwoods and mixed-

evergreen forest. You will enjoy a peaceful walk along the creek bank among the ferns, Solomon's seal, and other shade-loving plants. Early in the spring, trillium and redwood orchids bloom at the base of the young redwoods that have sprouted from the roots of trees that were felled during settlement of the valley in the 1850s.

3. **Coyote Peak Trail** climbs out of the canyon bottom offering views of the upper canyon and Napa Valley. Combining this trail with the Ritchey Canyon, Redwood and South Fork Trails makes a popular loop of 4.4 miles and reveals the variety of plant communities found in the park.

4. **South Fork Trail** goes up a canyon following a skid road used by early pioneers to haul out redwoods. After 0.4 miles the trail leaves the skid road and continues at an easier grade, passing a spur trail to a good overlook of Ritchey Canyon before rejoining the Spring Trail.

5. **History Trail** leads from the picnic area to the historic Bale Grist Mill. Near its beginning the trail passes through a pioneer cemetery and the site of the first church of Napa County, built in 1853. It was named after the Reverend Asa White, who gave sermons in a grove of trees on this site. A steep section of the trail climbs from the cemetery onto a ridge paralleling Highway 29.

The trail ends at the mill after passing the remains of the pond and ditches that brought water from Mill Creek to power the mill's overshot water wheel.

Robert Louis Stevenson State Park

3801 North St. Helena Highway
Calistoga CA 94515
707.942.4575
www.parks.ca.gov/default.asp?page_id=472

This undeveloped 5,000-acre park is seven miles north of Calistoga, and open during daylight hours only. There's a hiking trail to the top of Mount St. Helena, exhibits, a picnic area, and an historic landmark monument to Stevenson.

Bring your own drinking water for the long, sometimes very hot, climb up the mountain. Best time to visit is spring or fall. The view from the summit includes the nearby geyser country and, weather permitting, distant mountains such as Lassen, Shasta and the Sierra Nevada. Not only is there no water, there are no restrooms either. And only limited parking. Which probably explains why there's no entrance fee.

The park contains the old townsite of Silverado, and the tent site where Robert Louis Stevenson, author of *Kidnapped* and *Treasure Island* spent six weeks in the summer of 1880. Stevenson and his bride stayed in an abandoned mining building near the Silverado Mine. The building is long gone and a monument marks the site. While at the site, Stevenson kept a journal that he later used to write *The Silverado Squatters*.

Picnicking

Parks and wineries offer picnic locations throughout the valley. Unless you see an obvious picnic table in a vineyard near a winery's visitor area, avoid the vineyards. Growers don't take kindly to people tromping down the soil or "sampling" grapes.

Fortunately, a number of wineries provide picnic tables. As a courtesy to the winery that provides you with picnic facilities, and for your own enjoyment, we encourage you to purchase a bottle of wine from the winery to go with your lunch. Some of the wineries with picnic areas are:

Winery Picnicking

Casa Nuestra
Silverado Trail between Lodi and Bale Lanes
St. Helena
707.963.5783

Chateau Potelle
3875 Mt. Veeder Road
Napa
707.255.9440

A mountain setting on Mt. Veeder

Clos du Val
Silverado Trail between Oak Knoll and Yountville Cross Road
707.259.2200

Clos Pegase Winery
North side of Dunaweal Lane between Highway 29 and Silverado Trail Calistoga
707.942.4981

Picnic tables under a 300-year-old oak tree. Bring your own lunch or purchase cheese and other items at the winery.

Corley Family Napa Valley
Big Ranch Road south of Oak Knoll Crossroad
Napa
707.253.2802

Beautiful location with a Thomas Jefferson-style building.

Cuvaison Winery
Silverado Trail south of Dunaweal Lane
Calistoga
707.942.6266

Edgewood Estate
Highway 29 between Zinfandel Lane and downtown
St. Helena
707.963.7293

Louis M. Martini Winery
Highway 29 south of downtown St. Helena
707.963.2736

Madonna Estate (Mont St. John)
5400 Old Sonoma Road, at intersection with Highway 29 in the Carneros
707.255.8864

Napa Cellars
Highway 29, north of Yountville just past Mustard's Grill
707.944.2565

Nichelini Winery
2950 Sage Canyon Road
St. Helena
707.963.0717

In a canyon in the hills east of the Napa Valley.

Rubicon Estate
1991 St. Helena Highway
Rutherford
707.963.9099

On the grounds of movie director Francis Ford Coppola's winery.

Pine Ridge Winery
West side of Silverado Trail between Oak Knoll and Yountville Cross Road
707.253.7500

Picnic tables and barbecue grills

RustRidge Winery
Pope Valley
707.965.2871

Off the beaten path in Pope Valley east of the Napa Valley.

Rutherford Hill Winery
Silverado Trail north of Highway 128
Rutherford
707.963.1871

St. Clement Vineyards
2867 St. Helena Highway
St. Helena
707.967.3033

V. Sattui Winery
1111 White Lane at Highway 29
St. Helena
707.963.7774

Extensive delicatessen selection.

Sterling Vineyards
1111 Dunaweal Lane
Calistoga
707.942.3344

Other Great Picnic Spots

Old Faithful Geyser
Tubbs Lane in Calistoga. Admission charge

Yountville Park
North end of Washington Street in Yountville across from Napa Valley Lodge

Lyman Park
1300 Main St. in Downtown St. Helena at North end of business district

Vintage 1870
Center of Yountville

St. Helena Marketplace
Back of parking outlets at rear

Romantic Tips

More than half of the people who visit the Napa Valley arrive in pairs. With good reason: the Napa Valley is a romantic place. The views are gorgeous, the wine is both soothing and stimulating, the dining can be intimate and is always superb, the lodging is luxurious, and the mud baths, whirlpools and massages bring your body to full tingling alert.

Is there something special a couple should do in the Napa Valley? Actually a visit to the valley is almost foolproof for romance. But we can provide a few pointers.

1. Arrive in the valley in time for lunch, buy some goodies at one of the excellent delicatessens listed in this book, and picnic somewhere lovely and private. Or, as an

alternative, you could have lunch on the Wine Train.

2. Visit one or two wineries in the afternoon, but no more.

3. Spend a couple of hours at a Calistoga spa, preferably one that allows the two of you to take a mud bath, mineral bath and massage in the same private room.

4. Have a light dinner with just enough wine to feel very relaxed.

5. Stroll the sidewalks of Calistoga for a little fresh air and to work off the dessert you might have had after dinner.

6. Return to your room at one of the many hotels, B&Bs and resorts that offer rooms with their own whirlpool baths.

7. Pop open a bottle of champagne, pour two glasses and, while soaking in your bubbling bath, toast each other for your good sense in coming to the Napa Valley.

8. The rest is up to you.

Kids' Favorites

Here are some sights and activities of special interest to children. (Watching parents taste wine can get boring pretty quickly.)

Inside Napa Valley

Bothé-Napa Valley State Park (Calistoga)

Napa Firefighters Museum (Napa)

Napa Valley Museum (Yountville)

Napa Valley Wine Train (Napa)

Old Faithful Geyser (Calistoga)

Old Bale Mill (St. Helena)

Rutherford Grill (Rutherford)

Seguin Moreau cooperage (Napa)

Sterling Vineyards and Skytram (Calistoga)

Swimming Pools at Spas (Calistoga)

Yountville Park (Yountville)

Outside Napa Valley

Jelly Belly (Fairfield)

Safari West (Santa Rosa)

Discovery Kingdom (Vallejo)

Smith's Mount St. Helena Trout Farm (Calistoga)

Traintown (Sonoma)

Gay Information

Purple Roofs
www.purpleroofs.com/usa/californi a/canapa.html

Gay-friendly lodging in the Napa Valley

Nightlife

There's still not a lot. But it's better than it used to be.

Calistoga

Calistoga Inn & Brewery
1250 Lincoln Avenue
Calistoga CA 94515
707.942.4101
www.calistogainn.com

Open mike on Wednesday evenings from 8:30-11:00 p.m. Friday and Saturday evenings live acoustic music at the same hours. Some Sundays there's afternoon music in the beer garden.

Hydro Bar and Grill

1403 Lincoln Ave
Calistoga CA 94515
707.942.9777

Swing band Wednesday and Sunday evenings. Blues and R&B Friday and Saturday evenings.

Napa

Downtown Joe's

902 Main St.
Napa CA 94559
707.258.2337
www.downtownjoes.com

Open mike on Tuesdays. Live music Thursday through Saturday evenings. Cover charge Friday and Saturday.

Piccolino's Italian Cafe

1385 Napa Town Center (on First Street)
Napa CA 94559
707.251.0100
www.piccolinoscafe.com

Live keyboard and vocalist Friday and Saturday evenings. Jazz and contemporary.

River City

505 Lincoln Avenue
Napa CA 94558
707.253.1111
www.rivercitynapa.com

Live music Wednesday and Sundays from 5:30-8:30 p.m with dancing on the deck. Summer only.

Silverado Resort

1600 Atlas Peak Road
Napa CA 94558
707.257.0200
www.silveradoresort.com

Music and dancing Friday and Saturday evenings, and you don't have to be staying at Silverado to enjoy it. One of the few places in the valley where you'll want to dress up a little.

Uva Trattoria Italiana

2040 Clinton Street
Napa CA 94559
707.255.6646
www.uvatrattoria.com

Jazz in the dining room Wednesday and Thursday evenings, but you can enjoy it from the bar as well.

St. Helena

Ana's Cantina

1205 Main Street
St. Helena CA 94574
707.963.4921

Karaoke Thursday evenings, live bands Friday and Saturday evenings.

Silverado Brewing Company

3020 N. St. Helena Highway
St. Helena CA 94574
707.967.9876
www.silveradobrewingcompany.com
Live music Friday and Saturday evenings. No cover charge.

Relocation

Whether you're moving your family or your entire company to the valley, here is some useful contact information.

Economic Development

Napa Valley Economic Development Corporation
433 Soscol Avenue, Suite B131
Napa, CA 94559
707.253.3212
www.nvedc.org

American Canyon Chamber of Commerce
3429 Broadway, Ste. C-1
American Canyon, CA. 94503
707.552.3650
www.amcanchamber.org

Calistoga Chamber of Commerce
1458 Lincoln Ave #9
Calistoga, CA 94515
707.942.6333 Fax 707.942.9287
www.calistogafun.com

Napa Chamber of Commerce
1556 First St.
Napa CA 94559
707.226.7455
www.napachamber.org

The Napa Chamber offers a Relocation packet for $15 that includes maps, a business directory, and information on events, real estate, movers, education, employers, and much more.

St. Helena Chamber of Commerce
1010 Main Street Suite A
St. Helena CA 94574
707.963.4456 800.799.6456
www.sthelena.com

Yountville Chamber of Commerce
6516 Yount St.
Yountville CA 94599
707.944.0904
www.yountville.com

Schools

The Napa Valley has a number of public school districts, with the largest covering Napa, Yountville and American Canyon. St. Helena and Calistoga have their own districts. The valley also offers private schools, religious as well as secular such as Montessori and Waldorf. Napa Valley College in Napa is a two-year community college and Pacific Union College in Angwin is operated by the Seventh Day Adventist church.

For a complete list of school web pages, see www.napanow.com/localinfo.html#schools

Wine

Winewise Quotations

"Beer is made by men; wine by God."—Martin Luther

"I cook with wine. Sometimes I even add it to the food"—W. C. Fields

"Wine is the most civilized thing in the world."—Ernest Hemingway

"Wine cheers the sad, revives the old, inspires the young, makes weariness forget his toil."—Lord Byron

"Wine brings to light the hidden secrets of the soul, gives being to our hopes, bids the coward flight, drives dull care away, and teaches new means for the accomplishment of our wishes."—Horace

"A bottle of wine begs to be shared. I have never met a miserly wine lover."—Clifton Fadiman

"If food is the body of good living, wine is its soul."—Clifton Fadiman

"Wine is sunlight, held together by water."—Louis Pasteur

"In water one sees one's own face; but in wine, one beholds the heart of another."—Old French Proverb

"Penicillin cures, but wine makes people happy."—Alexander Fleming

The Paris Tasting

Napa Valley makes only four percent of the wine produced throughout California, but the quality of that wine has made California wines famous throughout the world. The Napa Valley itself is only one-eighth the size of France's Bordeaux region, but that hasn't kept its wines from besting the finest of France in prestigious wine tastings.

The most famous was the event that truly put the Napa Valley on the map. On May 24, 1976, in celebration of the American Bicentennial, a well-known British wine merchant named Stephen Spurrier conducted a blind tasting to see how well American wines held up against the most famous of the French wines. The tasting was held in Paris and was judged by a panel of nine highly respected French wine experts. The French wines included several Grand Cru Bordeaux and first-rate white Burgundies.

Although the bottles were covered, the judges knew that they were tasting both American and French wines and, indeed some judges made comments during the tasting about how obvious it was which wines were American and how inferior they those wines were.

When the results of the tasting were announced, many of the judges were horrified at what they had done. A few judges even tried to retrieve their tasting notes. The top red wine, surpassing the finest of French wine estates, was a 1973 Cabernet Sauvignon from Napa Valley winemaker Warren Winiarski and his Stag's Leap Wine Cellars. Winiarski's Cabernet edged out such highly-regarded entries as a 1970 Mouton Rothschild and a 1970 Chateau Haut Brion.

The top white wine, in an equally horrifying result for the French judges, was also from the Napa Valley. It was a 1973 Chardonnay from Chateau Montelena, made by winemaker Miljenko (Mike) Grgich (now co-owner of Grgich-Hills Cellars). In fact, six of the eleven highest rated wines were from California.

The wine world was stunned, the French were despondent, the Californians ecstatic. Napa Valley wines had truly arrived on the world scene. And things only got better after that.

Napa Valley Wines

The Napa Valley's climate and soil have made it one of the world's great winegrowing regions. It has long been famous for its ability to grow Bordeaux grapes such as Cabernet Sauvignon and Sauvignon Blanc. Later it was discovered that the southern part of the valley, particularly the Carneros region next to San Francisco Bay, was ideal for growing the grapes of Burgundy, including Chardonnay and Pinot Noir.

Other popular wines include Merlot, Zinfandel, Riesling, Petite Sirah, Gamay Beaujolais and Chenin Blanc, and some wineries are producing Semillon, Cabernet Franc and Muscat, Recently there has been a return to the old Italian grapes that were once grown in the valley, and wineries are beginning to produce such wines as Pinot Grigio, Sangiovese, Grignolino and Dolcetto.

There are also a number of wineries that produce sparkling wines, and a few produce *only* "sparklers.

Chief Grape Varietals

(Courtesy of the Napa Valley Vintners Association)

Cabernet Sauvignon is the acknowledged "king" of red grapes in Napa Valley. Some Napa Valley Cabernet vines from the 19th century are still producing, but most were replanted in the last 20 years. Cabernet Sauvignon is a complex grape; its character can emerge as black currants, green olives, herbs, bell peppers or combinations of these with mint and leather. These wines age beautifully. When young they are best matched with robust red meat dishes; older Cabernets are superb accompaniments to roasts and steaks, and also complement many cheeses.

Chardonnay is among the most widely planted grape variety in Napa Valley. In France, the great white Burgundies are made from the Chardonnay grape and Napa Valley labels have repeatedly won wine-tasting competitions against them, even in France! Napa Valley makes several types of Chardonnay, ranging from fresh, crisp wines to rich, complex wines with layers of flavors. With such a wide range of styles, Napa Valley Chardonnays accompany a variety of dishes, from simply prepared seafood to lighter red meats.

Merlot has long been available in Napa Valley. Traditionally used as a blending wine, Merlot gained popularity in the early 1970s. Wines made from Merlot show lovely cherry-like aromas with hints of their sibling Cabernet's herbaceousness. Because Merlot's tannins are softer than those found in Cabernet, the wines are drinkable at an earlier age than most Cabernets. At the same time, Merlots reward aging by gaining finesse and complexity much as Cabernets do. Serve Merlot with any dish that calls for Cabernet or try it with lighter meats such as pork or veal.

Pinot Noir has been called the fickle grape variety because it makes some of the world's best wines (Burgundian red) but is also one of the most difficult grapes both to grow and vinify. In France, these wines are exceptional only a few years in a decade. In California it has taken decades to make truly great Pinot Noir, and much progress has been made in the last eight to 10 years. Pinot Noir is less tannic and has less pigment than Cabernet and Merlot, so the wines are somewhat lighter. They can be very drinkable at two to five years of age and the best will improve for several years after that.

Sangiovese is an Italian varietal that has gone from cult status to full-blown success in the '90s. Napa Valley produces Sangioveses that are often ready to enjoy upon release. With hints of cherries, black tea and spice these wines enhance a wide variety of foods. Certainly with an array of creamy dishes and cheeses, mushrooms and game, this wine says mangia! In the mouth, Sangiovese is usually lighter than Cabernet, yet more full-bodied than its French cousins such as Gamay and can be as comfortable at a well-set table as at a picnic.

Sauvignon Blanc grapes make wines that appear under two names: Sauvignon Blanc and Fumé Blanc (a regional French nickname is "blanc Fumé"). These wines are increasingly popular as they have a distinctive character, often described as fruity with a touch of herbaceousness, and very good acidity. As with Chardonnay, you will find a range of styles - those that are crisp and "grassy" and others that have a ripe pineapple richness augmented by an oak bouquet. Because of their acidity, Sauvignon Blanc and Fumé Blanc are very enjoyable with shellfish and seafood.

Zinfandel, one of California's most versatile and friendly grape varieties, was the mainstay of 19th century winemaking. Much of the world's Zinfandel acreage is planted in the Napa Valley. This varietal is vinified as a light, easy-drinking red and a heavier, richly flavored version that rewards bottle aging, as well as a white or "blush" wine. With such a range of wine types, there is a Zinfandel for just about every wine enthusiast and for every imaginable food.

Rhone Varietals, chiefly Syrah among the reds and Viognier among whites, and Italian Varietals, chief among them, Sangiovese, as well as Barbera and Dolcetto, are increasingly popular.

Appellations / AVAs

Viticultural Areas

The Bureau of Alcohol, Tobacco and Firearms (ATF) started establishing viticultural areas in 1978, and their regulation became mandatory in 1983.

All American Viticultural Areas (AVA) were established by ATF until 2003 and are now determined by the Tax and Trade Bureau (TTB) of the

U.S. Treasury Department. If a wine is labeled with a viticultural area, at least 85% of the grapes used to produce that wine must have come from within the viticultural area.

Appellation vs. Viticultural Area

They're not the same. A viticultural area is a subset of appellation. It's just one kind of appellation. An appellation can also be the name of a country, a state (such as California) or a county (such as Napa County).

A viticultural area can be very small (such as Mendocino County's Cole Ranch AVA—150 acres) or very large (such as the Ohio River Valley AVA which includes all of Indiana, Kentucky, Ohio and West Virginia.) In Napa County they range from the largest (Napa Valley—25,280 acres) to the smallest (Stags Leap District—2,700 acres)

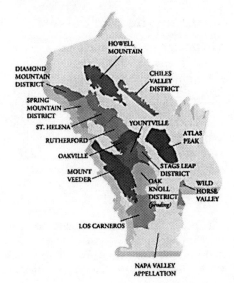

American Viticultural Areas in Napa County (Map courtesy of Napa Valley Vintners Association.)

Wine Bottle "Package"

A wine bottle consists of the glass bottle, front and back labels, a stopper (cork, synthetic or screw top) to close the bottle, and a capsule or foil to cover that stopper.

Bottle Sizes

Most wine bottles are 750 milliliters in size. They were originally called "fifths" because they contained a *fifth* of a gallon. Now wineries all use the metric system.

- Split (half-bottle/375 ml)
- Bottle (750 ml)
- Magnum (2 bottles)
- Jeroboam (double magnum/4 bottles)
- Rehoboam (6 bottles)
- Methuselah (Imperial/8 bottles)
- Salmanazar (12 bottles)
- Balthazar (16 bottles)
- Nebuchadnezzar (20 bottles)

Foil

The covering on the top (the neck) of a wine bottle is called a *foil* or *capsule*. Its purpose is to further seal the bottle opening and prevent leakage of wine or entry of air into the bottle. Originally the foil was made of metal, usually lead. The industry stopped using lead in 1993 to avoid the possibility of traces of lead ending up in the wine glass, and of contamination of landfills.

Today the capsule is made of tin, plastic or even paper. Should you encounter an older bottle of wine that has a lead foil, after removing the foil, carefully wipe the top of the bottle to remove any possible traces of lead before opening and pouring the wine.

Corks

For centuries, corks have been used to plug the opening of a wine bottle. Corks come from the bark of cork trees, usually from Portugal or Spain. Corks trees are around 35 years old before their bark can be used to make corks. It then takes another 7 to 10 years before the bark can be stripped again.

A cork prevents wine from spilling out of the bottle and most air from entering into the bottle.

However, corks vary in quality and can deteriorate over time. Eventually they can shrink enough to allow excessive air to enter the bottle, which negatively affects the taste of the wine. Corks can also develop mold. Wine with the taste of a moldy cork (or "wet newspaper") is said to be "corked."

Today more and more wineries, even ultra-premium wineries, are switching to corks made of plastic or a composite material, and even to screw tops.. While some purists still deride the change, the reality is that these solutions can prevent all of the problems associated with natural corks, with no apparent negative effects on the wine itself.

Inspecting the Cork

When the waiter at a restaurant opens a bottle of wine at your table and gives you the cork to inspect, you may, if you wish, sniff the cork to see if it smells okay. (In some restaurants the wait staff will snicker from a distance if you do it.) But it makes a lot more sense to simply try the sample of wine the waiter has just poured you, since you paid for the wine and not the cork.

The actual reason you're given the cork is historical rather than functional. There was a time in Europe when restaurants would attempt to pass off cheap wine as premium wine. To counter this, wineries started imprinting their name on the corks so that the customer could inspect the cork and see that it really did come from the winery whose wine he had requested.

Keeping the Cork Moist

When storing a bottle of wine, keep the bottle on its side, with the top a little lower than the bottom. This will keep the cork moist, and prevent it from drying out and allowing air to enter the bottle. (If your bottle has a synthetic cork, or screw top, this isn't necessary. The stopper won't dry out.)

Punt

The *punt* is the concave "dent" in the bottom of the wine bottle. There are a number of explanations as to why the punt is used. One is that in centuries past, it was created to provide more strength to bottles under pressure—champagne bottles. It then began to be used by all wine bottles.

Another explanation for its current use is to trap sediment along its edges as it sinks to the bottom, although most U.S. wine today is well filtered and has little, if any, sediment.

Another possible explanation is that in the days of hand-blown glass, leaving a concave dent in the bottom of the bottle minimized the possibility that the glass blower would end up making the bottom of the bottle *concave*, and thus unable to stand upright on the table.

Front Label

Due to bizarre U.S. laws going back to Prohibition, the production of wine fell until 2003 under the U.S. Bureau of Alcohol, Tobacco and Firearms (ATF). ATF (not so affectionately called "Drink, Smoke and Shoot" by some people) established the standards for what had to, or could, appear on wine labels, and approved each and every wine label before it could be used. That function moved to the U.S. Treasury Department's Tax and Trade Bureau in 2003.

ATF could even prevent a winery's use of a particular piece of art on the label if ATF found the art to be "inappropriate", i.e. risqué. It did this a number of times, even forbidding well-known European works of art.

Required/Permitted Label Information

Wines produced in the United States must have the following on their labels:

• *Brand Name*—The name determined by the bottler. It may, or may not, be the actual name of the winery.

• *Type of Wine*—Such as the variety (Sauvignon Blanc), generic (White Table Wine) or proprietary name (Ryan's Red).

• *Geographical Origin*—Country or state, vineyard or viticultural area. If a Viticultural Area, at least 85% of the grapes used in the wine must be from that area.

• *Bottle Size/Volume*—A standard bottle is 750 milliliters (750 ml)

• *Alcohol Strength by Volume*—Usually 11-15%. If 7-14%, it is not necessary to state the percentage. If it exceeds 14% alcohol, it must state the percentage.

• *Vintage Year*—The year the grapes for the wine were harvested. At least 95% of the wine must be from the designated vintage year. If it isn't, the year is omitted.

• *Bottling Information*—Where the wine was bottled. If 100% of the grapes were grown in vineyards owned or controlled by the winery, the label can say "Estate Bottled."

• *Vineyard*—If the label indicates a Vineyard Designation (such as Martha's Vineyard, or Winery Lake Vineyard), at least 95% of the wine grapes used to produce that wine must be from that vineyard. This is not an appellation but simply the winery's own term.

• *Name of the Wine*—Usually the variety of grape. Can also be the region where it was made or a name created by the producer (Mosaic) or by a group of producers (Meritage). If a varietal name such as Cabernet Sauvignon or Chardonnay is used, at least 75% of the wine must be from that variety of wine grape.

• *Health Warnings* (Required by U.S. government)

"GOVERNMENT WARNING: (1) According to the Surgeon General, women should not drink alcoholic beverages during pregnancy because of the risk of birth defects. (2) Consumption of alcoholic beverages impairs your ability to drive a car or operate machinery and may cause health problems."

"Contains Sulfites"—For those who may be hyperallergic to sulfites, which are a natural part of the grape, and which are also frequently used on grapes in the vineyard to prevent mildew, or at fermentation to prevent oxidation.

A Note about Sulfites

Some people (approximately .25 of 1%) are allergic to sulfites. Sulfites are an approved material used in the winemaking process. (Sulfur, which is different, is a pure, elemental form that is frequently sprayed in the vineyards to prevent mildew.) In the winery, sulfur dioxide can be added to the wine to prevent oxidation and to enhance the color and extend the shelf life of the wine.

Sulfites are also a natural component of the wine itself, produced in very small amounts during fermentation. They can sometimes be strong enough to cause an allergic reaction in some people.

If a wine contains 10 parts per million (ppm) of sulfites or more, it must state "Contains Sulfites" on the label. Federal regulations consider up to 350 parts per million as safe for non-hypersensitive wine drinkers. Wine yeasts naturally produce at least 10 to 20 parts per million, so almost every wine produced must carry the sulfite warning on its label.

These levels are far less than those frequently found in fresh and dried fruits and fruit juices, which can be as high as 150-330 parts per million.

Legally Meaningless Terms

The front label might also have terms such as *Private Reserve, Founder's Estate, Cask No. xx, Special Select, Vintner's Reserve,* and a variety of other phrases intended to give the impression that this wine is not just any ordinary wine. However, these words have no legal meaning, and their usefulness as an indicator of quality is directly proportional to the integrity of the winery.

Back Label

The label on the back of the wine bottle usually contains information about the vineyard, the vintage year, the winemaking process for that particular wine, recommended foods which it will complement, and anything else the winery feels will help sell the wine.

Other Statements

• *Produced By* or *Made By*—Means that the named winery fermented no less than 75% of the wine. This might not be where the grapes are actually from.

• *Cellared, Vinted* or *Prepared*—Means that the winery "subjected the wine to cellar treatment." There is no requirement that the wine/grapes actually come from the area where the winery is located.

• *Bottled For/Packed For*—Name and address of the entity for whom the wine was bottled or packed. Says absolutely nothing about where the wine came from.

Barrels

Barrels are used to store and age wine. The wine is "topped up" (the barrel is filled to the top) so that no air remains in the barrel to cause oxygenation of the wine. However, the porous nature of wood does allow a certain "breathing" to occur, which provides a slight exchange of air into the barrel and wine out of the barrel. You'll notice a very pleasant smell of wine in a winery's barrel room, so it's very obvious that a barrel isn't 100% tight.

Barrels are usually made of oak, either French or American. The oak imparts a desirable taste to the wine, particularly in heavier red wines that will age in the barrel for some years. Oak barrels are usually "toasted" on the inside. The current cost of a 55- to 60-gallon oak barrel is around $300-$450 for American oak and $600-$750 for French oak.

An oak barrel can be used for 3-5 years. After that, the barrel is no longer able to impart much of an oak taste to the wine.

In order to enhance the oak taste and add a "caramelized" taste to some wines, most wineries have their barrels "toasted." This slight burning of the inner side of the staves will give the wine tastes of vanillin, caramel, butterscotch and other flavors.

The cooperage will place an unfinished barrel over a hot fire so that the inside of the barrel is slightly burned. Levels of toast include light, medium, medium plus (currently the most popular) and heavy.

Wineries will frequently use a combination of barrels so that, for example, 1/3 might be brand-new, 1/3 three years old, and another 1/3 five years old. This gives a range of flavors of various wines, and also allows for blending wines with various levels of oakiness.

In order to save on the cost of new barrels, some wineries will "shave" the inside of used barrels, removing about 1/4 inch of the wood, revealing fresh wood, which will then impart the oak taste to the next wine that is put into it. They will likely also re-toast the barrel. This shaving can only be done once as the wood staves then become too thin to shave a second time.

Vineyards

Grapevines

Grapes are not planted from seed, but from shoots grafted onto roots (rootstock), usually obtained from a nursery that specializes in wine grapes.

Planting grapevines is expensive. In the Napa Valley, an acre of undeveloped vineyard property now goes for over $72,000. It costs more than $50,000 to turn that acre into vineyard. Then you have to wait five years for the vines to be in full production.

Because of the high cost of planting, and the fact that grapevines can last and produce for many decades, planting is done only when existing vines absolutely need to be replaced, or a new area is prepared for a vineyard.

Vines will be replaced for three reasons:

1. Old age. The vines are no longer producing sufficient yield

2. Disease. The vines have one or more diseases that cannot be successfully treated

3. New varietal. The grower decides to switch over to a different variety of grape.

Planting is usually done in the spring but can continue on into summer.

Growing grapes is a slow process, and requires a lot of patience. It takes three years for a vine to begin producing, and up to five years for it to reach full production. Add on additional years for the actual making and aging of wine before it's ready to sell, and you can see that no one goes into the wine business for quick profits.

Organic Vineyards

More and more organic winegrapes are being grown in the Napa Valley. Currently over 1,200 acres are organic, and other vineyards are being farmed organically but have not yet received certification.

Organic simply means that no chemicals can be used in the vineyard—no chemical fertilizers, weed killers or insecticides. The only substance that can be used is elemental sulfur, which is organic itself and is used to prevent powdery mildew in the fields.

Organic Wines

Organic wine is wine that is made from organically grown grapes, and that is also free from chemicals during the actual winemaking process.

Current federal law states that an organic wine cannot be subjected to sulfur dioxide during its fermentation process. It is, however, legal to use elemental sulfur in the vineyard.

Because sulfur dioxide is a necessary component during winemaking to prevent oxidation of the wine (which can cause discoloration and off-odors), no Napa Valley winery currently produces organic wine.

However, if you look for a phrase such as "Wine made from organically grown grapes" on the back label, you'll know that the grapes used in the wine were organic.

Kosher Wines

Kosher wine is a wine that has received special treatment and meets certain cleanliness and production standards so that it can be considered appropriate for use in Jewish religious practices. Its entire production has been supervised by a rabbi or a designated assistant. For the highest of the three levels of kosher wine, the wine must be pasteurized.

Kosher wine will have had no contact with animal byproducts (some wineries, for example, use gelatin to clarify the wine—a kosher wine would use a different clarification agent). It will also be made using special yeast and enzymes.

Currently only one winery in the Napa Valley makes kosher wine. All of the wines produced by Hagafen Cellars in Napa are kosher.

It should be noted, for those of you whose experience with kosher wines has been limited to Mogen David or other sweet East Coast wines, that Hagafen's wines are first and foremost Napa Valley wines. That is, they are delicious, premium wines. And they are *also* kosher.

Pierce's Disease / Glassy-Winged Sharpshooter

Pierce's Disease is a common bacteria-caused disease in the Napa Valley that has plagued grapegrowers for many years. Traditionally it has been spread by the *blue-green sharpshooter*, a small bug with a limited range whose habitat is along streams and creeks.

Growers have learned to live with Pierce's Disease (PD), and because the blue-green sharpshooter's range is so limited, PD usually affects only those sections of vineyards very close to water.

The *glassy-winged sharpshooter* (GWSS) has changed all this. Originally from Mexico, it moved into the southeastern part of the United States, and has now arrived in California—most notably Riverside County and other counties in Southern California, but in a number of other counties throughout the state as well.

The glassy-winged sharpshooter is about one-half inch long, more than twice the size of its blue-green cousin. It can fly much farther than

the blue-green sharpshooter, so that almost all vineyards in the Napa Valley would be within its reach. And it passes the bacterium (Xylella fastidiosa) that causes Pierce's Disease deeper into the system of the plant than does the blue-green sharpshooter. The bacteria multiply and block the water system of the plant, leading to its decline and death.

Sharpshooters also damage grapevines (and many other plants including almonds, citrus and alfalfa) by extracting fluids from the plant, eventually weakening the plant and leading to its death. An adult sharpshooter can extract fluids equal to 200 to 300 times its body weight in a single day. This is the equivalent of an adult human drinking about 4,300 gallons of water per day.

If the glassy-winged sharpshooter takes hold in the Napa Valley, it has the potential to wipe out our grape and wine industries. In the 1880s, the Los Angeles Basin had a thriving, and highly respected, wine industry. It was destroyed by Pierce's Disease, referred to at the time as *Anaheim Disease*.

State and local authorities are taking all possible steps to prevent the GWSS from spreading throughout California. Because the bug often "hitchhikes" on ornamental plants, all shipments from nurseries into Napa County are inspected. Residents and visitors are urged not to bring any plants into the Napa Valley from infected areas.

Scientists are conducting research and experiments to find biological, genetic and chemical ways of dealing with Pierce's Disease and the GWSS. Others are experimenting with various organic methods of dealing with the threat.

Traps have been placed throughout the county and special inspectors have been hired to monitor the traps as well as incoming shipments of grapes and plants.

For up-to-the-minute information on preventive efforts in Napa County, see www.bugspot.org.

Roses in the Vineyard

In the Napa Valley, as throughout the wine regions of France, you'll frequently see roses planted along the edge of vineyards. Traditionally they've served as an early warning system to protect the grapevines—the equivalent of a miner's canary.

Roses and grapevines are both susceptible to a fungus called powdery mildew. In fact, roses are more sensitive than grapevines.

Sulfur won't cure powdery mildew, but it can prevent it. So, if a grapegrower noticed that one day his roses had powdery mildew, he knew it was immediately time to spray sulfur on his grapes to prevent them from getting the same disease.

Roses also warn of other diseases and growing problems before they affect the grapevines, and they serve as a habitat for some beneficial insects that eat other undesirable insects.

And they're beautiful.

Seasons of the Vineyard

Winter

Ground cover, such as mustard or clover, is seeded in the vineyard to keep down weeds and provide nutrients to the soil. The vines are dormant.

Old branches are pruned, leaving only the basic trunk of the vine and whichever canes are desired. The smoke you may see coming from the vineyards is simply the controlled burning of old grapevines.

Spring

New vines are planted. You may see them wrapped in growing tubes that look like, and sometimes are, milk cartons. The tubes help train the vines and protect against rabbits and other hungry residents of the area.

Powdered sulfur, an organic fungicide, is sprayed on vines to prevent a fungus called powdery mildew. *Budbreak* takes place as the first small shoots burst forth out of the buds.

This is a time when frost can damage the new shoots, so growers prepare smudge pots (euphemistically called "orchard heaters" by some growers), wind machines and overhead sprinklers to protect against it.

Summer

New shoots appear. Vines begin to flower. Some shoots are pruned so that growth energy is focused on the remaining shoots. Shoots that are too long are trimmed, so that fewer, but higher quality, grapes will result. Some leaves are removed to increase the grapes' exposure to the sun and increase air circulation. This is done because moisture can lead to "bunch rot" or to mildew. Berries appear and begin to grow and swell. In the heat of the summer sun, sugar levels in the grapes begin to rise, and the amount of acid begins to decrease.

The grapes soften and approach full maturity.

Fall

Harvest (called "Crush"). The grapes are picked, brought to the winery and crushed, and the juice is fermented into wine.

After picking, the remaining leaves in the vineyards begin to change color. Yellow is normal, red leaves early in the season indicate a problem (disease or lack of appropriate nutrition.)

In the Napa Valley, Crush usually starts in August and goes through most of October. Sparkling wine producers pick first, as they use grapes with lower sugar levels and higher acids. Still wine producers usually start several weeks later. Thinner-skinned grapes ripen first, such as Chardonnay and Sauvignon Blanc. Thicker-skinned reds such as Cabernet Sauvignon are the last to ripen and be picked.

Crush / Making Wine

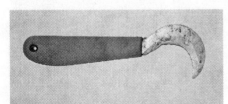

Most grapes are picked by hand with a special knife.

The grapes are picked one or more clusters at a time, and put into crates or bins, then dumped into open containers called *gondolas,* which are then taken to the winery.

Some vineyards now use mechanical harvesters. The harvester is particularly useful in large vineyards in flat areas, although smaller versions can be used on rather steep hills.

Not all grapes are picked by hand. Mechanical harvesting is becoming more common in some areas.

The harvester gently shakes the trunk or cordon of the vine, causing the grapes to fall from the vine into a catcher, which then moves them into a waiting gondola or other container.

However the grapes are picked, once they arrive at the winery, they are put into a destemmer/crusher, which removes the leaves and stems and crushes the grapes. Crushing doesn't mean pulverizing; it's done as gently as possible. Just enough to break the skins and allow the juice to come out.

The destemmer is a perforated, rotating drum. The juice and skins drop through the holes in the drum, while the leaves and stems are too big to fit through the holes so they continue on out of the crusher and into waiting trucks to be returned to the vineyard as compost.

The crushed grapes and juice, called *must*, are pumped into the winery.

Some winemakers may skip the crushing and destemming and move the grapes directly to a press for *whole berry* or *whole cluster* pressing. Or they may do *carbonic maceration* in which the weight of the grapes themselves gently crushes the grapes, releasing the juice.

Fermentation

Red Wine

The juice, skins and seeds from most red grapes (actually called "black" grapes by growers) go into large stainless steel fermentation tanks for primary fermentation, where yeast is added that breaks down the natural grape sugars into ethyl alcohol and carbon dioxide (CO_2). Fermentation is done at a temperature of approximately 85° Fahrenheit for four to six days.

After fermentation, red wines are pressed, and the grape skins and seeds are then separated from the wine. The skins, seeds and dead yeast cells are called "pomace", and can be used as compost.

White Wine

White grapes (which are actually green in color) are not immediately fermented but go first to a "press".

A wine press is a stainless steel cylinder containing an inflatable rubber bladder. The must is poured into the cylinder and the bladder is inflated with air. The bladder gently squeezes the skins against the sides of the cylinder, forcing the juice out. The *press juice* then goes to fermentation tanks. White wine is frequently fermented at around 60° for 12 to 18 days, although fermentation temperatures can range from 5° to 75° white wine takes longer because fermentation is slower at lower temperatures.

Sometimes white wines such as Chardonnay are fermented in oak barrels rather than stainless steel tanks. This is referred to as *barrel fermentation*.

Post-Fermentation

Settling and Aging

After fermentation, most red and white wines go into large stainless steel tanks, where *settling* takes place. After the skins, seeds, yeast and other particles settle to the bottom of the tank (creating the *lees*), the clearer wine is pumped out and put into small (55-60 gallon) oak barrels for *barrel aging*.

Most reds are barrel-aged to impart the oaky taste that many people find desirable. Many wineries also barrel-ferment Chardonnay. Lighter white wines, such as Sauvignon Blanc or Johannisberg Riesling are seldom, if ever, barrel-aged. An exception is Fumé Blanc, which is a barrel-fermented Sauvignon Blanc. Barrel aging can last from three to ten months for white wine, and anywhere from six months to three years for red wine.

Some red wines are subjected to *malolactic fermentation*. The winemaker adds a specific bacterium to the wine that breaks down the malic acid in the wine into lactic acid. This *secondary fermentation* can give the wine a creamy, buttery taste and texture. It is frequently done for red wines, and often for Chardonnay.

Clarification

During barrel aging, most wines "throw" sediments so that the wine must be "fined" and/or "filtered" to give it the clarity desired by most American wine drinkers. Filtration can also stabilize the wine, making sure that it does not continue to ferment in the bottle, by removing all yeast from the wine.

Several methods of fining are used. Traditionally in Europe, oxblood was poured on top of the vat and allowed to settle down to the bottom. As it settled, it attracted the sediment (yeast, seeds, and bits of skin) in the wine and pulled it down to the bottom of the vat.

Since blood passing through their wine is not something that appeals to most Americans—even though it didn't remain in the wine after the treatment—this method was long ago discontinued.

These days gelatin and egg whites, also traditional methods, are frequently used to fine the wine. Also, if the wine is run through a filtration machine, diatomaceous earth or filter pads are used in the filter to help remove very fine sediment.

Some winemakers prefer not to clarify their wines, subjecting the wines to as little physical treatment as possible.

After clarification, the wine is then bottled, corked and labeled. Some wines are then ready to drink; others, particularly heavier red wines, may undergoing aging in the bottle for as long as three years before being made available to consumers. Once sold to the customer, most wines are ready to drink, but some will still improve with age if the customer has the space and patience (and money) to store them.

Sparkling Wine

Sparkling wine (not referred to as *Champagne*, because that type of sparkling wine comes only from the Champagne district of France) is primarily made from Chardonnay and Pinot Noir grapes.

Grapes for sparkling wine (*sparklers*) are picked earlier in the season when sugar content is lower, usually starting in late July. Fermentation almost always takes place in stainless steel tanks over a period of two to three weeks.

After five months or so, selected wines are blended to form the *cuvee* that will be the basis for the final wine. After blending, the wine goes into its permanent bottle, and the *tirage* is added, which is a blend of sugar, wine and live yeast that will begin the wine's second fermentation. The bottle is then sealed with a temporary cap like that on a soft drink bottle.

Secondary fermentation takes place in the bottle. Because it is sealed, the carbon dioxide bubbles produced by fermentation remain in the bottle. This continues for at least a year.

During aging, the bottles are *riddled*. Riddling is the process of separating the clear wine from the sediment (primarily dead yeast cells) that forms in the bottle. The bottles are very gently shaken and twisted to allow the sediment to gradually settle at the top of the bottle. Riddling was historically done by hand, but today in most large sparkling wineries it is done by a machine that gently mimics the hand process.

When ready, the tops of the bottles are dipped into a solution to freeze the liquid and sediment in the bottle neck, but not in the rest of the bottle. The temporary bottle cap is removed and the pressure of the carbon dioxide forces out the frozen sediment. This is referred to as *disgorgement*.

The resulting empty space in the bottle is filled with a blend of wine and sugar called *dosage*. The bottle is then recorked, and the traditional cage and foil are placed over the top. Once sealed, the sparkling wine rests for additional months before it's made available for sale.

Wine Caves

The use of caves for storing and aging wine goes back, at least, to the Romans. In the 1800s, Chinese laborers using picks and shovels built the first Napa Valley wine caves. Jacob Schram constructed tunnels (at today's Schramsberg Vineyards) beginning in 1870 and the Beringer brothers began to do the same at their winery (now Beringer Vineyards) soon afterwards.

Today nearly 100 Napa Valley wineries have caves, and more are being created all the time—although the picks and shovels have been replaced by heavy-duty construction equipment. Originally built for the *storage* of wine barrels, some caves now contain a winery's entire operations.

Digging a cave is less expensive than constructing a building for similar purposes. Caves save energy costs by providing constant humidity (80-90%) and temperature (55°- 60° F), reduce evaporation of wine, and require less governmental approval. Plus they have less visual impact on the landscape, and offer a great—and often magnificent—location for tastings, dinners and musical events.

Caves can be humble tunnels for barrel aging or definitely *un*humble. For example, take Villa Amarosa in St. Helena. The cave sits below an 89,000 square foot "14th century" castle with three floors of wine cellars, more than 60 rooms, and a 1,000 square foot well-equipped medieval torture chamber (presumably for viewing only). Another is Palmaz Winery in Napa, owned by the co-inventor of the cardiovascular stent. The 50,000 square foot winery is completely underground, and includes a 50-foot high, 75-foot wide dome reminiscent of the interior of a mosque. Wine storage takes place 11 stories underground.

For detailed information on wine cave construction, we recommend this website: www.winecaves.com.

Here are some of the wine caves that can currently be visited.

Beringer Vineyards
2000 Main Street
St. Helena CA 94574
707.963.7115
www.beringervineyards.com

Daily tours. Hand-dug tunnels from the 1800s.

Castello di Amorosa
4045 North Saint Helena Hwy
Calistoga, CA 94515
800.286.7212
www.castellodiamorosa.com

107-room castle with seven levels and a dungeon.

Clos Pegase Winery
1060 Dunaweal Lane
Calistoga CA 94515
707.942.4981
www.clospegase.com

Daily tours of cave theater and dining room in 20,000 square feet of tunnels.

Cuvaison Winery
4550 Silverado Trail
Calistoga CA 94515
707.942.6266
www.cuvaison.com

Daily tours. 22,000 square foot cave.

Eagle and Rose Estate
1844 Pope Valley Road
Pope Valley CA 94567
707.965.9463
www.eagleandrose.com

Tours by appointment. 7,000 square feet of caves.

Jarvis Winery
2970 Monticello Road
Napa CA 94558
707.255.5250
www.jarviswines.com

Tours by appointment. Underground stream and waterfall.

Pine Ridge Winery
5901 Silverado Trail
Napa CA 94558
707.857.9777
www.pineridgewinery.com

Tours by appointment.

Robert Sinskey Vineyards
6320 Silverado Trail
Napa Ca 94558
707.944.9090
www.robertsinskey.com

Tours by appointment. 18,000 square feet of caves.

Rutherford Hill Winery
200 Rutherford Hill Road
PO Box 427
Rutherford CA 94573
www.rutherfordhill.com

Tours daily. One mile of wine caves.

Schramsberg Winery
1400 Schramsberg Road
Calistoga CA 94515
707.942.4558
www.schramsberg.com

Tours by appointment. Century-old wine caves have been extended to two miles of tunnels.

Shafer Vineyards
6154 Silverado Trail
Napa CA 94558
707.944.2877
www.shafervineyards.com

Tours by appointment. 8,000 square feet of caves with fresh underground springs.

Storybook Mountain

3835 Highway 128
Calistoga CA 94515
707.942.5310
www.storybookwines.com

Tours by appointment. Century-old wine caves.

Vine Cliff Winery

7400 Silverado Trail
Napa CA 94558
707.944.2388
www.vinecliff.com

Tours by appointment. 15,000 square feet of caves.

Von Strasser

1510 Diamond Mountain Road
Calistoga CA 94515
707.942.0930
www.vonstrasser.com

Tours by appointment. 6,800 square foot cave.

Wine Tasting

Ordering and drinking wine shouldn't be intimidating. But for many it is, largely because of all the hype and mystique that wine has endured in this country.

The simple method of wine tasting is:

1. Pour a glass of wine.

2. Drink it.

3. Did you like it or not?

That's really sufficient. However, by adding a few more steps, you can make the process of wine tasting much more interesting. And you can learn to determine which kind of wines you like, so that in the future you know what to look for in a store or restaurant.

Here are our suggestions on how to go about tasting a wine.

Look

1. Hold your glass by the stem so that your hand doesn't warm the bowl.

2. Hold the glass in front of your eyes, preferably against a white background, and look at the color and clarity of the wine.

Clarity—Wine should be clear and brilliant, unless the winemaker intentionally kept it unfiltered.

Color—With reds, the darker the color, the more intense the flavors and aromas are likely to be. Color can be red, ruby, purple, or brick red. Brown indicates oxidation. An older wine can be brick-brown. Too brown and it's probably over the hill. If a young wine is brown, it's likely oxidized. (If that is the case, let it sit in the glass for a while anyway. It's possible both taste and aroma will improve, possibly dramatically.)

With whites, the color can vary from almost clear to green to slightly yellow to straw colored to gold. Whites, too, should not be brown.

Blush wines, such as White Zinfandel or a Rose, are pink.

Swirl

1. Swirl the wine. Try to do it suavely without spilling, but if it flies out of the glass, you won't be the first. (If you pour a full glass for your dinner guests at home, they won't be able to enjoy swirling. Try not to fill the glass more than 1/3 to 1/2 full.)

2. Notice if the wine has "legs"—little streams of wine that cling to the

inside of the glass and slowly drip back down. "Good legs" indicate good body.

3. Swirl it again. Swirling doesn't just look cool. If you do it right it also "volatizes the esters" releasing aroma molecules into the air, which are somewhat contained in the bowl by the lip of the wine glass.

Sniff

1. Put your nose down into the bowl (where the aroma molecules are lingering) and take a good sniff.

2. See if you can match the various smells with smells from your past. Think of fruits, spices, herbs, and various plants.

Aroma—The smells that come from the characteristics of the grape itself, especially in a younger wine.

Bouquet—The smells that result over time, primarily from the winemaking process and aging.

Common off smells include:

Bitterness—Too heavy on tannins

Burning—Sulfur or excessive alcohol (alcohol is felt further back in the nose)

Nail polish/acetone—Excessive acetic acid

Rotten eggs—Excessive sulfur

You might also notice that you salivate, which indicates excessive acid.

Taste

1. Take a medium-sized sip, sucking air in through your teeth.

2. Swish the wine around in your mouth, "chew" it if you want, hold it in your mouth, and then swallow.

Flavors—Since the sense of taste is largely a result of the sense of smell, the nose of the wine will greatly affect the flavors you can taste.

Palate—Your tongue can notice sweetness, acid, alcohol, bitterness and astringency (tannin). They're sensed on different parts of the tongue and in the following order:

Sweetness—Tip of the tongue

Acid—Sides of the tongue

Vinegary—Acetic acid

Lemon/lime—Citric acid

Apple—Malic acid

Cream/yogurt—Lactic acid

Tannins—Puckery sensation at the back of the mouth and throat. Same as drinking black tea.

Bitterness—Very back of the tongue.

Alcohol—Can register as sweetness, viscosity of the wine, or warmth. Excessive alcohol results in a hot burning in the throat.

Feel

Pay attention to how it feels in your mouth.

Body—How is the "mouthfeel"? Is it light, medium or full? This is largely a function of alcohol content and any residual sugar, but there are other more subtle factors.

Finish—How long does the taste linger in your mouth after swallowing? What is the last taste you can sense? Fruit? Acid? Tannins?

Overall

Is it balanced? Do all the components—fruit, acid, alcohol, tannins and so on—work in harmony together?

Most importantly, did you like it? And why or why not?

Triangular Test

Long-time wine writer Dan Berger (www.vintageexperiences.com) suggests the *triangular test* as a simple, but effective, way to see if you can tell the difference between two different bottles of wine.

Take three identical glasses and label them A, B and C (Okay, use 1, 2 and 3 if you prefer numbers to letters) in a way that the people taking the test can't see the labels. Pour from one bottle of wine into A and B, and from a different bottle into C. Mix up the glasses and then sample each of the three glasses. All you have to do is determine which two glasses contain the identical wine.

Easy, right? Well, maybe. But the more similar the two wines are, the more difficult it will be. Differentiating between a Cabernet Sauvignon and a Sirah *might* be easy. Tasting a light, fruity Chardonnay from one winery and comparing it to a heavily-oaked Chardonnay from another *might* still be relatively easy. But how about two Chardonnays from the same winery that differ only in the year in which they were picked, or the vineyards from which their grapes came?

It's a simple, enjoyable and very educational experiment. Try it. Over time you'll sharpen your ability to pick up those subtle nuances of flavors and aromas that might have escaped you before.

Pronunciation

Varietal—Phonetic Pronunciation

Barbera—Bar-BEAR-ah

Cabernet Franc—CA-burr-NAY fronk

Cabernet Sauvignon—CA-burr-NAY SAW-vin-yown

Chardonnay—SHAR-dough-NAY

Chenin Blanc—SHEN-in-BLONK

French Colombard—COLL-om-BAR

Gewürztraminer—Guh-VERTZ-tra-MEEN-er

Merlot—MARE-low

Muscat—MUSS-cat

Pinot Grigio—PEE-no GREE-gee-o

Pinot Noir—PEE-no NWAHR

Riesling—REEZ-ling (Notice it is not RIZE-ling)

Sangiovese—San-gee-oh-VAY-zee

Sauvignon Blanc—SAW-vin-yown BLONK

Semillon—SEMM-e-yown

Sirah (Syrah)—Si-RAH (as in "Que sera, sera")

Viognier—V-OWN-yay

Zinfandel—ZIN-fan-dell

Glossary

Acid—A natural component of the grape, primarily tartaric acid. Acid adds flavor and crispness, and its tartness provides "backbone" to the wine.

Aging—Leaving the wine alone in a barrel or bottle for a period of weeks, months or years. This allows the wine to mature, and the flavors and other components to blend and harmonize.

Alambic—The pot, traditionally copper, which is used for distilling spirits such as brandy.

Alcohol—Ethyl alcohol. During fermentation, yeast breaks down the sugars in grapes and turns it into alcohol. Before fermentation, it's grape juice. Afterwards, it's wine. Napa Valley wine generally has anywhere from 10 to 14 percent alcohol. (Once a fermenting wine gets up to around 16 percent, which is possible if it started with very high sugar levels, the yeast dies and fermentation stops.)

Aperitif—A wine served before a meal.

Appellation—A particular wine-growing region that has been designated by the Bureau of Alcohol, Tobacco and Firearms as having shared characteristics of climate, soil or other conditions.

Aroma—The smell of a wine, particularly from the natural characteristics of the grape itself.

Astringent—Producing a puckering sensation in your mouth, such as you would experience when drinking tea. Comes primarily from tannins in the wine, which are found in grape skins, seeds and stems. Oak barrels also add tannins to the wine.

AVA—An "American Viticultural Area"; a more specific area than an "Appellation". Wines that have an AVA on the label must have at least 75 percent of the wine from that area.

Backbone—The acid in a wine. A wine that has insufficient acidity "lacks backbone".

Balance—When a wine is well-balanced, all its components—fruit, acid, alcohol, tannins, body—are in harmony, with no one component dominating the others.

Barrel—A wooden barrel, holding 55—60 gallons, used for aging, and sometimes fermenting, wine. Usually made of French or American oak.

Barrel Aging—Many wines are aged for a period of time in oak barrels, which allows a blending of the flavors in the wine as it matures, and also imparts the flavor of the toasted wood to the wine.

Barrel Fermentation - Converting grape juice to wine in a barrel rather than in a stainless steel fermentation tank. This imparts flavors and aromas to the wine from the oak wood. Often used for Chardonnay.

Black Grapes—The grapes used to make red wine are actually almost black in color. Examples are Cabernet Sauvignon and Merlot.

Blend—To mix together several lots of wine (perhaps from different vineyards and/or years, or even different varietals) in order to produce a desired wine.

Body—The "weight" of the wine, usually light, medium or full. A wine with a higher alcohol content and heavy tannins is felt to be full-bodied. Usually a fuller-bodied wine also has bigger "legs". Body is also a result of viscosity, which can be increased with higher residual sugar.

Botrytis—A fungus that can form on the skins of late harvested grapes, producing "bunch rot". It can ruin a crop or, under just right conditions, it can produce smaller grapes with intense flavors and high sugar content. Known then as the "noble rot", it results in highly-prized dessert wines.

Bottle Aging—Allowing wine to lie undisturbed in the bottle for a period of weeks, months or years. This allows the tannins in the wine to soften and the wine's components to further harmonize after barrel aging.

Bottle Sickness/Bottle Shock—Moving wine within the winery, bottling it, or transporting it to a different location can have a temporary negative effect on the flavor. After a period of time—a few days or weeks—it will be back to normal.

Bouquet—The smells from older wines, primarily resulting from the winemaking process and from aging.

Brix—A measurement of dissolved compounds in grape juice that approximately indicates the sugar content of unharvested grapes. Most grapes are picked between 21 and 25 degrees Brix. These will produce wines with an alcohol content between 12 to 15 percent.

Brut—French for "dry". A style of sparkling wine that has little, or no, residual sugar.

Bud Break—The time in early spring when new shoots emerge from the buds on a vine.

Bung—The stopper that goes in the "bung hole" in a wine barrel.

Buttery—A taste associated with Chardonnay after it has gone through Malolactic Fermentation. In extreme cases, it can taste like movie theater popcorn butter.

Cane—Older shoots on the vine that have become large and woody.

Canopy—The leaves and shoots of a grapevine.

Cap—When red wine ferments, carbon dioxide is produced which rises to the top of the tank. As it does, it pushes up the skins and seeds to the top, forming a "cap".

Capsule—The "wrapper" placed over the cork to help seal and protect it. Also called Foil. Originally of lead, now made of plastic, tin or paper.

Carbonic Maceration—Fermentation of whole grapes without crushing them.

Cask—A wooden barrel. Frequently used to refer to very large barrels.

Champagne—Sparkling wine made in the Champagne region of France.

Clarification—Making the wine clear by removing sediment.

Cluster—A single "bunch" of grapes.

Cold Stabilization—Lowering the temperature of a wine to 32°F causes the tartrates and other solids in the wine to precipitate and sink to the bottom of the tank, leaving a clearer (clarified) wine. This prevents the formation of tartaric crystals, sometimes called Wine Diamonds, in the bottle after the customer has purchased it.

Cooper—A person who makes or repairs barrels.

Cordon—A method of pruning leaving one cane (cordon) on each side of the trunk.

Cork—A wine bottle stopper made from the bark of oak trees, usually from Spain or Portugal.

Corkage—Fee charged by a restaurant for providing glasses to, and opening a bottle for, a customer who brings his own wine. Fees in the Napa Valley range from $5 - $50, although some restaurants have discontinued the charge.

Corked—A wine that has been tainted by a bad cork that has a mold that produces a chemical compound called TCA (Trichloroanisole). This "dirty sock" or "wet newspaper" smell results in a wine that is said to be "corked" or "corky".

Creamy—Wines that have undergone Malolactic Fermentation can have a rich, smooth feel that is referred to as "creamy".

Crisp—A young, fresh wine with good acid.

Crush—Harvest. When the grapes are picked and crushed. In the Napa Valley, this starts in late August (when grapes with low sugar levels are picked for sparkling wines) and usually goes through most of October, when thicker-skinned grapes finally mature.

Decant—Wine that was not filtered by the winemaker is often carefully poured into another container— usually a decanter—leaving the sediment at the bottom of the first container. Decanting can also aerate a wine, "opening up" its flavors and aromas.

(De)Stemmer Crusher—The machine, used by most wineries, which removes the stems from, and gently crushes the skins of, grapes that have just been harvested.

Dosage—A small amount of sweet wine added to the top of a bottle-fermented sparkling wine, to replace the yeast sediment that is removed just before final corking.

Dry—The absence of sugar in a wine. A wine with no residual sugar is totally dry. It is possible to have a slight amount of residual sugar, and still taste dry to most people.

Early Harvest—Wine made from grapes that are picked early in the harvest, when their acids are high and their sugar content is low.

Enologist—One who practices Enology.

Enology—The science and study of winemaking. Also spelled Oenology.

Estate Bottled—One hundred percent of the wine must be made from grapes grown in vineyards owned or controlled by the winery in the same appellation as the winery.

Esters—Chemical compounds responsible for much of the bouquet and aroma of wines. Swirling wine before tasting "volatizes the esters", enhancing the nose of the wine.

Fat—Rich and full-bodied wine.

Fermentation—The chemical process of converting grape juice to alcohol. This is done by yeast, which converts the natural sugar in the juice into alcohol—and also produces carbon dioxide, which is released out the top of the tanks. (In sparkling wine, the carbon dioxide is retained).

Filtering—Removing particles (yeast, pieces of skin) from wine by passing it through physical filters. This makes the wine clearer and prevents any further fermentation.

Fining—A technique for clarifying wine. Europeans used to use ox blood. Today common fining agents are egg whites, gelatin, bentonite or diatomaceous earth. The fining agent combines with particles in the wine, causing them to settle to the bottom of the tank.

Finish—The taste that lingers in your mouth after you've swallowed the wine. It includes both the type of taste and its length, i.e. a wine can have a "long finish".

Flabby — A wine that is too soft, lacks sufficient acidity, has no "structure".

Foil—Same as Capsule.

Fortified Wine—A wine to which alcohol has been added, such as Port.

Foxy—The distinctive character of wine made from *vinifera labrusca*, the native American grapes of which Concord grapes are an example.

Free Run—The juice released after the grapes are crushed. It is usually a higher quality than "press juice", which is obtained by squeezing the grapes.

Fruit—How grape growers usually refer to grapes.

Fruity—The natural taste of the grape, more obvious in younger wines. A dry wine can taste sweet due to its intense fruitiness.

Glassy-Winged Sharpshooter—An insect that spreads Pierce's Disease.

Glycerine—An alcohol, formed during fermentation from grape sugar, that contributes to the body of a wine.

Grafting—Splicing a vine of one type onto a rootstock of another type.

Harvest—The time of the year when the grapes are picked. Same as Crush.

Hot—A wine with overdominant alcohol.

Inoculation—Adding yeast to juice to start fermentation.

Late Harvest—Wine, usually dessert wine, produced from grapes picked late in the harvest, when their sugar content is high and their acids are low.

Lees—The sediment that accumulates in the bottom of a container during fermentation. Some wine is aged "on the lees" ("sur lie").

Legs—Also called "tears". The streaks of wine that form and slide down the inside of a glass after you've swirled the wine. An indication of "body". If the legs are wide and thick and move slowly down the glass, the wine can be said to have "nice legs".

Maceration—The extraction, during fermentation, of color, tannin and aromas from the skins and seeds to the juice. Wine juice itself has little color. The color comes primarily from the skins.

Magnum—A double-sized bottle holding 1500 milliliters of wine.

Malic Acid—The "apple" acid found naturally in grapes which can be converted to lactic acid during Malolactic Fermentation.

Malolactic Fermentation—Also known as "ML" or "Secondary Fermentation". A process by which the malic acid (as in apples) in wine is converted to lactic acid (as in the acid found in dairy products). This softens the acid, making the wine smoother and creamier.

Mature—A wine is mature when it is ready to drink. This can be a short time after fermentation for a light, fruity white wine, or many years later for a heavy red wine.

Mercaptans—A smell resulting from too much sulfur. Smells like garlic or rubber.

Meritage—A marketing name that the California wine industry invented for a Bordeaux-style wine that blends such varieties as Cabernet Sauvignon, Merlot, Cabernet France, Malbec and Petite Verdot.

Methode Champenoise—The classic Champagne method of making sparkling wine. Secondary fermentation takes place in the bottle, and the carbon dioxide produced is captured as bubbles.

Microclimate—A small area with unique climatic conditions. These conditions can be quite different from a neighboring area. They include temperature, sunlight, rain and fog.

Miniscus—The top line of liquid in a container. The miniscus in a wine glass should appear clear. (Note: This is a good "bar bet" item. You'll find very few wine drinkers who know what a miniscus is.)

Must—The skin, seeds and juice after the grapes have been crushed. Red wines are fermented as must. For white wines, the must is pressed and only the resulting juice is fermented.

Nose—The smell of a wine, including both Aroma and Bouquet.

Oaky—A strong taste of tannins in the wine due to its contact with oak.

Oxidized—Just as a slice of apple turns brown, so can wine be affected by oxygen. A little is good, too much isn't. A wine that has been exposed to too much oxygen is "oxidized". It tastes flat, tired and old.

Palate—One's ability to taste the subtleties and complexities of a wine. One is said to have a "good palate".

Phylloxera—A tiny louse that damages the roots of vines. During the 1990s, many thousands of acres of grapevines were replaced in the Napa Valley, and throughout California, due to phylloxera.

Pierce's Disease—A plant disease caused by a bacterium that attacks the vine's water-conducting system. Spread by the Blue Green and Glassy-Winged Sharpshooters.

Pomace—Grape skins, seeds, stems and pulp that remain after the grapes have been pressed. Often used as compost.

Press—The machine that gently presses the grapes to squeeze out their juice. Usually an inflatable rubber "bladder" press.

Press Juice—The juice obtained after grapes are pressed.

Pump Over—The process of pumping fermenting wine over the Cap. (This used to be done by hand and was called "punching the cap". It is still done this way in some wineries.) Pumping over gives the wine more contact with the cap, extracting more color, flavor and tannins from the skins and seeds in the cap.

Punt—The concave indentation in the bottom of a bottle.

Racking—Moving wine from one container to another. This is done to clarify wine, to aerate it, or to move it into another container for a different stage in the process, i.e from fermentation to barrel aging. Racking can be done by gravity or with a pump.

Reserve—A wine designated as special by the winery that produces it. There are no quality standards or regulations that apply to the use of "Reserve" or "Private Reserve" or "Vintner's Reserve".

Residual Sugar—The amount of sugar remaining in a wine after fermentation. For most dry wines, the residual sugar is so low that it is below the threshold of most people's ability to taste.

Riddling—In sparkling wine, the turning (traditionally by hand) of the bottle one-eighth of a turn every day. Over time this causes the yeast in the wine to end up in the neck of the bottle, from where it is eventually removed.

Room Temperature—The ideal temperature for serving red wine. This is probably not your room temperature. This is basically the room temperature of a European castle without central heating. Should be 55°-65°F.

Rootstock—The roots of a vine.

Rosé—A wine with very little red color and usually some slight carbonation. The light color results from minimal contact between the juice and the skins.

Rutherford Dust—The legendary reason why Cabernet Sauvignon grapes grown in the soil of the Rutherford area produce such excellent wines.

Second Label—A wine sold by a winery that has a different brand than that of the winery's main wines. It is usually less expensive and, although not always, of lesser quality.

Second Pick—Home winemakers and others will often be given the opportunity to have "Second Pick". They go through an already harvested vineyard and pick grapes that were missed or that matured after the first picking.

Secondary Fermentation—See Malolactic Fermentation

Sediment—Pieces of dead yeast cells, skin and other materials that can sink to the bottom of an unfiltered red wine.

Sommelier (som-MAL-ee-ay)- The knowledgeable person at better restaurants who can give you advice and answer questions about wine. Often wears the traditional *tastevin* cup attached to a chain around his neck.

Sparkling Wine—Bubbling wine made usually from Pinot Noir and Chardonnay grapes. When made in the Champagne region of France, it's called Champagne. Napa Valley vintners respect the French rights to that term, and call theirs "sparkling wine".

Stems/Stemmy—A tannic taste of stems in a red wine.

Still Wine—A wine with no carbonation. No bubbles.

Structure—All the components of a wine and how well they work together.

Sulfur/Sulfites—Elemental sulfur is used in the vineyards to prevent a fungus called powdery mildew. Sulfur dioxide (SO_2) is used during fermentation to prevent oxidation, to inhibit wild yeast, and as a preservative. (Too much sulfur can give a wine a "rotten egg" smell.) Sulfur is also used to clean barrels. Some people are allergic to sulfites in wine, which occur naturally at low levels. For this reason, the label must say "Contains sulfites".

Sur Lie (Sir-LEE)—French for "on the lees". Some white wines are barrel-aged in contact with dead yeast cells to produce a richer, yeastier-tasting wine.

Sweet—The impression of a sugary taste. It can come from residual sugar, or from the fruity flavor of the grape.

Tannin—Causes the astringent, mouth-puckering sensation. Much more predominant in red wines. Comes from skins, seeds, stems and oak. Helps preserve the wine and give it aging potential. With proper aging, tannins can soften to produce a velvety wine.

Tart—A wine that is too high in acid.

Tartrates—See Wine Diamonds

Taste—The sensation in the mouth of bitter, sweet or sour.

Terroir—French term for the growing conditions of a vineyard, including soil, elevation, climate, slope, and a variety of other factors.

Thief/Wine Thief—A glass tube used to sample wine directly from a barrel.

Thin—Lacking in body.

Tight—A closedness and underdeveloped quality of a wine where its flavors and aromas are not yet revealed.

Toast—To heat the inside of an oak barrel. This "caramelizes" its flavors.

Top Up—During barrel aging, wine can evaporate. Cellar workers "top up" the barrel by adding wine to replace the evaporated wine. This removes air from the barrel and prevents oxidation.

Trellising—Training a vine to grow on wires and stakes for better support and exposure to sunlight.

Unfiltered—Wine that has not gone through filtration. Many consumers and winemakers prefer wines that have had as little treatment as possible.

Ullage (UL-ij)—The space in a bottle between the wine and the cork. Also called "headspace". If there is too much, the bottle has obviously leaked.

Varietal—A wine made from one type of grape, such as Chardonnay.

Varietal Character—The unique character of a specific variety of grape. For example, Sauvignon Blanc is known for its "new-mown hay" or "grassy" character. Cabernet Sauvignon is associated with black currant, green olive, herb and bell pepper.

Variety—A particular type of grape, such as Cabernet Sauvignon or Chardonnay.

Veraison (Vay-ray-ZON)—The stage in the growing process when grapes begin to acquire their color. Takes place in the summer.

Vinification—The process of making wine from grape juice.

Vintage—The year in which a wine's grapes were harvested.

Vintner—Technically, the person who blends wine. Generally used these days for the person who owns the winery. In a small winery, this person might also be the winemaker.

Viticultural Area—See AVA

Viticulture—The study and practice of growing grapes.

Vitis labrusca—Native American grapes such as Concord grapes, that are considered of much lower quality for wine than *Vitis Vinifera*.

Vitis vinifera—European grape species to which most wine grapes belong.

White Grapes—Used to make white wines. Actually green in color.

Wild Yeast—Yeast that naturally occurs on grape skins.

Wine Diamonds—A romantic name for the crystals of tartaric acid (sodium bitartrate—the ingredient of Cream of Tartar) that can form in the bottle or on the cork. Although harmless, not everyone likes to see them, so many winemakers put their wine through Cold Stabilization to prevent this from happening.

Winemaker—The person who is in charge of the process of actually making the wine.

Yeast—Single-celled organisms that produce enzymes that convert sugar to alcohol and carbon dioxide. There is natural yeast on the grape skins, but most winemakers neutralize this "wild yeast" and use a commercial yeast of their choice.

Yield—The production of a vineyard in tons per acre. A lower yield is said to produce grapes of greater quality and intensity. Sometimes it's just a lower yield.

FAQ

We've listed some of the most common questions about wine and the Napa Valley.

How do I open a bottle of wine?

Use whatever tool you like best. There is a wide variety of corkscrews and other cork pullers out there. Some have one handle, some have two. Ask for suggestions at a wine shop, and experiment till you find one you really like. And you might want more than one type. Sometimes a dry cork needs one type of opener rather than another.

1. Take the blade of the opener or other type of foil cutter, cut the foil all the way around the neck, and remove the top portion of the foil.

2. Pull the cork with whichever device you settled on.

3. Pour the wine into a glass, no more than half full.

How should I store my wine?

If you don't have a wine cellar, and not many people do, try to keep it in a place that's cool and dark, and has a relatively constant temperature. The best place in most homes is in a closet in an interior room. Store it on its side so that the cork stays moist. This will prevent the cork from drying out, which could allow air to enter the bottle and spoil the wine. (This is not a problem with synthetic corks or screw tops.)

At what temperature should my wines be served?

"Room temperature" or "cellar temperature" is often given as an answer to this question. It's probably true, if you live in a European castle with no central heating. Your own room temperature is probably too warm. And not too many people have a temperature-controlled wine cellar.

Red wines should be served between around 65° Fahrenheit. If too cold, you won't be able to enjoy the full flavors and aromas. If too warm, the alcohol is more pronounced and the acids less noticeable.

White wines should be served between 55° and 60° Fahrenheit. If too cold, the fruitiness of the wine will be hidden. If too warm, it will seem less crisp and "dull".

But, as always, serve the wines the way you like them, even if it is not necessarily how the winemaker might prefer.

Should I let the wine breathe before drinking it?

Only if it needs it. Wines vary. Most wines are ready to drink when you pour them, or shortly thereafter. Some will improve after five or ten minutes, or even longer. And others will even go downhill over that period of time.

If the wine is "tight" or "closed", i.e. the flavors and aromas seem to be held in, let it breathe for a while—in the glass. The concept of letting the wine breathe in the bottle makes little sense. Not much air can contact the wine through the small opening in the bottle.

How many servings can I get from a bottle?

A 750 ml bottle is about 26 ounces, so you can pour about five 5-ounce servings, which is a generous serving. Six 4-ounce servings is probably a better idea. If you're doing a tasting, you could pour a dozen 2-ounce tastes.

Is wine really healthy?

A glass of wine a day is reported to reduce the risk of heart attack or stroke. All wines contain *reservatrol*, which can act as an effective preventative against coronary heart disease. It also increases levels of HDL, the "good" cholesterol that helps prevent clogging of the arteries. Wine also reduces the risk of certain types of cancer.

How do they make white wine from red grapes?

"Blush" wines such as White Zinfandel are made by separating the juice from the skins shortly after the grapes are crushed. Since the juice is clear, and the color comes primarily from pigments in the skins, this brief contact with the skins leaves the juice with only a slight pink color. The wine is then processed as a regular white wine would be.

Why are white wines fermented at cooler temperatures than red wines?

To retain the fruity flavors and aromas of the white grapes

What kind of champagne glass should I use?

There are two styles to choose from. One is the open, flatter style that legend says was based on the shape of Marie Antoinette's breast. The narrower flute style is considered the best, however, because it does a better job of retaining the carbon dioxide and aromas of the champagne.

How long can I keep a bottle of wine after opening it?

It depends how many minutes it takes you to drink it. However, if you really don't want to finish a bottle in one sitting, recork it and put it in the refrigerator, although we recommend this more with white wine than with red. (Red is probably better just left on the counter and drunk the next day).

White wine in the refrigerator should last two or three days. If you have any empty half bottles, pour the wine in one of them. That way there will be less air in the bottle, reducing oxidation and helping the leftover wine to last longer.

One new product that is highly recommended by Napa Valley wineries is "Private Preserve". It's a mixture of inert gases that protects open bottles of wine (and fine spirits) against oxidation for weeks and even months. You can find it at wine shops and winery sales rooms throughout the valley or at www.privatepreserve.com

Why do I get headaches from wine?

Assuming it isn't from drinking too much wine, it's most likely because of the histamines that are naturally present in wine. (And in cheese and other foods).

Red wine is much higher in histamines, so you might try switching to white wine. If that doesn't work, consider taking an anti-histamine. Just make sure the package doesn't say to avoid alcohol when using it.

What are the big fans in the vineyards? Are they to cool off the grapes in the summer?

Actually, no. They're to keep the grapes warm in the spring, when there is danger of frost which can damage the young shoots. When the temperature gets down to around 34° Fahrenheit, smudge pots (diesel heaters) are started to heat up the air. The fans then blow the warm air through the vineyard.

Another method of frost protection is the overhead sprinklers that you might have seen. The sprinklers spray the vines, covering the shoots with water, which then freezes. Interestingly, this insulated ice jacket protects the shoots, keeping them just warm enough to avoid freezing themselves.

Do the birds eat the grapes?

Yes and no. Interestingly enough, the large flocks of starlings that do eat grapes usually don't show up in the Napa Valley until after crush. They take the leftovers. And they create beautiful patterns as large flocks of them weave in and out in the skies over the vineyards.

Those birds that are around before harvest are kept away with owls—fake and real, mylar strips that are tied to vineyard trellises and flash in the sunlight, and machines that fire off blank cartridges that sound like shotgun blasts.

How long does a vine last?

After 30 or 40 years, a vine's yield starts to decrease, although its quality may still be excellent.

How long should I store wine before drinking it?

How long does it take you to drive home from the store? The average time that most Americans "lay down" wine is probably about half an hour. That's okay, because most wine, particularly white wine, is ready to drink when it is sold. But some wines, particularly red wines that are heavy on tannins such as a good Cabernet Sauvignon, will improve with age; often as much as ten or fifteen years—or more. Ask the winery and they'll tell you about a particular wine's aging potential.

Is it a good idea to buy wine at the winery?

You should know right off that you probably won't buy wine cheaper at a winery than at home. Most wineries sell at full retail and you probably have a discount house in your area. Does that mean you shouldn't buy wine at Napa Valley wineries? Absolutely not.

When did Robert Louis Stevenson say that Napa Valley wine was "bottled poetry"?

Actually, he didn't. He said that "wine" was bottled poetry. And he was referring to French wine when he wrote in his book *The Silverado Squatters*..."and the wine is bottled poetry."

But he wrote the book while he and his bride were staying on Mount St. Helena, so the Napa Valley claims him as one of its own. And he'd certainly say it about Napa Valley wine if he were around today.

What's a "wine brick"?

During Prohibition, most wineries closed. A few survived by making medicinal or sacramental wine. (Yes, there did appear to be an increase in the number of sick and deeply religious people during this time.)

In order to survive financially, some wineries also produced "wine bricks". These were bricks of compressed grapes that were shipped to customers around the country with a warning notice, which read: "Warning. Do not place this wine brick in one gallon of water, stir and let sit in warm temperatures for 10 days, or it might ferment and turn into wine."

Who made the Grapecrusher statue at the south end of the Napa Valley?

The Grapecrusher sculpture by Gino Miles is located on the Butler Bridge over the Napa River at the south end of Napa Valley.

It was designed by sculptor Gino Miles, and is actually a public relations coup for the industrial park developer whose logo it is.

Ten Reasons Why You Should Buy Wine at the Winery

1. You can find wines that are hard, if not impossible, to find in other parts of the country. With over 300 Napa Valley wineries, it's highly unlikely your local supermarket, or even specialty wine shop, is going to carry all the wines of all the wineries.

2. You can find wines that have a limited production and are sold only at the winery.

3. After tasting the wines, you can buy a bottle of wine that you know you like.

4. You'll get a great-tasting souvenir.

5. When you get home, you can pour the wine for friends and be able to tell them about the winery, how the wine was made, and, if it came from a small winery, possibly even that you met the winemaker.

6. Sometimes wines are on sale at the winery, and you can get an excellent price on an unusual or hard-to-find wine.

7. You can take the wine outside and have it with your picnic lunch.

8. You can take the wine to a Napa Valley restaurant, pay the corkage fee, and enjoy exactly the wine you want with your dinner.

9. If you're lucky enough to live in one of the right (wine-friendly) states, you don't even have to carry it home. The winery will ship it for you.

10. You're helping keep the winery in business, something that's particularly important for small, family wineries. The reason the Napa Valley isn't filled with houses—as is most of the San Francisco Bay Area—is that most of the valley has remained in agriculture. And it has remained in agriculture because that agricultural crop is winegrapes. (We had far fewer visitors when our main crop was prunes.)

Wine Trivia

Age of vine before producing useful grapes—3 years

Age of vine before full production—5 years

Productive lifetime of a vine—30-35 years—Although the quality can remain good, the yield begins to decrease after that

Grape clusters in bottle—7-8

Grapes in a bottle—500-600

Clusters on a vine—40

Grapes in a cluster—75-100

Grape clusters in a glass of wine—1

Vines per acre—400

Pounds of grapes produced by one vine—8-12

Tons per acre—5 (average—can vary greatly)

Gallons of wine per ton of grapes—120

Gallons of wine per acre—800

Barrels per acre—13.5

Bottles per vine—10

Bottles per ton—500–700

Bottles per acre—4,000

Cases per barrel—24.6

Glasses per acre—16,000

Glasses in a bottle—5-6

Bottles per 60 gallon barrel—300

Calories in a 5 ounce glass of dry wine—100-125

Fat in a 5 ounce glass of dry wine—0

Carbohydrates in a 5 ounce glass of dry wine—1-2

Average age of a French oak tree used to make barrels—170 years

Number of years an oak barrel is used—5-8

Year grapes first planted in Napa Valley—1838 (by George Yount)

First winery built in Napa Valley after Prohibition—Stony Hill (1951)

First large winery built in Napa Valley after Prohibition—Robert Mondavi (1966)

Biggest Napa Valley crop before grapes—Prunes

Wine Organizations

Association of African American Vintners
www.aaavintners.org

California Association of Winegrape Growers
www.cawg.org

Congressional Wine Caucus
www.house.gov/radanovich/wine/

Family Winemakers of California
www.familywinemakers.org

Napa County Farm Bureau
www.napafarmbureau.org

Napa Sustainable Winegrowing Group
www.nswg.org

Napa Valley Grape Growers Association
www.napagrowers.org

Napa Valley Vintners Association
www.napavintners.com

Wine America—The National Association of American Wineries (formerly the American Vintners Association)
www.americanwineries.org

Wine Institute of California
www.wineinstitute.org

WineSpirit
Institute for the Study of Wine and Spirituality
www.winespirit.org

Regional Associations

Appellation St. Helena (St. Helena Viticultural Society)
www.appellationsthelena.org

Carneros Wine Alliance
www.carneros.org

Mount Veeder Appellation
www.mountveederwines.com

Oak Knoll District
www.oakknolldistrict.com

Oakville Winegrowers
www.oakvillewinegrowers.org

Rutherford Dust Society
www.rutherforddust.org

Silverado Trail Wineries Association
www.silveradotrail.com

Spring Mountain District
www.springmountaindistrict.com

Stags Leap District Winegrowers
www.stagsleapdistrict.com

Yountville Appellation
www.yountvillewines.com

Winery List

We've included this list so you can track down a favorite winery. Not all of these wineries have tours or onsite sales. In fact, most don't. (The major ones that do allow you to drop in are listed in our *Town* sections.)

Some wineries have such limited production that they are not interested in any visitors. Most that are interested can have visits by appointment only. (This is due to the county's attempts to minimize automobile traffic in many areas.)

Most small, out-of-the-way, family-owned wineries give tours only by appointment. These are the wineries that can be the most interesting, and that will give you a chance to actually talk with the winemaker himself.

To visit these wineries, call in advance. While you may be able to set up an appointment the same day, or the next day if you're spending the night in the valley, you're better off phoning before you even come to the valley.

This also works even for the larger wineries that give public tours. You might have your local wine shop call the winery and tell them you're a special customer who would like a private tour.

Acacia Winery
2750 Las Amigas Road, Napa
707.226.9991
www.acaciawinery.com

Adastra Wines
www.adastrawines.com

Aetna Springs Cellars
7227 Pope Valley Road., Pope Valley
707.965.2675
www.aetnaspringscellars.com

Alatera Vineyards
2170 Hoffman Lane., Yountville
707.944.4005

Aloise Francisco Vineyards
1054 Bayview Avenue., Napa
707.252.4005

Altamura Vineyards and Winery
www.altamura.com

Amici Cellars
1109 Hudson Street St. Helena
707.967.9560
www.amicicellars.com

Amizetta Vineyards Winery
1099 Greenfield Rd, St. Helena
707.963.1460
www.amizetta.com

Ancien Wines
www.ancienwines.com

Anderson's Conn Valley Vineyards
680 Rossi Road., St. Helena
707.963.8600

Andretti Winery
4162 Big Ranch Road Napa
707.255.3524
www.andrettiwinery.com

Anomaly Vineyards
www.anomalyvineyards.com

Araujo Estate Wines
2155 Picket Road, Calistoga
707.942.6061
www.araujoestatewines.com

Arroyo Winery
2361 Greenwood Avenue, Calistoga
707.942.6995

Artesa
1345 Henry Road Napa
707.224.1668
www.artesawinery.com

Artistic Wines
www.artisticwines.com

Astrale e Terra
5017 Silverado Trail Napa
707.253.7643
www.astraleeterra.com

Atalon Winery
www.atalon.com

Atlas Peak Vineyards
3700 Soda Canyon Road., Napa
707.252.7971
www.atlaspeak.com

Azalea Springs
4301 Azalea Springs Way, Calistoga
707.942.4811

Bacio Divino
www.baciodivino.com

Ballentine Vineyards and Winery
2820 N. St Helena Highway St. Helena
707.963.7919
www.ballentinevineyards.com

Barlow Vineyards
4411 Silverado Trail, Calistoga, CA
94515
707.942.8742
www.barlowvineyards.com

Barnett Vineyards
4070 Spring Mountain Road., St.
Helena
707.963.0109
www.barnettvineyards.com

Bates Creek Winery
www.batescreek.com

Bayview Cellars
1202 Main Street, Napa
707.255.8544
www.bayviewwine.com

Beaucanon
1695 South St. Helena Hwy. St.
Helena
707.967.3520

Beaulieu Vineyard
1960 St. Helena Hwy. Rutherford
707.967.5411
www.bv-wine.com

Bell Wine Cellars
6200 Washington Street Yountville
707.944.1673
www.bellwine.com

Benessere Vineyards
1010 Big Tree Road St. Helena
707.963.5853
www.benesserevineyards.com

Beringer Vineyards
2000 Main Street St. Helena
707.963.4812
www.beringer.com

Bernard Pradel Cellars
2100 Hoffmann Lane Yountville
707.944.8720

Bettinelli Vineyards
www.bettinelli.com

Bighorn Cellars
1085 Atlas Peak Road Napa
707.224.6565

Blankiet Vineyards
www.blankiet.com

Bouchaine Vineyards
1075 Buchli Station Road., Napa
707.252.9065
www.bouchaine.com

Bressler Vineyards
www.bresslervineyards.com

Broman Cellars
www.bromancellars.com

Buehler Vineyards
820 Greenfield Road., St. Helena
707.963.2155
www.buehlervineyards.com

Burgess Cellars
1108 Deer Park Road., St. Helena
707.963.4766
www.burgesscellars.com

Cafaro Cellars
www.cafaro.com

Cain Vineyards & Winery
3800 Langtry Road., St. Helena
707.963.1616
www.cainfive.com

Cakebread Cellars
8300 St. Helena Hwy., Rutherford
707.963.5221
www.cakebread.com

Calafia Cellars
629 Fulton Lane., St. Helena
707.963.5221

Caldwell Cellars
www.caldwellcellars.com

Cardinale Winery
7585 St. Helena Highway Oakville
707.944.2807
www.cardinale.com

Carneros Creek Winery
1285 Dealy Lane., Napa
707.253.9463
www.carneros-creek.com

Carver Sutro Wine
3106 Palisades Road
Calistoga CA 94515
707.942.1029
www.carversutro.com

Casa Carneros
www.casacarneros.com

Casa Nuestra Winery
3451 Silverado Trail., N., St. Helena
707.963.5783
www.casanuestra.com

Caymus Vineyards
8700 Sage Canyon Creek Road., St.
Helena
707.967.3010
www.caymus.com

Ceja Vineyards
www.cejavineyards.com

Chalone Wine Group
www.chalonewinegroup.com

Chameleon Cellars
www.chameleoncellars.com

Chappellet Vineyard
1581 Sage Canyon Road., St. Helena
707.963.7136
www.chappellet.com

Charbay Winery & Distillery
4001 Spring Mountain Road, St.
Helena
707.963.9327
www.charbay.com

Charles Krug Winery
2800 St. Helena Hwy North St.
Helena
707.963.2761
www.charleskrug.com

Chateau Boswell
3468 Silverado Trail., St. Helena
707.963.5472

Chateau Chevre Winery
2030 Hoffmann Lane., Yountville
707.944.2184

Chateau L'Ego
www.westsong.com/chateau

Chateau Montelena Winery
1429 Tubbs Lane., Calistoga
707.942.5105
www.chateaumontelena.com

Chateau Potelle
3875 Mount Veeder Road., Napa
707.255.9440
www.chateaupotelle.com

Chateau Woltner
3500 Silverado Trail., St. Helena
707.963.1744

Chiles Lake Winery
www.chileslakewinery.com

Chiles Valley Wineyard
2676 Lower Chiles Valley Road., St.
Helena
707.963. 7294

Chimney Rock Winery
5350 Silverado Trail., Napa
707.257.2641
www.chimneyrock.com

Chinnock Cellars
www.chinnockcellars.com

Clark-Claudon Vineyards
www.clarkclaudon.com

Clos Du Val Wine Co., Ltd
5330 Silverado. Trail., Napa
707.259.2220
www.closduval.com

Clos Pegase Winery
1060 Dunaweal Lane., Calistoga
707.942.4981
www.clospegase.com

Colgin Cellars
7830-40 St. Helena Hwy Oakille
707.524.4445

Conn Creek Winery
8711 Silverado Trail., St. Helena
707.963.5133
www.conncreek.com

Corison Winery
987 St. Helena Highway St. Helena
707.963.0826
www.corisonwinery.com

Corley Family Napa Valley
4242 Big Ranch Road., Napa
707.253.2802
www.corleyfamilynapavalley.com

Cosentino Winery
7415 St. Helena Hwy, Yountville
707.944.1220
www.cosentinowinery.com

Costello Vineyards Winery
1200 Orchard Avenue, Napa
707.252.8483

Crane Family Vineyards
www.cranefamilyvineyards.com

Crichton Hall
1150 Darms Lane Napa
707.224.4200

Cuvaison Winery
4550 Silverado Trail., Calistoga
707.942.6266
www.cuvaison.com

D.R. Stephens Estate
1860 Howell Mountain Road St.
Helena
415.781.8000

Dalla Valle Vineyards
7776 Silverado Trail., Yountville
707.944.2676

Darioush Winery
4240 Silverado Trail Napa
707.257.2345
www.darioush.com

David Arthur Vineyards
1521 Sage Canyon Road, St. Helena
707.963.5190
www.davidarthur.com

Deer Park Winery
1000 Deer Park Road., Deer Park
707.963.5411
www.deerparkwinery.com

Del Dotto Vineyards
www.deldottovineyards.com

Destino Wines
www.destinowines.com

Diamond Creek Vineyards
500 Diamond Mountain Road
Calistoga
707.942.6926
www.diamondcreekvineyards.com

Diamond Mountain Vineyard
2121 Diamond Mountain Road.,
Calistoga
707.942.0707

Diamond Terrace
1391 Diamond Mountain Road
Calistoga
707.942.1189
www.diamondterrace.com

Dickerson Vineyard
www.dickersonvineyard.com

Dolce
www.dolce-farniente.com

Domain Hill & Mayes
1775 Lincoln Avenue, Napa
707.224.6565

Domain Carneros by Taittinger
1240 Duhig Road., Napa
707.257.0101
www.domainecarneros.com

Domaine Chandon
California Drive., Yountville
707.944.2280
www.chandon.com

Domaine Montreax
4101 Big Ranch Road., Napa
707.252.9380

Domaine Napa Winery
1155 Mee Lane., St. Helena
707.963.1666

Dominus Estate
2570 Napanook Road., Yountville
707.944.8954
www.dominusestate.com

Downing Family Vineyards
www.dfwines.com

Duckhorn Wine Company
3027 Silverado Trail. N, St. Helena
707.963.7108
www.duckhorn.com

Dusinberre Cellars
www.winecal.com

Dunn Vineyards
805 White Cottage Road., Angwin
707.965.3642

Dutch Henry Winery
4300 Silverado Trail Calistoga
707.942.5771
www.dutchhenry.com

Dyer Vineyard
1501 Diamond Mountain Road,
Calistoga
707.942.5502
www.dyerwine.com

Eagle and Rose Estate
1844 Pope Canyon Road Pope Valley
707.965.9463
www.eagleandrose.com

Edgewood Estates
401 St. Helena Hwy St. Helena
707.963.2335

Ehlers Grove Winery
3222 Ehlers Lane., St. Helena
707.963.3200
www.ehlersgrove.com

Eisele V & L Family Estate
3080 Lower Chiles Valley Road., St.
Helena
707.965.2260
www.volkereiselevineyard.com

Elan Vineyards
www.elanwine.com

Elke Vineyards
www.elkewine.com

Elkhorn Peak Cellars
200 Polson Road., Napa
707.255.0504
www.elkhornpeakcellars.com

El Molino Winery
P.O Box 306, St. Helena
707.963.3632
www.elmolinewinery.com

Elyse Wine Cellars
PO Box 83, Rutherford
707.963.5496

Emilio's Terrace
1496 Walnut Drive Oakville
707.944.2193
www.etvine.com

Etude Wines
1250 Cuttings Wharf Road, Napa
707.257.5300

Far Niente Winery
P.O. Box 327, Oakville
707.944.2861
www.farniente.com

Farella-Park Vineyards
PO Box 5217, Napa
707.254.9489

Fife Vineyards
www.fifevineyards.com

Flora Springs Wine Co.
1978 W. Zinfandel Lane., St. Helena
707.963.5711
www.florasprings.com

Folie a Deux
3070 N. St. Helena Hwy., St. Helena
707.963.1160
www.folieadeux.com

Fontana di Vita
www.fontanadivino.com

Forest Hill Vineyard
P.O. Box 96 St. Helena
707.963.7229

Franciscan Oakville Estate
1178 Calleron Road., Rutherford
707.963.7111
www.franciscan.com

Frank Family Vineyards
1091 Larkmead Lane St. Helena
707.942.859

Franus Wine Company
2055 Hoffman Lane Yountville
707.945.0542
www.franuswine.com

Frazier
40 Lupine Hill Road Napa
707.255.3444
www.frazierwinery.com

Freemark Abbey Winery
3022 North St. Helena Hwy. St.
Helena
707.963.9694
www.freemarkabbey.com

Freestone Wines
www.flywine.com

Frisinger Cellars
2277 Dry Creek Road., Napa
707.255.3749

Frog's Leap Winery
8815 Conn Creek Road., Rutherford
707.963.4704
www.frogsleap.com

Galleron Signature Wines
PO Box 2 Rutherford
707.265.6552
www.galleronwine.com

Golden State Vintners
www.gsvwine.com

Goosecross Cellars
1119 State Lane., Yountville
707.944.1986
www.goosecross.com

Grace Family Vineyards
1210 Rockland Drive., St. Helena
707.963.0808

Graeser Winery
255 Petrified Forest Road., Calistoga
707.942.4437
www.graeserwinery.com

Grandview Cellars
www.grandviewcellars.com

Green & Red Vineyard
3208 Chiles Pope Valley Road., St.
Helena
707.965.2346
www.greenandred.com

Greenfield Winery
205-B Jim Oswald Way, American
Canyon
707.552.0362
www.greenfieldwinery.com

Gregory Graham Winery
www.ggwine.com

Grgich Hlls Cellar
1829 St. Helena Hwy., Rutherford
707.963.2784
www.grgich.com

Groth Vineyards & Winery
750 Oakville Cross Road., Oakville
707.944.0290

Guilliams Vineyards
3851 Spring Mountain Road St.
Helena
707.963.9059

Gustavo Thrace Winery
1146 First Street. Napa
707.257.6796
www.gustavothrace.com

Hagafen Cellars
PO Box 3035, Napa
707.252.0781
www.hagafen.com

Hans Fahden Vineyards
www.hansfahden.com

Hanso-Hsieh Vineyard
1019 Dry Creek Road., Napa
707.257.2632

Harlan Estate Winery
PO Box 352, Oakville
707.944.1441
www.harlanestate.com

Harrison Vineyards
1527 Sage Canyon Road., St.Helena
707.963.8271
www.harrisonvineyards.com

Hartwell Vineyards
5795 Silverado Trail., Napa
707.255.4269
www.hartwellvineyards.com

Havens Wine Cellars
2055 Hoffman Lane., Yountville
707.945.0921
www.havenswine.com

Heitz Cellars
500 Taplin Road., Helena
707.963.3542
www.heitzcellar.com

Helena View Johnston Vineyards
3500 Highway 128 Calistoga
707.942.4956

Hendry Winery
3104 Redwood Road Napa
707.226.2130

Hess Collection
4411 Redwood Road., Napa
707.255.1144
www.hesscollection.com

Honig Vineyard and Winery
850 Rutherford Road., Rutherford
707.963.5618
www.honigwines.com

Howell Mountain
www.howellmountain.com

Jaeger Vineyards
www.jaegervineyards.com

James Creek Vineyards
Pope Valley
Jamescreek.getwebnet.com

Jarvis Vineyards
2970 Monticello Road., Napa
707.255.5280
www.jarviswines.com

Jessup Cellars
www.jessupcellars.com

Joel Gott
1458 Lincoln Ave. Railcar #15
Calistoga
707.942.1109
www.gottwines.com

Jones Family Vineyards
7830-40 St. Helena Highway
Oakville
707.942.0467
www.joneswine.com

Joseph Phelps Vineyards
200 Taplin Road., St. Helena
707.963.2745
www.jpvwines.com

Joya Wine Company
880 Vallejo Street., Napa
707.245.9548

Judd's Hill Winery
www.juddshill.com

Juslyn Vineyards
www.juslynvineyards.com

Karl Lawrence Cellars
4541 Monticello Road., Napa
707.255.2843
www.karllawrence.com

Kate's Vineyard
5211 Big Ranch Road Napa
707.255.2644

Kelham MacLean Winery
360 Zinfandel Lane St Helena
707.963.2000
www.kelhammaclean.com

Kent Rasmussen Winery
1001 Silverado Trail St. Helena
707.963.5667

Kirkland Ranch Winery
707.254.9100
www.kirklandranchwinery.com

J. Kirkwood
www.jkirkwood.com

Koves-Newlan Vineyards & Winery
www.kovesnewlanwine.com

Kuleto Villa
www.kuletovilla.com

Lail Vineyards
320 Stone Ridge Road Angwin
707.963.3329
www.lailvineyards.com

Laine Estate Wines
www.firstgrowth.com

Laird Family Estate
www.lairdfamilyestate.com

Lan Vieille Montagne
3851 Spring Mountain Road., St.
Helena
707.963.9059

Lakespring Winery
2055 Hoffman Lane., Yountville
707.944.2475

Lamborn Family Vineyards
2075 Summit Lake Drive, Angwin
707.965.2811
www.lamborn.com

Lang & Reed Wine Company
PO Box 662 St. Helena
707.963.7547

Larkmead Kornell Champagne
Cellars
1091 Larkmead Lane., St. Helena
707.942.0859

Larkmead Vineyards
1145 Larkmead Lane., Calistoga
707.942.6605
www.larkmead.com

Lewelling Vineyards
www.lewellingvineyards.com

Liparita Cellars
410 La Fata Street #200 St. Helena
707.963.2775
www.liparita.com

Littorai Wines
www.littorai.com

Livingston-Moffett Wines
1895 Cabernet Lane, St. Helena
707.963.2120
www.livingstonwines.com

Lokoya
7600 St. Helena Highway Oakville
707.944.2807
www.lokoya.com

Long Meadow Ranch
1775 Whitehall Lane St. Helena
707.963.4555
www.longmeadowranch.com

Lorenza-Lake Winery
1764 Scott Street St. Helena
707.963.8593
www.blockheadia.com

Louis M. Martini Winery
St. Helena Hwy., St. Helena
707.963.2736
www.louismartini.com

Luna Vineyards
2921 Silverado Trail Napa
707.255.5862
www.lunavineyards.com

Lynch Knoll
3305 North St. Helena Highway
Oakville
650.948.1344

Madonna Estate (Mont St. John)
5400 Old Sonoma Road Napa CA
707.255.8864
www.madonnaestate.com

Madrigal Vineyards
www.madrigalvineyards.com

Marilyn Merlot
www.marilynmerlot.com

Mario Perelli-Minetti Winery
1443 Silverado Trail, St. Helena
707.963.8762

Markham Vineyards
2812 N. St. Helena Hwy St. Helena
707.963.5292
www.markhamvineyards.com

Marston Family Vineyards
3600 White Sulphur Springs Road
St. Helena
415.931.0443

Mason Cellars
www.masoncellars.com

Mayacamas Vineyards
1155 Lokoya Road., Napa
707.224.4030
www.mayacamas.com

McKenzie-Mueller Vineyards
www.mckenziemuller.com

Mendelson Vineyard
www.mendelsonvineyard.com

Merryvale Vineyards
1000 Main, St. Helena
707.963.7777
www.merryvale.com

Michael-Scott
www.michaelscottwines.com

Milat Vineyards
1091 St. Helena Hwy., St. Helena
707.963.0758
www.milat.com

Miner Family Winery
7850 Silverado Trail Oakville
707.944.9500
www.minerwines.com

Monticello Brothers
707.255.9100

Montreaux
4242 Big Ranch Road., Napa
707.252.9380

Moon Vineyard
3315 Sonoma Highway, Napa
707.226.2642

Moss Creek Winery
6015 Steele Canyon Road., Napa
707.252.1295

Mt. Veeder Winery & Vineyards
1999 Mt. Veeder Road., Napa
707.224.4039
www.mtveeder.com

Mumm Napa Valley
8445 Silverado Trail., Napa
800.686.6272
www.mummnapavalley.com

Napa Cellars
7481 St. Helena Highway Yountville
707.944.2565
www.napacellars.com

Napa Redwood Estate
www.naparedwoodestate.com

Napa Wine Company
1133 Oakville Cross Road., Oakville
707.944.1710
www.napawineco.com

Neal Vineyards
www.nealvineyards.com

Newton Vineyard
2555 Madrone Avenue, St. Helena
707.963.9000

Nichelini Winery
2950 Sage Canyon Road., St. Helena
707.963.0717
www.nicheliniwinery.com

Nickel and Nickel
8164 St. Helena Highway, Oakville
707.944.0693
www.nickelandnickel.com

Noah Vineyards
www.noahvineyards.com

Oakford Vineyards
PO Box 150, Oakville
707.945.0445
www.oakfordvineyards.com

Oakville Ranch Vineyards
7781 Silverado Trail, Napa
415.284.1620

One Vineyard
3268 Ehlers Lane St. Helena
707.963.1123

Opus One Winery
7900 St. Helena Highway Oakville
707.944.9442
www.opusonewinery.com

Origin-Napa
PO Box 670, St. Helena
707.963.6134
www.originnapa.com

Paradigm Winery
683 Dwyer Road., Napa
707.944.1683

Pahlmeyer
PO Box 2410, Napa
707.255.2321
www.pahlmeyer.com

Palmaz Vineyards
4029 Hagan Road Napa
707.226.5587
www.palmazwinery.com

Paloma Vineyard
www.palomavineyard.com

Paoletti Estates Winery
4801 Silverado Trail Calistoga
707.942.0689
www.giannipaoletti.com

Paradigm Winery
683 Dwyer Road Oakville
707.944.1683
www.paradigmwinery.com

Parador Cellars
www.paradorcellars.com

Patz & Hall Wine Company
www.patzhall.com

Peju Province
8466 St. Helena., Hwy Rutherford
707.963.3600
www.peju.com

Perez and Sons Vineyards
707.963.8002

Pepi Winery
www.pepi.com

Peter Michael Winery
www.petermichaelwinery.com

Philip Togni Vineyard
3780 Spring Mountain Road.,
St.Helena
707.963.3731

Phoenix Vineyards
3175 Dry Creek Road Napa
707.255.1971
www.phoenixvineyards.com

Pillar Rock Vineyard
6110 Silverado Trail Yountville
630.293.1175
www.pillarrockvineyard.com

Pine Ridge Winery
5901 Silverado Trail. Napa
707.252.9777
www.pineridgewinery.com

Plam Vineyards
6200 Washington Street, Yountville
707.944.1102
www.plam.com

Plump Jack Winery
620 Oakville Cross Road Oakville
707.945.1220
www.plumpjack.com/

Pope Valley Cellars
6613 Pope Valley Road., Pope Valley
707.965.1438

Pope Valley Winery
www.popevalleywinery.com

Prager Winery & Port Works
1281 Lewelling Lane., St. Helena
707.963.7678
www.pragerport.com

Pride Mountain Vineyards
Spring Mountain Road., St. Helena
707.963.4949
www.pridewines.com

Quintessa
PO Box 407, Rutherford
707.963.7111
www.quintessa.com

Quixote Winery
6126 Silverado Trail Napa
707.944.2659
www.quixotewinery.com

Random Ridge
www.rnadomridge.com

Raymond Vineyard & Cellar
849 Zinfandel Lane, St. Helena
707.963.3141
www.raymondwine.com

Regusci Winery
5584 Silverado Trail Napa
707.254.0403
www.regusciwinery.com

Reid Family Vineyard
www.jkirkwood.com

Reverie on Diamond Mountain
1520 Diamond Mountain Road
Calistoga
707.942.6800
www.reveriewine.com

Reynolds Family Winery
3266 Silverado Trail
Napa CA 94558
707.258.2558
www.reynoldsfamilywinery.com

Ristow Estate
5040 Silverado Trail Napa
415.931.5405
www.ristowestate.com

Ritchie Creek Vineyard
4024 Spring Mountain Road., St.
Helena
707.963.4661
www.ritchiecreek.com

Robert Biale Vinyards
707.257.7555

Robert Craig Wine Cellars
830 School Road #14 Napa
707.252.2250
www.robertcraigwine.com

Robert Keenan Winery
3660 Spring Mountain Road., St.
Helena
707.963.9177

Robert Mondavi Winery
7801 St. Helena Hwy., Oakville
707.226.1335
www.robertmondavi.com

Robert Pecota Winery
P.O Box 303, Calistoga
707.942.6625
www.robertpecotawinery.com

Robert Pepi Winery
www.pepi.com

Robert Sinskey Vineyards
6320 Silverado Trail, Yountville
707.944.9090
www.robertsinskey.com

Rocking Horse Winery
www.rockinghorsewinery.com

Rombauer Vineyards
3522 Silverado Trail, St. Helena
707.967.5120
www.rombauervineyards.com

Ross Vineyards
www.rossvineyards.com

Round Hill Vineyards
1680 Silverado Trail., St. Helena
707.963.9503
www.roundhillwines.com

Round Pond
PO Box 556, Rutherford
877.963.9364
www.roundpond.com

Rowland Cellars
www.rowlandcellars.com

Rubicon Estate
PO Box 208, Rutherford
707.963.9435
www.rubiconestate.com

Rubissow-Sargent
www.rubissowsargent.com

Rudd Estate
500 Oakville Cross Road Oakville
707.944.8577

Rustridge Winery
2910 Lower Chiles Valley Road., St.
Helena
707.965.2871
www.rustridge.com/winery

Rutherford Benchmarks
www.rutherfordbenchmarks.com

Rutherford Grove Winery
1673 St. Helena Highway Rutherford
707.963.0544
www.rutherfordgrove.com

Rutherford Hill Winery
200 Rutherford Hill Road.,
Rutherford
707.963.7194
www.rutherfordhill.com

Rutherford Ranch
www.rutherfordranch.com

Saddleback Cellars
www.saddlebackcellars.com

Saintsbury
1500 Los Carneros Ave., Napa
707.252.0592
www.saintsbury.com

Salvestrin Vineyard & Wine
Company
www.salvestrinwineco.com

San Pietro Vara Vineyard & Wine
Company
1171 Tubbs Lane., Calistoga
707.942.0937

V. Sattui Winery
1111 White Lane, St. Helena
707.963.7774
www.vsattui.com

Sawyer Cellars
8350 St. Helena Highway
Rutherford
707.963.1980
www.sawyercellars.com

Schrader Cellars
2921 Silverado Trail Napa
707.942.1212

Schramsberg Vineyards
Schramsberg Road., Calistoga
707.942.4558
www.schramsberg.com

Schuetz Oles Winery
www.schuetzoles.com

Schweiger Vineyards & Winery
4015 Spring Mountain Road St.
Helena
707.963.7980
www.schweigervineyards.com

Scott Paul Wines
www.scottpaul.com

Screaming Eagle Winery
7557 Silverado Trail Oakville
707.944.0749
www.screamingeagle.com

Seavey Vineyards
1310 Conn Valley Road, St. Helena
707.963.8339
www.seaveyvineyard.com

Selene Wines
www.selenewines.com

Sequoia Grove Vineyards
8338 South St. Helena Hwy.,
Rutherford
707.944.2945
www.sequoiagrove.com

Selene Wines
PO Box 3131 Napa
707.258.8119

Shafer Vineyards
6145 Silverado Trail. Napa
707.944.2877
www.shafervineyards.com

Showket-Awni Wines
Oakville 707.944.9553
www.showketvineyards.com

Shypoke Vineyard
4170 St. Helena Highway Calistoga
707.942.0420
www.shypoke.com

Signorello Vineyards
4500 Silverado Trail, Napa
707.255.5990
www.signorellovineyards.com

Silver Oak Cellars
915 Oakville Cross Road., Oakville
707.944.8808
www.silveroak.com

Silverado Hill Cellars
3103 Silverado Trail., Napa
707.253.9306

Silverado Vineyards
6121 Silverado Trail., Napa
707.257.1770
www.silveradovineyards.com

Silver Rose Winery
400 Silverado Trail Calistoga
707.942.9581
www.silverrosewinery.com

Sjoeblom Winery
8060 Silverado Trail
Napa CA 94558
707.968.9395
www.sjoeblom.com

Sky Vineyards
Napa 707.935.1391
www.skyvineyards.com

Smith-Madrone Vineyards
4022 Spring Mountain Road., St.
Helena
707.963.2283

Sparrow Lane
www.sparrowlane.com

Spelletich Cellars
www.spellwine.com

Spottswoode Winery
1902 Madrone Avenue St. Helena
707.963.0134
www.spottswoode.com

Spring Mountain Vineyard
2805 Spring Mountain Road. St.
Helena
707.967.4188
www.springmtn.com

St. Andrews Winery
2921 Silverado Trail., Napa
707.259.2200

St. Clement Vineyards
2867 St. Helena Hwy.,
707.963.7221
www.stclement.com

St. Supéry Wine Discovery Center &
Winery
8440 St. Helena Hwy., Rutherford
707.963.4507
www.stsupery.com

Stag's Leap Wine Cellars
5766 Silverado Trail, Napa
707.944.2020
www.stagsleapwinecellars.com

Stag's Leap Winery
6150 Silverado Trail, Napa
707.944.1303
www.stagsleap.com

Staglin Family Vineyard
P.O. Box 680, Rutherford
707.963.1749
www.staglin.com

Star Hill Winery
1075 Shadybrook Lane., Napa
707.255.1957
www.starhill.com

Steltzner
5998 Silverado Trail, Napa
707.252.7272
www.steltzner.com

Sterling Vineyards
1111 Dunaweal Lane., Calistoga
707.942.3344
www.sterlingvyds.com

Stonefly Vineyards
www.stoneflyvineyard.com

Twomey Winery
1183 Dunaweal Lane., Calistoga
707.942.6500
www.stonegatewinery.com

Stoneheath Wines
www.stoneheath.com

Stonehedge Winery
401 South St. Helena Highway St.
Helena
323.780.5929
www.stonehedgewinery.com

Stony Hill Vineyard
3331 North St. Helena Hwy., Napa
707.963.2636
www.stonyhillvineyard.com

Storybook Mountain Winery
3835 Hwy. 128, Calistoga
707.942.5310
www.storybookwines.com

Strack Vineyard
4120 St. Helena Hwy., Napa
707.224.5100

Stratford Winery
1472 Railroad Avenue, St. Helena
707.963.3200

Streblow Vineyards
1455 Summit Lake Drive, Angwin
707.963.5892

Sullivan Vineyards Winery
1090 Galleron Road., Rutherford
707.963.9646
www.sullivanwine.com

Summers Winery
1171 Tubbs Lane Calistoga
707.942.5508
www.sumwines.com

Summit Lake Vineyards & Winery
2000 Summit Lake Drive, Angwin
707.965.2488

Sutter Home Winery
277 St. Helena Hwy., St. Helena
707.963.3104
www.sutterhome.com

Swanson Vineyards
1271 Manley Lane,Rutherford
707.944.1642
www.swansonvineyards.com

Titus Vineyards
PO Box 608, St. Helena
707.963.3235
www.tituswine.com

Tom Eddy Wines
www.tomeddywines.com

Tongi Philip Vineyard
3780 Spring Mountain Road., St.
Helena
707.963.3731

Trinchero Family Estates
(See Sutter Home)

Traulsen Vineyards
2250 Lake Country Hwy., Calistoga
707.942.0283

Trefethen Veneyards
1160 Oak Knoll Ave, Napa
707.255.7700
www.trefethen.com

Truchard Vineyards
3234 Old Sonoma Road., Napa
707.253.7153

Tudal Winery
1015 Big Tree Road., St. Helena
707.963.3947
www.tudalwinery.com

Tulocay Winery
1426 Coombsville Road., Napa
707.255.4064
www.tulocay.com

Turley Wine Cellars
3358 St. Helena Hwy.,
707.963.0940
www.turleywinecellars.com

Turnbull Wine Cellars
8210 St. Helena Hwy., Oakville
707.963.5839

V. Sattui Winery
South St. Helena Hwy., St. Helena
707.963.7774
www.vsattui.com

Van Asperen Vineyards
1680 Silverado Trail St. Helena
707.968.3200
www.vanasperen.com

Van Der Heyden Vineyards &
Winery
4057 Silverado Trail., Napa
707.259.9473
www.vanderheydenvineyards.com

Venge Vineyards
7802 Money Rd., Oakville
707.944.1305

Viader Vineyards
1120 Deer Park Road., Deer Park
707.963.3816
www.viader.com

Vigil Vineyards
3340 Highway 128 Calistoga
707.942.2900
www.vigilwine.com

Villa Andriana
1171 Tubbs Lane Calistoga
707.942.5508

Villa Encinal
620 Oakville Cross Road, Oakville
707.944.1465

Villa Helena Winery
1455 Inglewood Ave, St. Helena
707.963.4334
www.wineweb.com/villahelena.html

Villa Mt. Eden Winery
PO Box 350, St. Helena
707.944.2414
www.villamteden.com

Vincent Arroyo Winery
2361 Greenwood Avenue, Calistoga
707.942.6995

Vine Cliff Winery
7400 Silverado Trail., Yountville
707.944.1364
www.vinecliff.com

Vineyard 29
2929 Highway 29 North St. Helena
707.963.9292

Volker Eisele Family Estate
3080 Lower Chiles Valley Road., St.
Helena
707.965.2260
www.volkereiselevineyard.com

Von Strasser Winery
1510 Diamond Mountain Road.,
Calistoga
707.942.0930
www.vonstrasser.com

W Winery
1001 Silverado Trail St. Helena
707.259.2800

Wermuth Winery
3942 Silverado Trail., Calistoga
707.942.5924

White Cottage Ranch Winery
www.whitecottageranch.com

Whitehall Lane Winery
1563.S St. Helena Hwy., St Helena
707.963.9454
www.whitehalllane.com

White Rock Vineyards
www.whiterockvineyards.com

Whitford Cellars
4047 East 3d Avenue, Napa
707.257.7065

William Hill Winery
1761 Atlas Peak Road, Napa
707.224.4477
www.williamhill.com

Winter Creek Winery
PO Box 2847, Napa
707.252.8677

Woltner Estates Winery
150 White Cottage Road. South,
Angwin
707.965.2445

X Winery
www.xwinery.com

Young Ridge
www.youngridge.com

Yverdon Vineyards
3787 Spring Mtn. Road., St. Helena
707.963.4270

Zahtila Vineyard
2250 Lake County Road Calistoga
707.942.9251
www.zahtilavineyards.com

ZD Wines
8383 Silverado Trail, Napa
707.963.5188
www.zdwines.com

Local Information

Emergency

Emergency Phone Number
(Fire, police, ambulance)
Dial 911

Poison Control Center
800.523.2222

Medical

Queen of the Valley Hospital
1000 Trancas St.
Napa CA 94558
707.252.4411
Emergency Room: 707.257.4038
www.thequeen.org

Kaiser Permanente
(members only)
3285 Claremont Way
Napa CA 94558
707.258.2500
Clinic only . No emergency room

St. Helena Hospital
PO Box 250
650 Sanitarium Road
Deer Park, CA 94576
707.963.3611
Emergency Room: 707.963.6425
www.sthelenahospital.org

Newspapers

Angwin Reporter
(online only)
www.angwinreporter.com

Calistoga Tribune
(weekly)
Mud City Weekender
1360 Lincoln Avenue
Calistoga CA 94515
707.942.5181
calistogatribune@aol.com

Napa Sentinel
(weekly)
1627 Lincoln Avenue
Napa CA 94558
707.257.6272
www.napasentinel.com

Napa Valley Register
(daily)
1615 Second St.
Napa CA 94559
707.226.3711
www.napanews.com

St. Helena Star
(weekly)
1328 Main Street
St. Helena CA 94574
707.963.2731
www.sthelenastar.com

Weekly Calistogan
(weekly)
1328 Main St.
St. Helena, CA 94574
707.942.6242
www.weeklycalistogan.com

Yountville Sun
(weekly)
6795 Washington St.
Yountville CA 94599
707.944.5676

Radio Stations

KVON - 1440 AM
(local news and weather)
www.kvon.com

KVYN - 99.3 FM
(music)
www.kvyn.com

Television Stations

Commercial

There are no local commercial television stations. Main Bay Area stations are channels 3 (NBC), 5 (CBS) and 7 (ABC). PBS stations are Channels 9 and 22.

Community

Napa Channel 28
Public Access TV
707.257.0574
www.napatv.org

Cable TV

Comcast
2260 Brown St.
Napa CA 94558
800.945.2288

Serves all cities in Napa County.

Napa Valley Trivia

Bigfoot

Even Bigfoot allegedly visits the Napa Valley. The large, hairy creature, also known as a *Sasquatach* (or *Yeti in the Himalayas)*, was reportedly seen a number of times in the Pope Valley area over the period 1978-1989.

Bigfoot was occasionally observed running in the distance. Other incidents involved footprints, screams and smells. It was described as about seven feet tall and covered head-to-toe with grayish-brown hair. One resident even stated that one "had tried to enter their house but was frightened away with a gun blast."

Sightings usually occurred in early evenings, but sometimes in the early morning just before daybreak.

Mary Ellen Pleasant

Mary Ellen Pleasant (1814? – 1904)

Mary Ellen Pleasant is perhaps better known as "Mammy Pleasant", but it was a name she detested. She was born a slave in Georgia some time between 1814 and 1817, the illegitimate daughter of an enslaved Vodou priestess from Haiti and a Virginia governor's son, John Pleasants. She was bought out of slavery by a planter and indentured for nine years as a store clerk with abolitionist Quakers in Massachusetts.

Around 1841 she married a wealthy mulatto merchant and contractor from Ohio and Philadelphia named James Smith, who was also a slave rescuer on the Underground Railroad. The two worked to help slaves flee to safety in Canada and safe states. Smith died in 1844, leaving her a $45,000 fortune and a plantation run by freedmen near Harper's Ferry, Virginia.

Because of slaver reaction to her own ongoing Underground Railroad activities, she was forced to flee to New Orleans in 1850 where she met the Vodou queen Marie Laveau who trained her in how to "pressure the powerful to help the powerless" — blacks and poor women—gain rights and jobs. She then went to San Francisco, arriving in April 1852. Because she had no "freedom papers" she passed herself off as white, while she worked as a steward and cook in a white boardinghouse and invested in real estate and various business activities.

Pleasant's training with Marie Laveau proved beneficial. Pleasant became so successful at leveraging social change that many called her San Francisco's "Black City Hall". Her activities and her money helped ex-slaves avoid extradition, start businesses and find employment in hotels, homes and on the steamships and railroads of California.

In 1858 she returned to the East, bought land to house escaped slaves, and aided abolitionist John Brown both with money and by riding in advance of his famous raid at Harper's Ferry encouraging slaves to join him.

She went back to San Francisco where her investments with an influential business partner helped her amass a joint fortune estimated at $30 million. She later led the Franchise League movement in San Francisco that earned blacks the right to testify in court, and to ride the trolleys. Her lawsuit in 1868 in San Francisco against the North Beach and Mission RailRoad was used as a precedent in 1982 to achieve contemporary civil rights.

Mary Ellen Pleasant died in San Francisco in 1904. Her body was taken by friends to Napa and buried in Tulocay Cemetery. On her tombstone is inscribed "the mother of civil rights in California."

For more information, incuding a book on Mary Ellen Pleasant by Susheel Bibbs, we recommend http://hometown.aol.com/mepleasant.

POW Camp

At the end of World War II, a farm labor camp on the Silverado Trail was converted to a camp for German prisoners of war. The camp was established to provide agricultural labor as many of the usual farmworkers were away on duty with the military. The POW camp was located north of Yountville on the east side of the Trail, where Rector Creek flows down from Rector Dam. The compound was surrounded by barbed wire, had lookout towers with machine-guns and searchlights, and was patrolled by heavily armed guards. Every day, just after dawn, the prisoners were loaded into open trucks and taken to work in prune orchards and vineyards in the valley.

The first 250 German POWs did not arrive until August 14, 1945, over three months after the surrender of Germany, and the same day the Japanese agreed to unconditional surrender.

As an interesting sidenote, during the war German and Italian "enemy" aliens *and citizens* (All Japanese-Americans had been moved to camps east of the Sierra Mountains) were not allowed within a certain distance from the California coast. The line went approximately through the middle of the Napa Valley. The result was that one German-American resident of the valley, a baker, found his home on one side of the line and his bakery on another. After a number of confrontations, he was finally allowed to pass freely between his home and his workplace.

Invention of the Loudspeaker

Edwin Pridham and Peter Jensen moved to Napa in 1911 and set up a research lab. They invented the "Magnavox" loudspeaker, the first public address system.

Their first public demonstration was in San Francisco's Golden Gate Park on December 10, 1915. On December 25, they played music to a crowd of 100,000 people in front of San Francisco City Hall. Their Magnavox company gained national attention when they provided loudspeakers for

a 1919 speech in San Diego by President Woodrow Wilson.

Tribute in downtown Napa's Dwight Murray Plaza to the inventors of the loudspeaker.

Shipbuilding During World War II

From 1940 to the end of the war, Basalt Rock Company's Steel Division built 115 barges and 40 other ships for the U. S. Navy. The shipyard was located south of the city of Napa on the Napa River, where Napa Pipe Corporation is located today. (You can see the facilities when looking north from the Butler Bridge, which carries Highway 29 over the river.) Ships were as large as 1,700 tons and included self-propelled freighters and fuel oil tankers. LSTs (tank landing ships) were also repaired at the shipyard.

Historical Landmarks

Courtesy of the Office of Historic Preservation - California Department of Parks and Recreation http://ohp.parks.ca.gov/

No. 359 **OLD BALE MILL** - This historic gristmill was erected by Dr. E.T. Bale, grantee of Carne Humana Rancho, in 1846. The mill, with surrounding land, was deeded to the Native Sons of the Golden West by Mrs. W. W. Lyman, and was restored through the efforts of the Native Son Parlors of Napa County.

LOCATION: Bale Grist Mill State Historic Park, Hwy 29, 3369 N St. Helena Hwy, 3 mi NW of St. Helena

No. 547 **CHILES MILL** - Joseph Ballinger Chiles, who first came to California in 1841, erected the mill on Rancho Catacula 1845-56. The first American flour mill in Northern California, it was still in use in the 1880s. Chiles served as a vice president of the Society of California Pioneers, 1850-53.

LOCATION: SW corner on hillside, Chiles and Pope Rd and Lower Chiles Valley Rd, 3.6 mi N on Hwy 128, Chiles Valley

No. 563 **CHARLES KRUG WINERY** - Founded in 1861 by Charles Krug (1825-1892), this is the oldest operating winery in Napa Valley. The pioneer winemaker of this world-famous region, Krug made the first commercial wine in Napa County at Napa in 1858.

LOCATION: Krug Ranch, 2800 Main St, St. Helena

No. 564 **GEORGE YOUNT BLOCKHOUSE** - In this vicinity stood the log block-house constructed in 1836 by George Calvert Yount, pioneer settler in Napa County. Nearby was his adobe house, built in 1837, and across the bridge were his grist and saw mills, erected before 1845. Born in North Carolina in 1794, Yount was a trapper, rancher, and miller. He became grantee of the Rancho Caymus and La Jota. He died in Yountville in 1865.

LOCATION: NE corner of Cook Rd and Yount Mill Rd, 1 mi N of Yountville

No. 565 **PETER LASSEN GRAVE** - In memory of Peter Lassen, the pioneer who was killed by the Indians April 27, 1859, at 66 years of age.

LOCATION: 2550 Wingfield Rd via Richmond Rd, 5 mi SE of Susanville

No. 682 **SITE OF YORK'S CABIN, CALISTOGA** - Among the first houses in this area was John York's log cabin, constructed in October 1845. Rebuilt as part of the home of the Kortum family, it was used as a residence until razed in 1930. Nearby was the cabin of David Hudson, also built in October 1845. Calistoga was named by Samuel Brannan.

LOCATION: SW corner Hwy 29 (Foothill Blvd) and Lincoln Ave, Calistoga

No. 683 **SITE OF HUDSON CABIN, CALISTOGA** - David Hudson was one of the early pioneers who helped develop the upper portion of Napa Valley by purchasing land, clearing it, and planting crops and building homes. Hudson built his cabin in October 1845.

LOCATION: NE corner of Hwy 29 (Foothill Blvd) and Lincoln Ave, Calistoga

No. 684 **SAM BRANNAN STORE, CALISTOGA** - Sam Brannan arrived in Napa Valley in the late 1850s and purchased a square mile of land at the foot of Mount St. Helena. This is the store he built, in which he made $50,000 in one year.

LOCATION: NW corner of Wappo Ave and Grant St, 203 Wapoo Ave, Calistoga

No. 685 **SAM BRANNAN COTTAGE, CALISTOGA** - Sam Brannan arrived in Napa Valley in the late 1850s with the dream of making it the "Saratoga of California." In 1866 cottages were built and palm trees planted in preparation for the grand opening of the resort. This is the only cottage still standing.

LOCATION: 1311 Washington St, Calistoga

No. 686 **SITE OF KELSEY HOUSE, CALISTOGA** - Nancy Kelsey arrived in California in 1841 with the Bidwell-Bartleson party and settled with her family south of present-day Calistoga. Now the hearthstone is all that can be seen of the house. The property is owned by the Rockstrohs.

LOCATION: 500 ft NW of intersection of State Hwy 29 and Diamond Mtn Rd, 1.1 mi S of Calistoga

No. 687 **NAPA VALLEY RAILROAD DEPOT, CALISTOGA** - The Napa Valley Railroad depot, now the Southern Pacific depot, was built in 1868. Its roundhouse across Lincoln Avenue is gone. On its first trip, this railroad brought people to Calistoga for the elaborate opening of Brannan's summer resort in October 1868.

LOCATION:1458 Lincoln Ave, Calistoga

No. 693 **GRAVE OF GEORGE C. YOUNT** - George Calvert Yount (1794-1865) was the first United States citizen to be ceded a Spanish land grant in Napa Valley (1836).

Skilled hunter, frontiersman, craftsman, and farmer, he was the true embodiment of all the finest qualities of an advancing civilization blending with the existing primitive culture. Friend to all, this kindly host of Caymus Rancho encouraged sturdy American pioneers to establish ranches in this area, so it was well populated before the gold rush.

LOCATION: George C. Yount Pioneer Cemetery, Lincoln and Jackson Sts, Yountville

No. 710 **ROBERT LOUIS STEVENSON STATE PARK** - In the spring of 1880, Robert Louis Stevenson brought his bride to Silverado. He and Fannie Osbourne Stevenson lived here from May 19 until July, while he gathered the notes for Silverado Squatters.

LOCATION: Hwy 29 (P.M. 45.5), 75 mi NE of Calistoga

No. 814 **BERINGER BROTHERS WINERY** - Built by Frederick and Jacob Beringer, natives of Mainz, Germany, this winery has the unique distinction of never having ceased operations since its founding in 1876. Here, in the European tradition, were dug underground wine tunnels hundreds of feet in length. These maintain a constant temperature of 58 degrees, a factor considered necessary in the maturing and aging of fine wines.

LOCATION: 2000 Main St, St. Helena

No. 828 **VETERANS HOME OF CALIFORNIA** - This home for California's aged and disabled veterans was established in 1884 by Mexican War veterans and members of the Grand Army of the Republic. In January 1897, the Veterans Home Association deeded the home and its 910 acres of land to the state, which has since maintained it.

LOCATION: SW corner of California Dr and Hwy 29, Yountville

No. 878 **FIRST PRESBYTERIAN CHURCH BUILDING** - Designed by pioneer architects R. H. Daley and Theodore Eisen, this church is an outstanding example of late Victorian Gothic architectural styling. It is the best surviving example in this region of the early works associated with Eisen, who later became an important Southern California architect. The church has been in continuous use since its construction in 1874, longest pastorates were those of Richard Wylie and Erwin Bollinger.

LOCATION: 1333 Third Street between Randolph and Franklin Streets, Napa

No. 939 **TWENTIETH CENTURY FOLK ART ENVIRONMENTS (Thematic) - LITTO** - This is one of California's exceptional Twentieth Century Folk Art Environments. Over a period of 30 years, Emanuele "Litto" Damonte (1896-1985), with the help of his neighbors, collected more than 2,000 hubcaps. All around Hubcap Ranch are constructions and arrangements of hubcaps, bottles, and pulltops that proclaim that "Litto, the Pope Valley Hubcap King," was here.

LOCATION: 6654 Pope Valley Rd (P.M. 14.3), 2.1 mi NW of Pope Valley

Napa Walking Tour

Historic Buildings and Points of Interest

* (asterisk) Indicates the structure is individually listed on the National Register of Historic Places.

This walking tour takes approximately 45 minutes.

Dwight Murray Plaza
First Street (North side between Main and Coombs Streets

Formerly called "Clocktower Plaza" until the long-maligned (by most people in Napa) clocktower on the site was torn down. At the southeastern corner of the plaza is a monument to Napa's contribution to the invention of the Magnavox loudspeaker.

The plaza is a controversial testament to the City of Napa's redevelopment plan begun in the 1970s. Numerous historic buildings were demolished to make way for a downtown shopping center. This prompted a group of concerned citizens to form Napa County Landmarks. Thanks in part to their efforts, the City's redevelopment program now emphasizes building *on* Napa's past, not simply over it.

First National Bank* (1916-1917)
1026 First Street On the east side of the plaza

Napa County Landmarks revived this handsome Neo-Classical building in 1994 after it stood vacant for five years. Now known as the John Whitridge III Community Preservation Center, after Landmarks' founder and longtime president, it serves as a gathering place for civic activities. The style reflects the appearance of strength and stability long favored by American banks. In 2002, it was converted to an Italian restaurant.

Waterfront Mural
On Main Street on the northwest corner of Main and First Street

Numerous local groups collaborated to start Napa's downtown mural project. This first mural (see page 55), dedicated in 1994, depicts the Napa River waterfront (circa 1900) with its wharfs, mills, wineries, schooners and steamships.

Opera House* (1879)

1018 Main Street Across the street and slightly north of the mural

Painstakingly restored by local preservationists, the Opera House (see page 63) never really presented classical opera; instead, it offered such notables as John Phillip Sousa and Jack London along with travelling vaudeville shows. Due to the unpredictable nature of the entertainment business, the ground level was devoted to commercial uses in order to provide a steady source of income.

The symmetrical façade, large brackets under the eaves, and tall rectangular, pedimented windows are all indicative of the Italianate style. The Opera House reopened in 2002 for the first time since 1914. The upstairs theater is now known as the *Margrit Biever Mondavi Theatre* at the Napa Valley Opera House. Downstairs is the *Café Theatre*.

Underneath Main Street, as it crosses over the Napa Creek, are the remnants of a stone bridge dating from the 1860s. Some long-gone businesses were built over the creek and had trap doors that allowed the merchants to do a little fishing on the job.

Kyser-Williams Buildings (c. 1886)
1124-1142 Main Street

Designed by Wright and Saunders of San Francisco for the Williams Brothers, this native stone structure was the first multi-tenant building north of Napa Creek. The building was covered by a false front of metal, stucco and mission tiles for almost 50 years before restoration in 1999. David Sterling Kyser (mayor in 1907) purchased the building some time after 1900 for his furniture and undertaking business.

Napa Firefighters' Museum
1201 Main Street

The museum (see page 57) features an outstanding collection of vintage equipment and accessories.

Pfeiffer Building (1875)
1245 Main Street

This is Napa's first stone building (feel the texture of the native sandstone) and oldest surviving commercial structure. Bavarian immigrant Phillip Pfeiffer built it as a brewery. In the 1880s it became the Stone Saloon. Pioneer Chinese businessman Sam Kee later converted it to a laundry. The false front, customarily made of wood, was a common practice in early western towns to give the impression of a larger building.

For those with extra time and interest, two treasures lie several blocks further north: the Lisbon Winery (1880), now the Jarvis Conservatory, a jewel-box theater devoted to the performance of Zarzuela Opera and Baroque Ballet, at 1711 Main Street; and the Hennessey House (1889), 1727 Main Street. Otherwise, retrace your steps back down Main Street to the intersection of First Street.

Semorile Building* (1888)
975 First Street

Napa's foremost architect, Luther Turton, designed this building for Italian immigrant grocer Bartolemeo Semorile. It is Napa's finest brick structure, beautifully blending in features such as the cast iron balcony railing, balustrade, and Corinthian columns. Look through the front windows to see the old style of seismic retrofitting.

Winship Building* (1888)

948 Main Street

Financier E.H. Winship hired Luther Turton to design this Italianate style building, which was once the tallest on Main Street until the tower that crowned its bay window was removed in 1910. (It was restored in 2003.) Many such towers were removed after the 1906 earthquake for protection.

The Winship Building—more than 100 years at First and Main in Napa.

The building had a variety of tenants over the years—including a drug store, dentists, and a pawn shop—before it was restored in the 1980s. The sunburst in the arched pediment along the Main Street façade was a feature repeated in many of Napa's finer homes.

Oberon Building (1934)

902-912 Main Street

The colorful tiles, some of which create stylized Ionic columns, make this the best example of Art Deco architecture in Napa. The various establishments on this site have been serving drinks for well over a century, which is only fitting given that the first commercial building in Napa, the Empire Saloon, was located just a block south.

Bank of Napa* (1923)

903 Main Street

Inspired by the Ecole des Beaux Arts in Paris, this Classical Revival building has six colossal Doric columns framing the windows along Main Street. Don't miss the chandeliers, marble wainscoting and plaster ceiling in the lobby.

Veterans' Memorial Park

On the east side of Main Street between Downtown Joe's restaurant and the Third Street bridge.

This site was once full of turn-of-the-century commercial buildings that were razed in the 1970s to create the park. The Third Street Bridge (since replaced) once served as a crossing for electric rail cars, much to the dismay of other travellers who were occasionally jolted by the electric lines.

Chinatown Site

Located near the first street bridge where Napa Creek meets the Napa River

Arriving as early as 1851, the Chinese were instrumental in many early trades and industries and built many of the wine caves and stone walls found throughout Napa Valley. Their settlement along the bend in the Napa River once numbered more than 500 residents. The site was razed in 1930 to make way for a yacht harbor that never materialized.

Fagiani's Bar (1908)
813 Main Street

One of the few remaining commercial buildings built with native stone, the less visible side walls are brick. The ground-level façade was covered in Art Moderne tiling in the 1940s. The bar has been closed since the 1970s when one of the owners was found murdered inside. The case remains unsolved.

Center Building (1904)
816 Brown Street

William Corlett, who along with Luther Turton created many of Napa's finest buildings, designed this fine example of native stone architecture that features the use of contrasting colored stone radiating from the window heads.

Courthouse * (1878)

825 Brown Street

Built on land donated by Napa founder Nathan Coombs, the courthouse is a large-scale version of the popular Italianate style. Rich in 19th century charm, the building has been used as a set for several Hollywood films. There is an excellent photo exhibit of historic Napa County on the first floor. Look for the picture of the courthouse when it had a towering cupola evoking Russian and Gothic styles. The onion-shaped dome was removed in 1931.

The Hall of Records on the west end of Courthouse Square was restored in 1996 after Napa County Landmarks led an effort to save it from the wrecking ball. On the east end of the square is a flag pole

(1892) modeled after the Eiffel Tower and a grinding rock used by the Wappo Indians. There were perhaps several thousand Wappo living in the area when the city was established. Through disease and violence their numbers were drastically reduced within a generation of the arrival of the first pioneer settlers. In 1897, California's last public hanging took place here. It was an invitation-only event!

First Presbyterian Church * (1874)
1333 Third street

This California State Landmark church, constructed entirely of wood, is an exceptional example of the late Victorian Gothic architecture.

United States Post Office (1933)
1351 Second Street

Designed by William Corlett during the Great Depression, this is a fine example of a restrained Art Deco style that came to be known as WPA Moderne after the federal government program that put unemployed Americans back to work. Don't miss the glazed terra cotta work, including the rams' heads, along the roof line. Take a look inside.

Goodman Library * (c.1901)
1219 First Street

George Goodman, the co-owner of Napa's first bank, built this native stone structure for $15,000. The

building was designed with the
rough and heavy feeling of the
Romanesque style by Luther Turton.
It served not only as a public library,
but also as a tea room and social
gathering spot. It is now the home of
the Napa County Historical Society.

Napa Register Building
(1905)
1202 First Street

The *Napa Register* (now called the
Napa Valley Register), the city's
oldest newspaper, occupied this
Italianate building until 1965 when
the paper moved to a more spacious
production facility several blocks
away.

Gordon Building* (c.1929)
1146, 1142 and 1130 First Street

The glazed terra cotta tiles of the
commercial façade exemplify the
Spanish Colonial Revival influence
that was an attempt to recreate the
romantic look of the days of
California's ranchos.

Acknowledgment

The above tour is reprinted courtesy
of the *Napa Downtown Association*
and *Napa County Landmarks*.
This is just one of five walking
tours (including Napa's famous
Victorians). For a brochure with all
five tours, contact:

Napa County Landmarks
1026 First St. Napa CA 94559
707.255.1836 888.255.1836
www.napacountylandmarks.org

Brochures can also be purchased at
the Visitors Center (see page 62) of
the Napa Valley Conference and

Visitors Bureau in downtown Napa,
and in local bookstores and other
shops.
Napa County Landmarks offers
scheduled walking tours of valley
towns throughout the year.

Napa Downtown Association
707.257.0322
www.napadowntown.com

For a free map of the historic Napa
downtown area, send a self
addressed stamped envelope (SASE)
to:
Napa Downtown Association
Downtown Map Request
1556 First Street, Ste. 102,
Napa, CA 94559 USA

Napa WineWalk

Downtown Napa has the biggest and most centralized collection of wine tasting shops anywhere on the planet. You can walk from one to another in minutes (sometimes it's almost door-to-door), and experience wines from more than **150** different wineries. You'll notice that as you walk, you'll also pass most of Napa's finest restaurants. Do yourself a favor, and stop in during or after your walk for a thoroughly enjoyable meal, whether it be lunch, dinner or a midafternoon snack.

Most wines available for tasting on the **Napa WineWalk**^{sm} are from small, low-production wineries in the Napa Valley—many of them hard-to-find "cult" wines. Others are from the Pacific Northwest, Europe, South America and elsewhere.

The **Napa WineWalk**^{sm} focuses on "wine bars", which give you the opportunity to taste wines from a number of wineries at a single location. The **Napa WineWalk**^{sm} also includes several winery tasting rooms, where a single winery pours samples of the various wines that it makes.

Wine samples on the *Napa WineWalk*^{sm} can vary from an ounce to a full glass. There's a fee, of course, but the **Napa WineWalk**^{sm} is a rare opportunity to not just sample but purchase some of the finest wines in California and in the world. The wine shops and tasting bars will be happy to deliver your wine purchase to your hotel, or arrange for shipment to your home or office, assuming you live in a state where direct delivery is legal. (See www.freethegrapes.org for more information.)

Nowhere else can you try so many wines so conveniently. And nowhere else can you buy so many hard-to-find wines knowing that you just tried them and liked them.

Join us on the **Napa WineWalk**^{sm}.

Note: Many of these businesses accept the "Taste Napa Downtown" card which for one fee lets you taste wines at many different places. For more information, see www.napadowntown.com.

When you actually do the walking, you can start your **Napa WineWalk**^{sm} anywhere on the route you wish, but with these directions we'll start you off at the Vintner's Collective, at Main Street and Clinton on the edge of Downtown Napa.

Vintner's Collective

1245 Main Street
Napa CA 94559
707.255.7150 Fax: 707.255.7159
www.vintnerscollective.com

A co-op tasting room representing a number of Napa Valley boutique wineries. This is the only place in the valley you can sample these excellent wines.

When you're ready to journey on, go out the front door, cross Main Street to the other side, and turn right to walk along the sidewalk. Your next stop is Rocca Family Vineyards. On the way you'll cross Pearl Street and pass by Annalien Restaurant. Rocca is just before Cole's Chop House.

Rocca Family Vineyards
1130 Main Street
Napa CA 94559
707.257.8467
www.roccawines.com

Although their vineyard is in Yountville, Rocca offers tasting and sales at their tasting room in Napa. By the tasting, glass or bottle. Cabernet Sauvignon, Merlot, Syrah. They're currently closed Sundays but open afternoons other days.

Time to leave Rocca? Go back out to Main Street and turn left. Go to First Street (you'll pass the Napa Valley Opera House), and see the Napa River mural across the street at the corner of Coombs and First) and turn right. Walk down one full block (you'll pass Ristorante Allegria and nv at the back of the plaza) to the intersection of First and Coombs. You're at Napa Wine Merchants.

Napa Wine Merchants
1146 First Street (corner of Coombs)
Napa CA 94559
707.257.6796
www.napawinemerchant.com

A shared tasting room offering wines from more than 12 different wineries. Closed Sundays. (Web site has complimentary tasting coupon)

Ready for more? Turn right on Coombs along the pedestrian street, then turn left into the Napa Town Center walkway just past Buckhorn Grill. Continue walking between the shops to the rotunda. On your right is the Napa Valley Conference and Visitors Bureau. Stop here if you wish, then continue a few steps and turn at the street (You'll see Gillwoods Cafe on your left). You're now at Wineries of Napa Valley.

Wineries of Napa Valley
1285 Napa Town Center
Napa CA 94559
707.253.9450 800.328.7815
www.napavintages.com

Open daily with sales, tasting and concierge services located very close to the Visitors Center in downtown Napa. Wines from Burgess Cellars, Dusinberre Cellars, Girard Winery, Goosecross Cellars, and Ilona Howell Mountain Winery. Free wi-fi Internet.

Time to move on. Walk out of the tasting room (you'll see the Independence Day Parade mural across the street at Randolph and Clay), turn left, continue just on the edge of the rotunda (the front of Gillwoods will be on your right) and go directly along the pedestrian walkway (with Napa Valley Jewelers on your right) to First Street. Turn right on First Street, walk one block (you'll pass Piccolino's Italian Café) and turn left on Franklin to cross First Street. A few more steps on Franklin and you're at Back Room Wines.

Back Room Wines
974 Franklin Street
Napa CA 94559
707.226.1378 877.322.2576
www.backroomwines.com

Between First and Second Streets in Downtown Napa.

A wine shop and tasting bar. Winetasting by the half-glass or glass, as well as artisan cheeses and charcuterie. Tasting flights of six wines are also available on scheduled evenings. Free wi-fi Internet access.

On to the next stop. Leave Back Room Wines, turn right on Franklin, go to First Street and turn right.

Walk two and a half blocks (along the way you'll pass Annette's Chocolates, Caffe Cicero, and the historic Goodman Library, built in 1901 and now home to the Napa County Historical Society), and you'll come to Stave Wine Lounge.

Stave Wine Lounge
1149 First Street
Napa CA 94559
707.259.5411
www.stavewinelounge.com

Wine bar with automatic wine dispensers. Buy a card, then use it to pour yourself one of the many available wines from small Napa Valley producers and elsewhere. The dispensers automatically give you a one-ounce taste. You can also buy a bottle of any of the tasting wines, and take it home or sit back and enjoy it in Stave's comfortable surroundings.

Thirty-two wines available for tasting, including eight international wines. Cost per ounce tasting ranges from $1.10 to $9.00. By the bottle from $10 - $100. Local wineries include Venge, Igneous, Macauley, Punk dog, Parallel, Trespass and Terraces. Free wi-fi.

Coming out of Stave, turn right (you'll pass by the Hispanic Americans of Napa County mural) and continue to Main Street. At the corner, where Tuscany is located, turn right and walk south on Main. Along the way you'll pass Zuzu and Pilar restaurants. Continue for a total of about three blocks (the river is on your left and you'll pass the new courthouse and jail on your right) until you come to the Napa Mill.

The mill was originally a flour mill and a feed and grain business, but is now a hotel, restaurants and shops, including Sweetie Pies bakery and Vintage Sweet Shoppe. Your next stop, the Naps General Store, is almost at the end of the brick building.

Napa General Store
500 Main Street
Napa CA 94559
707.259.0762
www.napageneralstore.com

A specialty market and cafe. Visitors can choose from a daily selection of a dozen or more reds and whites, most from Northern California vineyards. Current price is $7 for three wines.

Leave the General Store and retrace your steps back to First Street, the main street of downtown Napa (just past Veterans Park you'll see Downtown Joe's, the only brew pub in the city of Napa). Turn right on First and you'll immediately come to the Bounty Hunter, on your right just before the river.

Bounty Hunter Rare Wine & Provisions
975 First Street
Napa CA 94559
707.255.0622 800.943.9463
www.bountyhunterwine.com

Mark Pope focuses on rare, limited-production wines, primarily from California but his wines—and wine paraphernalia—come from all over the world. He's in the historic Semorile Building, constructed in 1888 and located between Main Street and the river.

Mark also offers a wine bar (more than 40 wines by the glass) and bistro fare for tasting and fine snacking. Open until 1 a.m. Friday and Saturday nights, the Bounty

Hunter has become a lively and popular hangout.

Leave the Bounty Hunter, turn right, and cross the First Street Bridge over Napa Creek. Continue several blocks on First until you come to Copia (across the street on the north side of First Street). (There are several crosswalks you can use to cross First, but you should still watch out for traffic.)

Copia (Wine Spectator Tasting Table)

500 First Street
Napa CA 94558
707.259.1600 (tickets) 707.265.5900 (admin)
www.copia.org
Adults: $5.00 ; Seniors/Students: $4.00; Children 12 and under: Free.

Half-price Wednesdays for Sonoma and Napa County residents. Annual memberships available. Day pass is not required to visit the Café, Julia's Kitchen or the store, but is required for the Wine Spectator Tasting Table.

Copia is situated on 12 acres on the banks of the Napa River, a short walk from downtown Napa. The center celebrates America's contributions to wine, food and the arts.

It offers a variety of wine education classes with such titles as The ABCs of Starting a Wine Cellar and The Carpenters of Wine: All About Wine Barrels and Cooperage, as well as Wine Certificate programs in partnership with the Wine and Spirits Education Trust. Over 40 different wine courses are offered, most paired with food. It also offers more than 200 food classes, including both cooking and non-cooking programs.

Visit the Wine Spectator Tasting Table from 11:00 - 4:00 pm daily for complimentary tastings from a different winery every week.

Walk out of Copia, and turn left on First, heading westward toward the hills. Cross the bridge and you'll see JV Wine & Spirits on your left.

JV Wine & Spirits

First Street and Silverado Avenue
Napa CA 94559
707.253.2624
www.jvwineandspirits.com

The place where Napans go for good prices on wine and spirits. It's just over the river from Copia. The largest wine selection in the Napa Valley, with over 1200 different wines, including more than 250 Cabernets, 320 Chardonnays, 120 Zinfandels and 140 Merlots. If that's not enough for you, try one of the more than 115 different micro and imported beers. Wine tasting every day from 2-7 p.m. with a rotation of 40 different wineries. There's a $5 tasting fee, but it's refundable with your purchase of wine.

You can also order many of their wines online at www.jvwine.com

———————————

And that's the **Napa WineWalk**[sm]. We hope you enjoyed it. We also hope you simply tasted, rather than totally indulged. The wines are too good not to be able to savor each taste and aroma.

No matter how you chose to experience the walk, it makes sense to have a room at one of the hotels, inns or B&Bs in the downtown area. With a convenient location like that, you can can have a great meal at one of the downtown restaurants, walk back to your room, have a good night's sleep, and do it all again tomorrow, trying some of the wines you missed today.

Thanks for joining us on the **Napa WineWalk**^{sm}

Index

Printed in the United States
131763LV00005B/6/A